EU Law and the Social Character of Health Care

P.I.E.-Peter Lang

Bruxelles · Bern · Berlin · Frankfurt/M · New York · Oxford · Wien

Elias MOSSIALOS & Martin McKEE

With Willy PALM, Beatrix KARL & Franz MARHOLD

EU Law and the Social Character of Health Care

"Work & Society"
No.38

© P.I.E.-Peter Lang S.A.
PRESSES INTERUNIVERSITAIRES EUROPÉENNES
Brussels, 2002 – Second printing 2004
E-mail: info@peterlang.com
www.peterlang.net

ISSN 1376-0955
ISBN 90-5201-110-9
D/2002/5678/25 – Printed in Germany

Die Deutsche Bibliothek – CIP-Einheitsaufnahme

EU law and the social character of health care. / Elias Mossialos & Martin McKee with Willy Palm... . – Bruxelles ; Bern ; Berlin ; Frankfurt/M. ; New York ; Oxford; Wien : PIE Lang, 2002
(Work & Society ; No.38)
ISBN 90-5201-110-9

*CIP available from the British Library, GB
and the Library of Congress, USA.*
ISBN   0-8204-4691-2

Table of Contents

List of Boxes and Tables

Acknowledgements

We would firstly like to thank Mr. Frank Vandenbroucke, Minister for Social Affairs and Pensions, Federal Government, Belgium, for inviting us to write this book[1] and for his constructive comments on earlier drafts.

Our thanks also go to Mr. Jo De Cock, Director-General, National Sickness and Disability Insurance Institute (RIZIV-INAMI), Brussels, Belgium for co-organising with the Ministry of Social Affairs, the conference on "European Integration and National Health Care Systems: A Challenge for Social Policy", facilitating the meetings between the authors of this book and for commenting on several drafts.

We particularly appreciated the detailed and very constructive comments of our reviewers: Professor Danny Pieters, Institute of Social Law, Catholic University of Leuven, Professor Reinhard Busse, Department of Health Care Management, Technical University of Berlin, and Dr. Josep Figueras, Regional Adviser for Health System Analysis, WHO, Regional Office, Europe.

Moreover, our special thanks go to Professor Christa Altenstetter, Professor of Political Science at the Graduate School and Queens College of The City University of New York, US, Mr. Alain Coheur, Project Director, Association Internationale de la Mutualité, Brussels, Belgium, Professor Leigh Hancher, Professor of European Law, Catholic University Brabant, Tilburg and partner, Allen & Overy, Amsterdam, The Netherlands, Dr. Vassilis Hatzopoulos, Lecturer of EC law at the Democritus University of Thrace, Greece, Professor Yves Jorens, Professor of Social Security Law, University of Ghent, Belgium, and Mr. Jason Nickless, Barrister at Law and member of the Honourable

---

[1] This project was commissioned and financed by the Belgian Presidency of the European Union, with the support of the Belgian Ministry of Social Affairs, Public Health and Environment, the European Commission and the Belgian National Sickness and Disability Insurance Institute. The results were first presented at the conference on "European Integration and National Health Care Systems: A Challenge for Social Policy", organised by the Belgian Presidency of the European Union on 7th-8th December, 2001 in Ghent, Belgium. This volume incorporates both the original project results and subsequent discussions at the conference.

Society of Gray's Inn, Cheshire, UK, for reviewing particular sections of the book, which benefited greatly from their specific expertise.

Professor Jos Berghman, Professor of Social Policy, Catholic University of Leuven, Department of Sociology, Mr. Herwig Verschueren, Deputy Head of Unit "Free Movement of Workers and Co-ordination of Social Security Schemes", DG Employment and Social Affairs, European Commission, Mr. Eric Marlier, Task Force Europe of the Ministry of Social Affairs, Brussels, Belgium, Mr. Bart Vanhercke, Cabinet of the Minister of Social Affairs, Brussels, Mr. Paul Belcher, European Affairs Manager, European Health Management Association, Brussels and Mr. Michel Eggermont, Ministry of Social Affairs, Brussels, Belgium also offered thorough and detailed feedback on earlier drafts of this book and we extend to them our appreciation.

We would also like to extend our gratitude to Mr. Eric Teunkens at RIZIV-INAMI for organising all the meetings in Brussels and for his valued feedback on our work, Ms. Caroline White of the European Observatory on Health Care Systems for diligently retrieving many often obscure references, Ms. Valérie Cotulelli for preparing the text, Ms. Anna Maresso of the European Observatory on Health Care Systems for editorial assistance and Mrs. Dorothy McKee for diligently proof reading the manuscript. Beatrix Karl would like to thank the Austrian Programme for Advanced Research and Technology of the Austrian Academy of Sciences for supporting her work.

Last, but not least, we would like to thank the *Observatoire social européen* (OSE) for their overall co-ordination of this study, and in particular, Ms. Rita Baeten for her constructive feedback as well as her unique skills in successfully managing to bring together a myriad of time-challenged individuals on so many vital occasions.

It remains the case that the views expressed in this book are those of the authors alone and should not be taken as representing those of any of the organisations with which they are affiliated.

Elias MOSSIALOS, Martin MCKEE,
Willy PALM, Beatrix KARL and Franz MARHOLD

Foreword

Frank VANDENBROUCKE

Minister for Social Affairs and Pensions,
Belgian Federal Government

Despite the fact that Member States have, in principle, sole respon-sibility for health care policy, decisions taken by European Union (EU) institutions in the context of European integration increasingly influence national policy-making in that field. A myriad of technical norms, procedural obligations and other elements have an impact on national health care systems. Additionally, judgements of the European Court of Justice (ECJ), applying the basic principles in the Treaty to specific cases, illustrate the impact of the internal market on these systems, even if many uncertainties about how to interpret them in other situations remain.

Inevitably, growing EU integration has an increasing impact on health care systems. The political challenge is to guarantee that this growing impact does not unbalance basic social features that national health care systems should meet – namely solidarity, equity, acces-sibility and quality – but, on the contrary, supports these social features in the context of the Single European Market.

Under the Belgian Presidency during the second half of 2001, a con-ference was organised in Ghent in December 2001 "European Integra-tion and National Health Care Systems: A Challenge for Social Policy". The aim of this conference was to assess the various and complex issues at stake. Firstly, it was necessary to map out the issues and to put the debate into a broader perspective. Secondly, the findings were discussed with those responsible for the daily management of the health care systems in the Member States. And thirdly, questions were raised that will need a political answer. This conference allowed significant pro-gress to be made on understanding the impact of European integration on national health care systems.

In order to facilitate the debate at the conference and to provide the required material for policy-making, I asked Dr. Mossialos, together with Professor McKee, Mr. Palm, Dr. Karl and Professor Marhold, to produce a Report on "The Influence of EU Law on the Social Character of Health Care Systems in the European Union", which was presented at the above conference. This book is based on that Report and I want to congratulate the authors for producing this excellent publication. This is the first time the impact of European integration on health care systems has been mapped out so systematically in all the domains of health care. It is not just pioneering work on a very large issue; their analytical approach to social issues is innovative. This book has also profited from the many solid papers, drafted by all the speakers at the conference, which have helped to make it so comprehensive.

Testing theory by practical experience, by what is happening in the field and by the impact on the social systems has been illuminating. We were given many examples showing that the impact is different on the different health care systems, but that there is a common concern in all Member States.

But the process of stocktaking is not yet finished. We will have to study further the impact of European integration on each of the Member States, on the different models of health care systems, on each of the involved players and on the relationship between the players, namely public authorities, insurers, patients, health care providers, social partners and industry.

Market Rules and Health Care: Not an Easy Combination

It would certainly be simplistic to blame "Europe" for the problems we are confronted with; we need a more sober assessment of the nature of the issues. Fundamentally, the problem is that market rules and health care are never an easy combination, either at the national level, or at the European level.

The health care sector represents between 7 and 10% of gross domestic product (GDP) in EU Member States. Segments of the health care system interact with important markets in national and European economies. These interactions involve pharmaceutical products, medical devices, health care insurers and health care providers, but also medical staff and patients. The Treaty guarantees freedom of movement. Europe has been tackling health care issues for quite a long time within this economic context.

However, health cannot simply be treated as any other commodity. As the authors have underlined in this book, individuals may not always be in the best position to assess their health needs, whether because they are unaware of the nature of their health needs or are simply unable to voice it. Health care is increasingly complex and patients do not have access to all the necessary information to make an informed decision about the care they need. Fundamental economic theory teaches that the information asymmetry between patients and health care providers makes it impossible to achieve an efficient "market" for health care. This explains why European health care systems are, to a large though varying extent, organised and funded by public authorities, and why – again to a large though varying extent – we plan and control services and prices, in order to prevent exploitation of our systems.

As this book illustrates, Member States vary considerably in the detailed organisation of their health care systems but, underlying all of them, is a common perspective based on social solidarity and universal coverage. All our health care systems aim for solidarity between ill and healthy people, between the poor and the rich and between the young and the old. They try to guarantee financial accessibility to a broad package of quality care for the whole population. In order to do so, public authorities must be able to limit the price of the care they pay for, to guide choices between comparable treatments and to guarantee the financial sustainability of their systems. Health authorities need to take measures to prevent health care insurers from only selecting the wealthy and healthy, since this would make it impossible to guarantee access to good quality care for the less wealthy and healthy.

The basic argument that, both from an efficiency and a social perspective, market principles cannot and should not automatically apply to health care holds both at national and European levels; that is, it holds also at the level of the single market.

Although it was clear from the outset that single market rules would be applied to some aspects of health care, not all the possible consequences have been properly thought through with a long-term perspective. One third of the European decisions concerning health care are decisions of the ECJ. The ECJ can only apply the Treaty provisions, but cannot create policy as such. The ECJ tries to balance the social objectives of the national systems when deciding upon the applicability of market rules, but it is not able to take into account all the possible consequences of its decisions – both direct and mainly indirect consequences.

In search of more effective cost control, many Member States have introduced market mechanisms and more competition into their systems. In some national health systems we see the introduction of the purchaser/provider split. In insurance-based systems, competition between insurers has been introduced. Introducing market mechanisms into national systems makes them vulnerable to the application of EU market rules. But the application of internal market rules can also enhance dynamism and offer new perspectives to citizens.

Internal Market Rules: New Perspectives for Citizens

The ECJ rulings are the result of actions that citizens bring against the organisers of national health care systems. Evidence shows that the demand for cross border care is higher where the satisfaction with the national system is lower. The judgements can therefore stimulate the authorities to better adapt their systems to the needs of citizens. And, as this book stresses, Member States could also develop a more proactive policy concerning cross-border access, integrating foreign supply into national health care planning and procurement. European cross-border contracting could become an instrument to improve access to health care while maintaining control over the cost and quality of care. In border areas, contracting across the border could complement a limited regional supply of medical services. Some countries explore cross-border care to ease existing waiting lists due to a shortage of staff or other resources. In tourist areas, cross border contracting can offer culturally and linguistically appropriate facilities. EU-wide planning of internationally renowned centres of excellence could offer a more cost-effective way of ensuring highly technical care in a few specialised areas. I fully agree with the authors of this book that the necessary complementarity between people seeking treatment and facilities capable of treating them can be seen as a promising dimension of European integration.

This evolution will undoubtedly bring about the need for a European framework providing benchmarks for health care quality, medical training and practice, licensing and accreditation, and patient rights.

Certainly, we have to make sure that further health care integration does not increase social inequalities in access to care, as wealthier and better-informed citizens will be most likely to benefit from extended rights to health care abroad.

The application of market rules to other aspects of health care can also create new possibilities. The public procurement rules enhance transparency in public spending; parallel imports can limit the price of pharmaceuticals, and so on.

Some Important Issues

Reflecting the book's conclusions let me focus on three particularly important issues:

- We have to examine how cross border free movement of patients can remain compatible with the evidence-based standards of care and quality standards of care that we uphold – or endeavour to uphold – within our national systems. The rights patients can claim from the internal market should be clarified in national and EU legislation.

- It is necessary to incorporate explicitly issues of professional quality in the EU regulations on free movement of professionals, in order to ensure the continuing quality of the professionals involved.

- In the pharmaceutical sector, some aspects such as the supply of medicines have been harmonised, with the pharmaceutical industry largely in the driving seat. While Europe should support Research and Development in the pharmaceutical sector and access to new therapies, at the same time there is a need to ensure that only real innovation is supported and that new products are cost-effective and contribute to the improvement of health care systems.

In this context, along with the authors, I am concerned about direct-to-consumer advertising. The headline of an advertisement in the US on an antibiotic for the treatment of acute ear infection provides a convincing illustration: "Your son has another bacterial ear infection. He may need an antibiotic, and remember, he has to take all of it". In a country like Belgium, where we have too much consumption of antibiotics, one should certainly send a rather different message to the public; and I take it that from a public health point of view nobody would want to signal the quoted message to the public.

Moreover, I am concerned that direct-to-consumer advertisements might inappropriately increase patient demand for specific, generally costly, agents (the antibiotic I just referred to was indeed more costly than the traditional treatment). There are some figures to corroborate this concern. For instance, prescriptions for the top twenty-five drugs directly marketed to consumers in the US rose by 34% from 1998 to 1999, compared with a 5.1% increase for all other prescription drugs. Also, the demand for more costly drugs might have a negative effect on medical practice and, as a matter of fact, also on the physician-patient relationship. Therefore, direct-to-consumer prescription drugs advertising is not in the public interest, and does not serve the purpose of informing the patient. It is commonly misleading, and as a source of information it performs poorly.

On issues where Europe has created a proactive policy to apply the principle of free movement to health care services and products, there still is a need for more transparency and political guidance. In a sense, European policy is multiplying some well-known problems of political transparency concerning health care policy at the national level. A myriad of committees of civil servants or external experts take decisions on very technical aspects with sometimes far-reaching consequences for publicly organised health care systems – for instance concerning pharmaceutical products or medical devices. The decision-makers themselves are not always aware of these consequences. Given this lack of transparency, these committees are vulnerable to lobbying of – often powerful – interest groups. The involvement of politically responsible actors is too limited on these issues.

Few aspects of our societies are so embedded in our nations' histories and cultures as health care. Thus, it is very understandable that Member States have not transferred competencies, as such, to the EU in the area of health care. The Treaty states that: "Community action in the field of public health shall fully respect the responsibilities of the Member States for the organisation and delivery of health services and medical care". This explains also why there is no specific forum at EU level to discuss health care issues. At EU level, health care issues are usually tackled from an internal market perspective and therefore are debated within the "Internal market" EU Council of Ministers. Ministers in charge of Health or Social Affairs are not involved.

This problem is compounded, as health care is a shared competence of those responsible for social policy and those responsible for public health in the European institutions, as well as at national level in some Member States. Some Ministers responsible for health care are members of the Health Council; others are members of the Council for Social Affairs and Employment. They do not meet at European level to discuss their common problems. Again, there is no clear platform at European level to discuss the problems outlined here and to react politically to how these problems have evolved.

Increasing Political Awareness and Perspectives for the Future

Recent discussions have demonstrated an increased willingness to put the issue of health care on the EU political agenda.

The European Parliament adopted in 2000 a Resolution on supplementary health insurance, in which it calls on the Commission to analyse how health care systems can meet the objective of providing access for all to high-quality treatment for which there is a need, and within reasonable time limits.

The EU Charter of Fundamental Rights states that "everyone has the right of access to preventive health care and the right to benefit from medical treatment" and that "the Union recognises and respects this entitlement to social security benefits and social services providing protection in cases such as maternity, disability, illness, industrial accident, dependency or old age".

The May 2000 Communication of the Commission on Health Strategy has the potential to create a forum to discuss the issues raised in this book. The Ministers of the Health Council decided to undertake discussions on patient mobility during a high level event in Malaga (Spain) in February 2002.

The Göteborg European Council (June 2001) asked the Council to prepare an initial report for the spring 2002 European Council on the way forward in the field of health care and care for the elderly. The Social Protection Committee and the Economic Policy Committee, who will write a joint report, will do this work. The results of this work should be integrated into the Broad Economic Policy Guidelines (BEPGs).

In addition, and as a direct reaction to the conference mentioned above, the Laeken European Council in December 2001 highlighted the importance of tackling the issue of health care and care for the elderly and concluded that: "particular attention will have to be given to the impact of European integration on Member States' health care systems".

A Commission Communication was adopted in December 2001 that identifies three common objectives for European health care systems:

– guarantee access for all to health care of good quality;
– improve the transparency and quality of health care systems;
– ensure the financial viability of the health care systems.

This Communication and its objectives are a first concrete step towards an EU approach to better tackle the common health care challenges confronting Member States. And I am pleased to hear of support for the development of systems for assessment of medical treatment, and for common standards for quality in health care.

The method suggested by the Commission in its Communication is close to the "Open Method of Co-ordination" (OMC), which is already underway in the area of social inclusion and, since the EU Council of Ministers' meeting of 3 December 2001, in the area of pensions. Open co-ordination is a process where explicit, clear and mutually agreed objectives are defined, after which peer review enables Member States to examine and learn from good practices in Europe

It respects local diversity, is flexible, and simultaneously wants to ensure progress in the social sphere.

Open co-ordination is not just a learning process. It is certainly more than a defensive process: open co-ordination can and should be a creative process because it will enable us to translate the much discussed but often unspecified "European social model" into a tangible set of agreed objectives, to be entrenched in European co-operation (Vandenbroucke, 2002).

The first aim of open co-ordination applied to health care, therefore, should help us to identify the basic values that underlie European publicly organised health care systems and the values to be safeguarded: solidarity, equity, accessibility and quality of health care.

Moreover, open co-ordination can be an important research tool, helping us to discover tensions within our legal architecture. Efficient EU co-operation can help identify and prepare the legislative work both at national and EU level.

In order to tackle the problems discussed in this book, exchanging experiences and good practices will not be sufficient. It will have to be accompanied by legislation.

It is no longer possible to state that health care systems are purely a national matter given that Member States have, to a certain extent, devolved responsibility, notably when single market rules apply. I concur with the authors of this book that it is necessary to agree on a statement of fundamental principles that enshrine the values and objectives of European health systems, thus creating a common framework, without however diminishing the Member States' current degree of autonomy in shaping and reforming their health care systems. These principles could be incorporated in a future Treaty, thus balancing the internal market with social goals. This could be an element to introduce into the preparatory negotiations for the coming Intergovernmental Conference.

In the meantime, it is essential to deal with some of the problems which this book raises through secondary legislation; that is, on the basis of the existing Treaty. Decision procedures must be made more transparent and subject to more political guidance.

At the political level more communication is necessary between policy makers responsible for economic policy and social policy, for public health and for social affairs. There is a lack of communication and consultation on issues of EU policy at European level but also at the level of Member States. A health and social impact assessment of EU decisions for the creation of the single market could be useful.

Therefore, I would conclude with a statement that may sound like a paradox. In order to safeguard the social features of our systems, as we cherish them in our nation states, it is necessary to discuss health care policy both at national and European level. I hope progress will soon be made on the issue of health care policy. What is at stake is nothing less than fundamental social justice.

Introduction

EU Member States organise their health care systems in many different ways but all provide near universal coverage based on social solidarity. Of course, the way in which they ensure these characteristics varies. Countries in which health care is funded from taxation usually base entitlement on residence within the country in question. The situation is more complex with social insurance, especially where there are multiple funds. However, each country has made membership compulsory, other than the few countries that exempted or excluded the wealthy, taking the view that they will obtain alternative cover; but even in such circumstances governments may make special arrangements for catastrophic illness, as in the Netherlands. Consequently, over recent decades health care coverage of EU citizens has become almost universal, although there are still a few gaps for certain groups such as illegal migrants.

Yet the European social model is concerned with more than simple coverage. Social protection is also a means of promoting social cohesion and economic growth. If these goals are to be achieved health systems must be organised so that they deliver equitable access to effective care. As a consequence, health systems must go beyond the simple meeting of demand expressed by individuals. They must develop mechanisms to assess the health needs of their populations, with an emphasis on those that are not otherwise met, and they should ensure that effective policies are put in place to meet them. Member States have differed in their success in implementing this model but all EU health care systems aspire to it. Thus, the European social model is based on the belief that health care is not a normally traded good. As access to health care is a fundamental right, funding is based on a complex system of cross-subsidies, from rich to poor, from well to ill, from young to old, from single people to families and from workers to the non-active. This model continues to attract overwhelming popular support, reflecting the shared historical circumstances from which it emerged as well as the deeply rooted values of solidarity in Europe.

A market for health care delivery is inevitably imperfect as individuals are often unable to assess their health needs. They may be unaware of the nature of their health need or may be unable to articulate it effectively. The increasing complexity of health care creates major asymmetries in information providing scope for exploitative opportunistic behaviour by providers. This necessitates effective regulatory systems that can provide oversight. As a consequence, governments in all industrialised countries have played an active role in the organisation of health care. Even the US has a large public sector that covers about 40% of the population, thus providing some albeit basic and fragmented health care for the poor. For these reasons, Member States have explicitly stated in the EU Treaties, that they will retain national responsibility for the organisation and delivery of health services.

This guarding of national control does not, however, take account of the complexity of the situation. Many elements of health care are traded commercially. Thus, with a few exceptions such as some vaccines, governments do not produce or distribute pharmaceuticals. Medical equipment, whether clinical or otherwise, is purchased on the open market. Many health professionals are self-employed, under contract to health authorities or funds. Patients may obtain private treatment outside the statutory health care system, either in their own country or abroad.

All of these issues are entirely legitimately subject to the rules of the internal market and the fundamental freedoms enshrined in the Treaty require that the transactions involved are transparent and non-discriminatory. For this reason alone, health care managers must be aware of the implications of EU law. But other developments, in particular the growing role of market-based models in the delivery of health care within publicly funded systems, mean that the consequences for health services have become, directly and indirectly, ever greater.

This creates certain challenges. Policies that were developed to promote the principle of solidarity, with its complex system of cross-subsidies, become vulnerable to policies based on market principles. Unregulated competition in health care can be expected to reduce equity as organisations are stimulated to select those whose health needs are least, with those whose need is greatest finding it difficult or expensive to obtain care. While risk adjustment systems exist they have many limitations, especially where the environment is highly competitive.

Policies to contain costs may be based on restrictions on the supply of expensive equipment to health care facilities. This may be undermined if patients can insist that their funders pay for treatment elsewhere. Policies promoting effective care may involve selective contracting with providers but this requires the existence of transparent, and uniform standards. European governments have rejected direct-to-consumer advertising of pharmaceuticals, which is lawful in the United States, on the basis of the evidence that it often misleads, increasing health care costs while bringing few if any benefits to patients. Yet this is obviously an interference with the working of the market. Thus, even where aspects of health care are covered by provisions of the internal market, Member States and the European Union have insisted on constraining the effects of the market.

The consequence is that health and social policy in Europe has emerged in a disconnected fashion. Member States choose the goals they wish to pursue, such as equity and more effective care, but must then identify mechanisms that will achieve these goals that are consistent with European law. As much relevant European law has emerged from rulings that relate to other sectors or address those issues arising within a particular case, major issues of applicability remain unresolved. Health policy makers are therefore faced with a mass of contradictory advice from those who take either a restricted or expansive view of the scope of European law in health care.

This is illustrated by the evolving issue of free movement of patients. Two rulings of the European Court of Justice (ECJ) required the Luxembourg social security system to reimburse unauthorised health care in another Member State as these were covered by the principles of free movement of goods and services. The rulings clarified that certain aspects of social security systems are not exempt from European law. In subsequent cases the ECJ determined that all medical services, including hospital treatment, are covered by the definition of services, as used in the EC Treaty as, in one way or another, providers are remunerated for the service delivered. Whether reimbursement is claimed under a system that operates through a benefits in-kind approach or straightforward reimbursement is not relevant.

European law is thus an increasingly important factor in the development and implementation of national and local health policy. Yet for many it remains shrouded in mystery. This is hardly surprising as the European legislative process appears remote, with little coverage by either the popular or professional media. But the situation with regard to laws impacting on health care is especially problematic as, typically, consequences arise from policies designed primarily to address problems in other sectors, which then establish general principles whose applicability to health care only becomes apparent once interpreted by rulings of the European Court of Justice. As the Court can only rule on the precise situation that has been presented to it, this means that the broader implications for health care are unclear, and often highly contentious.

In December 2001, during the Belgian Presidency of the European Union, Mr. Frank Vandenbroucke, the Belgian Minister for Social Affairs, convened a conference in Ghent on the implications of European law for the social nature of health care.

Two complementary books emerged from this process. In this volume, written with the health and social policy community in mind, we have attempted to explore what the issues mean for the social nature of health care in Europe. In a sister volume, leading commentators provide their perspectives from the legal profession on the current situation and prospects for the future.[1] Despite differing in the detail of how they are organised, Europe's health care systems are united by the principle of solidarity. Yet, as these books show, there are often tensions between free movement and social solidarity. How can these tensions be resolved? Is the present legal basis of the European Union sufficient to achieve this? We argue that it is not, and we also argue for the development of an explicit European health policy, based on a revision of the Treaties, and incorporating formal systems for co-ordination of national health policies so that all can benefit from best practices wherever they arise.

Specifically, we explore how European law on a series of issues relevant to the organisation of health care has evolved so far and how it supports or impairs the ability of Member States to ensure high quality care. We begin by exploring in detail the policy-making context within which policies related to health and health care are developed.

Chapter 2 analyses how health policy has grown from its modest beginnings in the Treaty of Rome, indicating the role of the EU's decision-making framework in this process. This analysis demonstrates some of the reasons why it has not been possible so far to develop a comprehensive basis for health policy action.

In subsequent chapters, the impact on health care of the freedoms enshrined in the Treaty is examined in detail. These are freedom of movement of people, in this case health professionals and patients; freedom of movement of goods, here pharmaceuticals and medical devices; and freedom of movement of services, here health insurers. Two subsequent chapters examine specific aspects of European law that have relevance for health systems. The first is competition law. A single market can only operate in the presence of open competition across borders, which means that national transactions must not unfairly discriminate on grounds of nationality. This is an extremely complex area because of the many ways in which discrimination may take place, involving the creation of cartels or abuse of a dominant position, as well as the many exemptions, especially where policies involve sovereign actions of governments or social goals. The second examines the development of

---

[1]   McKee, M., Mossialos, E. and Baeten, R. (eds.) (2002), *The Impact of EU Law on Health Care Systems*, P.I.E.-Peter Lang, Brussels.

information technology law and the growth of electronic commerce. Electronic commerce makes cross-border trade much easier, so furthering the goal of a single market, but at the same time it raises issues of regulation where services (such as medical advice) or goods (such as pharmaceuticals) may pose a risk to the consumer. It also has implications for social inclusion, as those in greatest need may be least able to access this mode of communication.

The book concludes by exploring where the EU should go next, to ensure that the single market enhances health protection in Europe rather than undermines it.

This book cannot hope to be an exhaustive analysis of every aspect of European law that might have an impact on health systems. We do, however, hope that it provides a comprehensive assessment of the main implications of EU law in certain key areas.

CHAPTER 1

A European Social Model?

Introduction

Health care policy in the European Union has, at its centre, a fundamental contradiction. On the one hand, recent Treaties, which are the definitive statements on the scope of European law, state explicitly that health care is a responsibility for Member States. On the other hand, as health systems involve interactions with people (staff and patients), goods (pharmaceuticals and devices) and services (health care funders and providers), all of whose freedom to move across borders is guaranteed by the same Treaty, it is increasingly apparent that many of their activities are subject to European law. Yet the picture is far from straightforward. The European Union (EU) has both economic and social goals and, since the Treaty of Maastricht, it has been required to "contribute to the attainment of a high level of health protection".

But Member States, reflecting the societal preferences of their citizens, have chosen different ways to organise their health care systems. These reflect many factors. The overall design often reflects history, so commonly accepted norms are important. For example, social insurance systems require an existing set of relationships between employers, trade unions and government. National health services imply a different relationship between the individual and the state, in which the social partners play a less prominent role. Levels of funding reflect views about the balance between individual and collective financing of health services, as well as the amount of redistribution that is desirable. Methods of provision reflect views on the balance between professional and organisational autonomy on the one hand and the role of the state in ensuring effective treatment and an equitable distribution of facilities. The ways in which these varying goals are achieved reflects views about the legitimacy of regulation, incentives, or other levers.

These decisions have combined in ways that mean that, while they are often thought of as falling within broad categories, each national health care system in Europe is unique. Furthermore, given their grounding in national culture, institutional frameworks, and contemporary political choices, there is no obvious reason to seek to harmonise them. Indeed, any attempt to do so would almost certainly end in failure, as well as potentially provoking widespread popular dissent.

For these reasons, the application of a uniform legal framework, as set out in the EU Treaties, will inevitably be problematic. But the challenge is even greater. Achievement of the single market, through the promotion of free movement, must proceed but where policies have implications for national health care systems, legislators and the European Court have no framework of reference with which to work, other than general statements about ensuring high levels of health protection.

This book will argue that such a framework is needed. By exploring the evolution of European law on movement of patients and professionals, pharmaceuticals and medical devices, insurers and health care providers, it will show that the existing situation has created uncertainty and, in places, confusion. Health care policy makers are frequently forced to speculate about the application of European law to their actions on the basis of judgements made in other sectors, or in systems whose relevance to their own is far from clear. This creates the worst of all worlds; the potential benefits that the single market might bring are not realised and the unintended consequences of laws drafted to achieve a quite different objective may impair the ability to provide effective services.

The remainder of this chapter will explore the extent to which there is consensus on the goals of health care in Europe. In other words, might it be possible to produce a fundamental statement about what they seek to achieve? Before doing so, however, it is necessary to describe, briefly, the legislative framework of the EU.

The primary legal basis for EU legislation is a series of Treaties, beginning with the 1957 Treaty of Rome, which established the European Economic Community (EEC) (Craig and de Burca, 1998). This provided the basis for a common market, characterised by four fundamental freedoms of movement, of people, goods, services and capital. These four freedoms have continued to lie at the heart of the European idea and, as shall become apparent later, have important implications for the development of health policy in Europe.

Since then, there have been periodic revisions to take account of changing circumstances, the most recent examples being the Treaties of Maastricht, Amsterdam and Nice. Treaties are agreed by Member States and, once ratified, they determine the scope for legislative action by the EU, defining what lies within its competence and what is the responsibility of individual Member States. While the Treaties identify the goals to be pursued by the EU, and do have direct force of law in Member

States once ratified, the detailed implementation of policy is based predominantly on secondary legislation, enacted on the basis of the Treaties by the institutions of the EU.

Three European bodies, the Commission, the Parliament, the Council of Ministers, dominate the legislative process, although, as will be seen, the legal basis for action is shaped powerfully by the accumulated case law of the European Court of Justice and is also influenced by other bodies, such as the Committee of the Regions, which have a consultative role in some cases. Although there are a variety of mechanisms, depending on the topic involved, the usual one is for secondary legislation to be initiated by the Commission and sent to the Council of Ministers (representing the governments of the Member States) and the Parliament (consisting of elected representatives of the EU population). Approval is subject to agreement by both bodies, with provisions for conciliation in case of disagreement when matters involving co-decision are involved. Depending on the topic, the Council of Ministers may determine their support or otherwise by unanimity or by qualified majority voting, where each country is allocated a particular quota of votes reflecting its size.

A range of possible legislative instruments is available. Regulations are specific measures that have immediate and direct force of law, so that, as with the Treaty provisions, an individual can seek redress in a national court. They do not need to be adapted to take account of national circumstances, so they are most appropriate in areas such as the EU's external trade relationships. For many issues this is not possible. National structures and circumstances influence how a measure will be implemented in each country. Consequently, a more common device is the Directive. This sets out goals to be achieved but allows each Member State to draft legislation in a manner appropriate to its circumstances. The national legislation must be in place within a fixed time period and, if not, an individual can seek redress against the state in question or any public authority within it, in which case the national court is obliged to rule on the basis of the earlier Directive as long as its provisions are sufficiently clear to do so. In all cases, EU law takes precedence of national law in the event of a conflict.

Both Regulations and Directives are applicable to all Member States. There may, however, be circumstances in which legislation is required to address an issue affecting only some Member States, individuals or organisations. In this case the appropriate device is a Decision that, like a Regulation, has immediate force of law. The EU can issue Recommendations and Opinions, which while setting out goals that it would be desirable to achieve, do not have force of law.

Finally, in the public health field, the mechanisms of integration used have not typically been "classic" harmonisation through the application of Community law or Community-level (minimum) regulatory standards (Hervey, 2002). The Community institutions have sought to use persuasive methods of integration in this field, such as financial support and measures of "soft law" (*i.e.* Commission Recommendations and Opinions) (Hervey, 1998) (see Chapter 2).

As noted above, there are inevitable disagreements about whether a particular law applies in certain circumstances. The final arbiter is the ECJ, which has the power to both interpret and, in certain circumstances, rule unlawful secondary legislation. The latter course is open to it where either its content or the process by which it was agreed is inconsistent with the Treaties. Thus, a Directive banning tobacco advertising was ruled unlawful because it was agreed as an internal market matter, subject to qualified majority voting in the Council of Ministers, whereas the Court accepted the arguments of the German government, acting with a group of multinational tobacco companies, that it should have been a public health matter and so subject to unanimity[1].

Article 152 (ex 129) of the EC Treaty does not give any mandate to the Community to bring forward legislation concerning the organisation and delivery of health services, and explicitly excludes measures aimed at the harmonisation of the laws and regulations of the Member States (with the exception of measures in the field of veterinary and phytosanitary legislation, and measures in relation to the quality and safety of organs and substances of human origin, blood and blood derivatives). Furthermore the Duphar Case[2] has been widely invoked to support the argument that Community law does not detract from the powers of the Member States to organise their social security systems (Pieters and van den Bogaert, 1997).

However, as the ECJ and Courts in Member States are bound to follow precedent, successive rulings of the Court have been extremely influential in the development of the accumulated body of European law. The Court is required to interpret secondary legislation in the light of the Treaty provisions, in particular the pursuit of the four fundamental freedoms. Consequently, rulings have frequently gone beyond what some Member States anticipated when they agreed particular pieces of legislation. This is particularly well illustrated by the evolving situation with regard to movement of patients (see Chapter 4).

---

[1] European Court of Justice, C-376/98, Judgement of 05/10/2000, Federal Republic of Germany *v.* European Parliament and Council of the European Union.

[2] European Court of Justice, C-238/82, Judgement of 07/02/1984, Duphar and Others.

The complex relationship between primary and secondary Community law can be depicted as "stage working". Secondary Community law encompasses those provisions established by Community institutions on the basis of primary Community law (the Treaties). Any legislation enacted as secondary law must be based on primary law. Any secondary law that conflicts with the guarantees provided by primary Community law must give way. Thus, primary Community law is simultaneously the basis for, as well as the limit to acts of secondary Community law (see Chapter 4).

This relationship has important implications for social security in general, and health care in particular, because of the lack of guarantees for social security in primary Community law. In contrast, basic economic freedoms and European competition law are part of primary Community law and so prevail in any legislation in the field of social security or health care. For many years the legal competence of the European institutions to address health care was restricted to the co-ordination of the social security systems of Member States. It is only relatively recently, in the framework of protocol 14 of the EU Treaty on social policy and subsequently through Article 137.3 of the EC Treaty (ex 118.3), that it has been argued that the Community has achieved competence to harmonise social security and, as part of it, health care systems.

The result of this legal situation is a continuous victory for basic economic freedoms and competition law in cases where social security instruments, principles and legislation contradict them. Some degree of EU competence in the area of social security seems to be necessary in conflicts between basic economic freedoms and social security. The ECJ has seldom taken this path. As long as there is no counterbalance to the way social policies are defended in primary European law there will be concerns about the unanticipated consequences for social security systems in light of the freedom to transfer goods and services, the freedom to migrate and the restrictions to exclusive rights (Marhold, 2001a).

I. The Development of a European Social Model

Any attempt to define a European social model must start by differentiating it from potential alternative models. On the assumption that models implemented in developing or middle-income countries are of limited relevance to this discussion, the most obvious comparator is that of the US. As the remainder of this section will show, its approach to social policy differs greatly from that seen in Europe, in many different ways, but one simple comparison suffices to illustrate the fundamental nature of this difference. While all European countries have ensured universal, or near universal health care coverage for their populations, the US has singularly failed to do so. In this way it stands apart from all advanced industrialised nations. Others outside Europe, such as Japan, Australia and Canada, stand with Europe on this fundamental issue.

But is this sufficient to define a specific European model? And if so, where do the boundaries of this model lie, and by extension, where might consensus on the goals of the health care system be reached?

To answer these questions it is necessary to look to history. A concern by the state for the health of its population is relatively recent, emerging identifiably in the nineteenth century. By the end of that century welfare states were beginning to spread across Europe. The spread of health care coverage was, however, slow, beginning with coverage of industrial workers in Germany in the second half in the eighteenth century and only including agricultural workers in some countries in the 1960s (Flora and Alber, 1982). This pattern was related intimately to the process of industrialisation. Industrialisation, and the consequent division of labour, changed the social structure fundamentally (Durkheim, 1984). Existing social support systems, based on relationships within families and local communities in agrarian societies, were replaced by new systems of inter-dependence that met the needs of the many individuals who found themselves in unfamiliar and often hostile settings in the newly industrialised towns and cities. And their needs were often great, as is apparent from evidence of worsening of the already poor health of the English working class in the late 19th century (Engels, 1987).

It soon became clear that a response by the state was required to address these new needs. From an economic perspective, health care was a public good; under normal market conditions an insufficient amount was produced. Those whose need was greatest did not have the purchasing power to create effective demand, so that illness reduced productivity, and thus earnings of employers, and the state was unable to draw on a sufficient healthy pool of manpower in the event of war. It was subject to externalities; the middle classes had an interest in ensuring that they did not contract disease from freely roaming fever victims and were not murdered by those with psychiatric illnesses, although some were also motivated by altruism (Jessop, 1990).

Importantly, these factors were much less important in North America, and in particular in the US. Under-performing workers could always be replaced by the continuing tide of immigrants from Europe, with the barriers placed in their way acting to select only the fittest (with the health examinations on Ellis Island the most explicit of these). And unlike the relatively crowded countries of North-Western Europe, the

US had what seemed to be almost unlimited space, so that the middle classes could isolate themselves from the poor by distance, a phenomenon illustrated graphically by the film "The Great Gatsby", where the rich insulated themselves in their mansions on Long Island.

The next major extension of the welfare state in Europe came after the Second World War (WWII). One major factor was the shared experience that had affected entire populations but attitudes were also shaped by the reaction to the social forces that had given birth to extremism, which in turn had contributed substantially to the war. Once again, North America did not share directly in these experiences. The collective trauma of the depression of the 1930s might have led to universal coverage; indeed there was considerable enthusiasm for it among both the public and medical profession. However, a small group of predominantly urban doctors within the American Medical Association were able to block reform until 1938, by which time Roosevelt's efforts were focused on foreign affairs and the political make-up of Congress had become unfavourable to social reform (Starr, 1982). It was not until 1965 that another Democrat President was able to introduce a limited extension of coverage, again in the face of sustained opposition from the medical profession (Marmor, 2000). Canada, which shared many of the historical experiences of the US, only achieved universal coverage in 1972.

In the space available it is not possible to engage in a detailed comparison of the wide range of health care systems that exist in Europe, which anyway have been described in detail elsewhere. Instead, the remainder of this section will explore the extent to which they share common features.

As is apparent from the preceding discussion, the fundamental distinguishing feature of European health care systems is the provision of near universal coverage. The precise nature of entitlement varies. In countries with a single national health system funded from taxation, entitlement is usually straightforward, based on residence within the country in question. In social insurance systems the situation is more complex, especially where there are multiple funds, but all Member States with such systems have made membership of a sickness fund compulsory, although a few countries have exempted the wealthy, assuming that they can make alternative arrangements. Governments may, however, require cover against catastrophic illness, as in the Netherlands. They have also made arrangements for those who would otherwise not be covered, although it must be recognised that these may be less than satisfactory for certain groups such as illegal migrants.

In spite of the important differences among the European health systems, all EU Member States endorse the fundamental goal of access to necessary health care for the whole population, irrespective of individual health and financial status. This is based on the principle of solidarity, in which contributions are according to ability to pay (a vertical dimension) and benefits are according to needs (a horizontal dimension). This principle is applied in different ways.

* In terms of integration into the system:
    – inclusion of all citizens (universality)
    – mandatory affiliation for the citizen (prohibition of opting-out from the statutory scheme), requiring his/her financial participation in the public system;
    – an obligation of acceptance of the administering bodies (prohibition of exclusion).
* In terms of funding:
    – a progressive income-related contribution;
    – a contribution independent of individual risk factors (*i.e.* medical history, age, sex);
    – cross-subsidisation among schemes.
* In terms of benefits:
    – equal treatment for equal need;
    – progressive cover according to needs (positive discrimination in favour of those in greatest need).

However the European social model goes beyond just access to health care, seeing social protection as a means of promoting both social cohesion and economic growth. To do so requires that the organisation of health systems promote equitable access to effective care. However, health systems should do more than simply meet expressed demand by individuals. Specifically they should actively assess the health needs of their populations, in particular those that are not being met, and ensure that effective policies are provided equitably to meet them (van Herten and van de Water, 2000). The extent to which this approach has been implemented does vary but it is a clearly identifiable aspiration in all EU health care systems. One manifestation is the increasing interest in the concept of targets for health improvement (McKee and Fulop, 2000).

Other shared features of European health systems are more difficult to measure but can be implied from the arrangements put in place by Member States. Europe has not seen the growth of vast for-profit chains of health care providers or insurers seen in the US. This appears to reflect a more fundamental belief, that health care is not simply a typical industrial concern. Many of the factors that led to the creation of the

European welfare state in the 19th century, including the characteristic of health care as a public good and the existence of externalities, still apply, with others, such as the asymmetry of information between consumer and provider becoming even more important. This does not mean a rejection of market principles in the delivery of health care; it is apparent that some activities, such as the production and distribution of pharmaceuticals are best undertaken as a commercial activity, as are many other aspects of procurement of (non-clinical) services, but it does mean that Europeans are unwilling to go down the path taken by the US. As this book will show, this creates difficulties when European law is being applied to activities that impact on the organisation of health care as nowhere in the Treaty are these principles enunciated in a way that would provide context for policies that seek to promote free movement of people, goods or services.

In summary, the main message of this section is that Europe's historical collective experience, and the consequent emergence of institutions and shared beliefs about the role of the state, differs fundamentally from that of North America. However it is important to know whether these factors remain applicable today. This will be explored in the next section.

II. The European Social Model: Popular Acceptance

Social policy is embedded in broader considerations about how people organise their lives. Thus, the US has achieved a higher level of economic attainment (as measured by GDP) than Europe but has done so primarily by increasing the number of hours worked per year. Partly because of its lower investment in capital, labour productivity per hour worked is somewhat lower than in Europe. In other words, Europeans have, to some extent, chosen to trade income for leisure (Turner, 2001). Europeans are also more willing to forego some degree of economic growth to ensure, through strict application of planning laws, the preservation of the environment. The US has chosen a model that tolerates wide variations in income, while accepting (perhaps reluctantly) the social consequences such as high levels of violent crime. In contrast, all European governments, while maintaining minor differences according to their political complexion, have embraced the need to tackle social exclusion.

However, there is compelling evidence that, at least in the field of health care, the European model continues to have more widespread popular support in Europe than its American alternative has in the US. Public opinion surveys undertaken in the 1970s showed that, among western European countries, approval for the performance of government in the provision of medical care exceeded that seen in the US in all countries except Italy, with the other European countries included (Switzerland, the Netherlands, Austria, Germany, Finland and United Kingdom) all recording approval ratings of over 70% (Pecosolido *et al.*, 1985). A later survey, undertaken in 1990 in ten industrialised countries, found the US to have the lowest percentage of respondents stating that their health care system required only minor changes (Blendon *et al.*, 1990). The US also had the highest percentage of respondents who believed that their system needed to be completely rebuilt (29%).

A nascent neo-liberal political agenda in the 1980s began to challenge the prevailing view, in particular seeking to reduce the role of the state in areas such as health care. Such moves attracted little enthusiasm. A survey in all fifteen EU countries in 1996 found, overall, that 84% of respondents across all countries favoured either the same or higher levels of expenditure, ranging from 74.6% in Austria to 96% in Sweden (Mossialos, 1998). In response to a question about the obligation by the government to provide health care for all, only 4% across all countries took the view that the government need not provide for those on low incomes. Only in Belgium (15.7%) was this view held by more than 5% of respondents.

Of course, some commentators have always challenged the idea of a sustainable welfare state, arguing that the European social model was a temporary phenomenon that would eventually collapse in the face of economic reality. Some of the earliest warnings came in the mid-1970s, largely as a result of the economic shock following the 1974 Middle East War, with its accompanying worldwide recession. More recently, pressures imposed by the convergence criteria for joining European Monetary Union have been an important factor. However, perhaps the most important is the challenge posed by the post-industrial society. The traditional model of employment and family life, with male industrial workers in life long employment and supported by non-working wives, is disappearing (Esping-Andersen, 1996).

Politicians feared that systems will become unsustainable but they adopted a wide range of cost containment strategies so that, by the 1990s, most European countries had reduced the rate of growth in expenditure on health care as a percentage of national wealth (Mossialos and Le Grand, 1999).

Some of the methods involved the introduction of market-based reforms. Thus, some tax-based systems, such as the United Kingdom and Sweden, separated purchasers and providers of health care (Bartlett *et al.*, 1998). Some with social insurance systems, such as Germany, introduced competition between insurance funds. Many increased direct payments by patients, by removing certain drugs from lists of those that can be prescribed or by introducing co-payments for certain services. Some also increased the amount of care provided by the private sector (Saltman and Figueras, 1997).

While many other factors played a part, including shortages of key workers because of demographic changes and rising public expectations, these policies were linked, by the media and ultimately by health professionals and the public, with a decline in the quality of care in some countries. This was particularly true for countries with tax-funded systems that had tended to spend less on health care than did those with social insurance systems.

By the late 1990s it was apparent that a backlash was occurring in many countries. The United Kingdom abandoned some of its market-based reforms. A British civil servant has noted, "The British public's sense of justice and fairness was not consistent with the concept of maximising private advantage that underlies the competitive model" (Smee, 2000). In France, the government constrained the system that had permitted physicians in certain areas to charge higher fees (Poullier and Sandier, 2000). In Germany the Social Democrat led government reversed many of the pro-competitive elements introduced by its predecessor (Pfaff and Wassener, 2000).

The public perception of these changing policies has been plotted in Sweden, which has experienced substantial changes (Bergmark, 2000). During the period of relative affluence in the early 1990s a majority of the population favoured a reduction in public sector expenditure but, by the late 1990s, when the quality of services had deteriorated visibly, this changed, and more people favoured an increase in expenditure.

Taken together, these findings indicate that, while greater efficiency is welcomed, there is little appetite in Europe, across countries with quite different health systems, for radical reforms that are seen as undermining the welfare state.

At the same time many policy-makers are looking at evidence from the former socialist countries in Central and Eastern Europe that has cautioned against leaving health care (or other elements of social policy) to the ravages of the market. Rapid introduction of market-based systems had calamitous consequences for health, as well as for economic development. The clear message from this period is that while markets may have a place in social policy they must be embedded within a strong institutional framework (EBRD, 1999).

In summary, there is a high degree of popular satisfaction with existing European health care systems. These systems have survived intact in the face of changing economic fortunes and, where fundamental changes have been attempted they have failed or been rejected by a public that places a high value on their underlying concept of social solidarity.

III. The Political Embodiment of the European Social Model

In the mid-1990s, a series of developments placed social protection more centrally on the EU political agenda. One factor was the perception that the EU was increasingly seen as a solely economic entity, with the implementation of the single market and competition by countries to attract investment potentially driving down social protection. Another was the recognition that changes in age structure, labour force participation, and gender roles were forcing a rethink of some existing systems of financing the welfare state. Confronted with the same challenges over the past two decades, health policy makers learned from the experience of others. This was first stimulated by a sharp rise in health expenditure resulting from several factors such as implementation of new and costly medical technology, the high cost of new medicines and the medicalisation of social problems. Secondly, a slowdown in economic growth, a quest for fiscal stability, and the desire to reduce labour costs to encourage employment have exerted greater pressure on collective funding. Finally, an increase in the dependency ratio, with more old people and fewer of working age, is challenging collective financing, both in terms of the amount needed now and for investment in new services for a changed population in the future.

This led to a reassessment of the role of the EU in the field of social protection, which has received widespread support from governments of Member States. The European Social Charter (1989) gives the Community the role of supporting activities of the Member States in this area (Hantrais, 2000). The 1992 European Council Recommendation concerning the convergence of social protection policy objectives (Council of the European Communities, 1992a) is an example. In the area of health it calls on the Member States:

- under conditions determined by each Member State, to ensure for all persons legally resident within the territory of the Member State access to necessary health care as well as to facilities seeking to prevent illness;
- to maintain and, where necessary, develop a high-quality health-care system geared to the evolving needs of the population, and especially those arising from dependence of the elderly, to the development of pathologies and therapies and the need to step up prevention;

- to organise where necessary the rehabilitation of convalescents, particularly following serious illness or an accident, and their subsequent return to work;
- to provide employed persons forced to interrupt their work owing to sickness with either flat-rate benefits or benefits calculated in relation to their earnings in their previous occupation, which will maintain their standard of living in a reasonable manner in accordance with their participation in appropriate social security schemes.

Subsequently, the European Commission has taken a more active role in creating a common framework for social protection while respecting the competences of the Member States. Since 1993 it has regularly reported to the European institutions on the progress made by social protection systems towards attaining the goals set by the 1992 Recommendation. To deal with the obstacles presented by socioeconomic, social and demographic changes, the Commission launched a debate on the future of social protection. In its Communication "Modernising and improving social protection in the European Union" (European Commission, 1997a), it argued for modernisation of social protection systems so that they could continue to play a crucial role in promoting social cohesion and preventing social exclusion. In a recent Communication "A concerted strategy for modernising social protection" (European Commission, 1999a) the Commission, with the support of the Council (Council of the European Union, 1999), entered a new phase, aiming to increase co-operation between the Member States, centring on four objectives including "to ensure high quality and sustainable health protection". This states "everyone should be in a position to benefit from systems to promote health care, to treat illness, and to provide care and rehabilitation for those who need it".

In 2000 the Lisbon European Council agreed on a new strategic goal for the Union, to become the most competitive and dynamic knowledge-based economy in the world, capable of sustainable economic growth with more and better jobs and greater social cohesion. One element of this strategy is to modernise the European social model and to adapt social protection systems to ensure that work pays, to secure their long-term sustainability in the view of an ageing population, to promote social inclusion and gender equality, and to provide quality health services. To achieve these aims, co-operation between Member States should be strengthened by exchanging experiences and best practices through improved information networks.

To implement this strategy the Lisbon Council introduced the "Open Method of Co-ordination" as a means of spreading best practice and achieving greater convergence.

This method involves:

- fixing guidelines for the Union combined with specific timetables for achieving the goals;
- establishing indicators and benchmarks as a means of comparing best practice;
- translating these European guidelines into national and regional policies by setting specific targets and adopting measures, taking into account national and regional differences;
- periodic monitoring, evaluation and peer review organised as mutual learning processes.

In the absence of a legal basis in the Treaty to act on this issue, the "Open Method of Co-ordination" can be seen as a compromise between pure integration and simple co-operation. A Social Protection Committee with high level civil servants from the Member States was created to activate this social protection strategy. It was formalised during the Nice Summit and was integrated into the Treaty (Article 144). The long-term aim is to draw up European guidelines for social protection.

However, the mechanism that has, in practice, been used until now is that of dialogue, in other words, co-operation rather than co-ordination. This involves the exchange of views with the hope that this will be beneficial to all Member States; but there are no common objectives, no guidelines, no recommendations, no peer review, and no sanctions. This reflects national government's fear of intrusion by the European Union in their national arrangements. While the fundamental goals are similar, the detailed organisation of welfare states among EU Members differs widely. Another reason is that existing data on social protection provide a somewhat unclear picture of the true scope of social protection throughout the EU (de la Porte *et al.*, 2001).

So far the "Open Method of Co-ordination" has been used to examine social exclusion and pensions. Since the Göteborg European Council, in June 2001, the process was applied to health care. This European Council called on the Council in conformity with the Open Method of Co-ordination and on the basis of a joint report of the Social Protection Committee and the Economic Policy Committee to prepare a report on health and care for the elderly, to be integrated in the Broad Economic Policy Guidelines (BEPGs). The Presidency conclusions of the Laeken Summit in December 2001 added to this, stating: "particular attention will have to be given to the impact of European integration in Member States' health care systems".

To begin this process, the Commission adopted on 5 December 2001 a Communication that identifies three common objectives for European health care systems:

- guarantee access for all to health care of good quality;
- improve the transparency and quality of health care systems;
- ensure the financial viability of the health care systems (European Commission, 2001a).

In a related action, the EU has since signalled its intention to monitor the impact of the single market on health policy (European Parliament and Council of the European Union, 2002).

Conclusion

There is compelling evidence of a shared set of values that have given rise to the welfare state in all EU Member States, which are distinct from those in, for example, the US. While these values may fluctuate from time to time they appear to be relatively stable. While some politicians have advocated radical reforms from time to time, it is notable that no European country has dismantled its health care system as was done by Pinochet in Chile, with disastrous consequences (Reichard, 1996). Indeed EU Member States have now explicitly stated that equitable effective health care systems are a means of promoting both economic growth and social cohesion in Europe.

The challenge facing the EU is how to take advantage of the Single European Market to promote this goal and not to undermine it. As already noted, while Member States have clearly committed themselves to the provision of high quality health care, as Pieters and van den Bogaert (1997) have noted elsewhere, they have not so far found a way of including it in a Treaty. As a consequence, legislators and the Court have so far been guided primarily by the imperative to promote free movement. The newly established system of enhanced co-operation does, however, provide a basis from which a future Treaty revision could emerge and is highly likely to promote development of a shared, more concrete vision of how the EU might proceed.

CHAPTER 2

The Theoretical Basis and Historical Evolution of Health Policy in the European Union

Introduction

Originally embarked upon as an exclusive organisation of six west European states with common economic interests in two industries, the European experiment has come a long way since the visions of Jean Monnet and Robert Schuman were first put on paper in the Schuman Declaration of 1950. Having expanded well beyond the comparatively limited scope of the European Coal and Steel Community (ECSC) established in 1952, the European Union (EU) now wields authority in many areas, social, political and economic. Health policy is one such area, though it is undoubtedly the case that EU competencies in health policy are considerably less developed than those in other areas. This was recognised during the June 1999 European Council Meeting in Luxembourg, when incoming European Commission President, Romano Prodi, announced his intention to establish a new, separate Directorate-General (DG) for Health and Consumer Protection matters (Prodi, 1999). The new DG was established as part of the reform of the European Commission in late 1999. Admitting the need for such a body is one thing: whether it will be able to take account of and effectively deal with all Community health and health care related matters is, of course, another.

It has long been recognised that many other areas of Community policy (such as agriculture, the environment and industry) do impact on health. So although not its primary purpose, this chapter inevitably tackles many of the more important questions that face the European Union in the area of health policy.

43

I. Theoretical Reflections on EU Health Care Policy-making

The evolution of the European Community into an organisation with supranational qualities has been explored extensively in the academic literature on European integration. The aim of securing peace in post-WWII Europe was actively pursued by the region's politicians and supported by many of its academics – the latter having sought to articulate the political systems necessary for achieving this goal. Though not offering a detailed analysis of the theories and debates that emerged, this section aims to offer a theoretical perspective on the consolidation of a EU role in health policy.

Beginning with neo-functionalism and intergovernmentalism as the two most influential integration theories, we then turn to meso-level analysis in order to pick up on specific aspects of the policy process. The reason is that although macro theories are germane to "history-making decisions", they "tend to lose their explanatory power" *vis-à-vis* policy decisions (Peterson, 1995). While it may be possible to establish linkages both between and amongst the broader theories and levels of application, this chapter does not seek to make them. Instead, accepting that such an integrated approach does not do justice to the EU as a complex polity unto itself (Puchala, 1972) – predominantly because of the generalisations it assumes – we turn our attention to specific instances of where each approach is valid and what it helps to explain about the EU health policy-making process. This reflects a tacit acceptance of the EU as a new system of governance (Peterson, 1995; Sbragia, 1991; Mazey and Richardson, 1993), and one which does not readily lend itself to any singular theoretical categorisation. We do not aim to provide a coherent theory of EU health policy developments, and we do not endeavour to examine the relative merits or flaws of the approaches themselves. Rather, we aim to show where and how EU competencies in the health field have developed, by referring to different theoretical approaches where relevant, and why; therefore, there is no singular direction for health policy at Community-level.

II. The Relevance of Traditional Integration Theory

Depending on their point of departure, the early integration scholars of the 1940s tended to follow one of two main lines. The federalists and functionalists were led by the visions of Jean Monnet and the work of David Mittrany (1966) respectively. Their focus was on the end product of political integration in Europe, that is, what form the integrated Europe should take. The transactionalists meanwhile, headed by Karl

Deutsch (1966), sought to understand the conditions requisite for political integration to be possible in the first place (Cram, 1996). Both approaches served to generate the academic debate that would later culmi-
nate in the development of neo-functionalism as the (then) leading
theory of European integration.

A. Neo-functionalism – The "Spill Over" Effect

During the 1950s and 1960s, as a critique of deficiencies in the functionalist conception, neo-functionalism became the theory of choice for
academics, particularly amongst American social scientists, with Ernst
Haas (1968) at the fore. By combining the competition element in the
political process of traditional pluralist thinking with the (necessarily)
gradual nature of political change understanding proffered by Mittrany,
the neo-functionalists sought to show how the European political process was dependent as much on political action as economic determinism.

Central to this understanding was disproving the functionalist idea
that a meaningful and lasting distinction could be made between policies
involving functional or technical questions, and those which were more
political or constitutional in nature. Health policy proves their point.
Although the distinction may initially seem applicable – at least in ideal
circumstances – health policy is not a uni-dimensional concept or policy
field. So although it might be the case that health issues are indeed
specific and sensitive enough to merit attention of their own, in practice,
health policy proves to be as much a political as a technical (and economic) issue. Member States are, therefore, particularly sensitive where
health matters are concerned (Mossialos and Permanand, 2000).

Neo-functionalist theory helps explain how health came to be part of
the Community agenda. What is arguably its best-known premise, the
concept of "spill over" – where Community authority develops or
evolves as a result of policy developments in related fields – is particularly relevant. The idea of integration taking place in small steps where
"pressure in one sector could demand integration (or changes in standards) in order to complete the process of policy change" (Church,
1996) coincides with efforts to establish a health policy role for the
Community. While it has been shown that EU health competencies have
developed primarily to promote a common market (McKee *et al.*, 1996),
we argue that some aspects (though not all) of the present Community
framework seem to have evolved as "spill over" from other provisions
relating to this process.

Crucial to the "spill over" premise was that the integration process
would prove self-sustaining. In developing this idea as an inheritance
from Mittrany, the neo-functionalists attempted to gauge the relevance

and role of the new European Community institutions to the integration process. They argued that these new bodies could (and did) foster integration of their own accord as supranational constructs. While the role of the ECJ as guardian and instigator of Community law, which supersedes national legislation, may have been the embodiment of this idea, the Luxembourg Compromise of 1966 shattered it. French President de Gaulle precipitated a constitutional crisis over the use of qualified majority voting *vis-à-vis* common market decisions, which culminated in agreement on the need for unanimity to pass legislation in instances where "very important [national] interests are at stake". Health and welfare policy fall within this caveat. Without engaging the specifics of the Luxembourg Compromise, it did serve to underline the point that the integration process was not entirely self-sustaining, and that the Member States remained very much in charge of their own destiny; especially where sensitive matters of national interest were implicated. Later, however, with the Single European Act (SEA) of 1986, the integration process was revived, leading to neo-functionalism and its brand of "spill over" specifically.

Several health and health care-related areas within the mandate of the EU can be explained by "spill over". It would appear that these single market aspects of health policy have (necessarily) developed because of Community activities in the broader field of social regulation. The two are, of course, related but Community competencies in the two areas have developed quite separately (Huelshoff, 1992). It is, however, worth noting that social regulation aspects of the single market framework are considerably more developed (Majone, 1993).

For instance, in the area of occupational health and safety regulation, the Community had to establish uniform workplace safety (and environment) standards in order to ensure the working of the single market. The post-1985 Directives on health and safety were passed primarily because the Community wanted to avoid the danger of "social and ecological dumping" (Eichener, 1997), where business would be able to take advantage of differences in standards, and hence costs, between Member States. The Community thus sought pre-emptively to avoid a weakening of health and safety measures resulting from increased competition, by regulating occupational health and safety standards upwards. European policy-makers from both the Commission and national governments recognised that extending the Community's competencies into social areas would in turn benefit its economic functioning. In other words, by trying to establish a "level playing field" for business, it would advance the progress of a single market. This generalisation does not, however, account for differing interests within the wider business community, and in this vein it has been argued elsewhere that larger firms have tended to support higher levels of protection as a means of keeping ahead of smaller competitors less able to meet stricter standards (Scharpf, 1997).

Another example of this interpretation of "spill over" in the health field, and one in keeping with more contemporary events, is the current degree of attention being paid to food safety. The recent occurrence of food scares in Europe – Bovine Spongiform Encephalopathy (BSE) and New Variant Creutzfeldt-Jakob Disease (nvCJD), dioxin contamination, and the use of sewage slurry in animal feed – has in part undermined consumer confidence in food safety regulation (whether at national or EU-level) (Smith *et al.*, 1999), and in turn has (had) ramifications for the single market *i.e.* the world-wide ban on British beef, or the recalling of a cola drink from the Belgian market. Here it is interesting to note that the media have tended to refer to the new Directorate-General established under the Presidency of Romano Prodi as simply the "DG for Food Safety" rather than acknowledging its more complete role in health and consumer protection. It would appear to be the case, therefore, that food safety has come to dominate the EU health agenda largely as the result of the "spill over" from single market (trade) issues.

B. Intergovernmentalism – Retaining National Control

Despite the numerous health-related developments created by the "spill over" effect, it is obviously not the sole determinant of the Community's health competencies. It is clear that the Member States do retain a considerable degree of autonomy where important national interests such as health are concerned. That European integration does not succeed without Member State support – that "spill over" does not have unchecked momentum – is one of the key tenets of intergovernmentalism as the other main theory of European integration.

Developed out of the realist position in traditional international relations theory, with Stanley Hoffmann (1966) as its leading proponent, the intergovernmentalist perspective evolved as a critique of neo-functionalism. In seeking to maintain a lid on the potential intergovernmental "can of worms" – for there are varying interpretations relating to institutions ("institutional intergovernmentalism"), area fields ("functional intergovernmentalism"), and the "three pillars" of the Treaties (formal "intergovernmentalism") (Haltern, 1995) – we remain within a simple understanding which asserts the pre-eminence of the Member States over the Community institutions in the integration process. That said, it should be borne in mind from the outset that one of the major flaws in this conception is that the intergovernmental focus on individual actors (Member States) pursuing self-interested goals may serve to elucidate their behaviour in the integration process, but does not necessarily explain policy outcomes.

Health policy in the Community thus raises several important points. First, the issue of national self-interest may (implicitly) help to explain, in general terms, why health policy has not been devolved to Community authority by the Member States. For the Community to exercise a wider role in health policy would require a new Treaty provision. It would necessarily be one that recognised public health as a multidimensional concept – both in theory and practice – rather than limiting it only to tackling specific diseases and "taking health into account in other Community policies". Member States are not prepared to give the Community such a role primarily because they themselves have not been able to address some of these key issues themselves. Notwithstanding their acceptance of concepts such as solidarity and universal health care coverage, it is noteworthy that, historically, European governments have, for political and practical reasons, been unable – if not unwilling – to institute the changes that a wider health policy framework would require (Mossialos and Permanand, 2000).

For many European governments since the Second World War, especially those that were liberal or right wing, the more centralised state role this type of framework would necessitate proved ideologically untenable. Accordingly, they did not attempt to make the connection between the wider determinants of health and a comprehensive health policy framework. As has been summarised elsewhere, "pursuing a social agenda in a world dominated by neo-liberal assumptions about the primacy of needs of the economy has not proven easy for health advocates" (Baum, 1999). In the UK for instance, although a national health system (NHS) was already in place, the pro-market, conservative government of Margaret Thatcher did not seek to address the question of social inequalities in health. Even where ideology was not so much the mitigating factor, and social democratic parties were in power such as in Germany, Austria and the Netherlands, the social insurance-based health care systems they employed were unable to accommodate the changes a wider health policy approach would involve (Mossialos and Permanand, 2000).

A second way, in which intergovernmentalist theory provides a useful backdrop to health policy in the Community, is via Hoffmann's division between matters of so-called "high" *versus* "low" politics (Hoffmann, 1966). The former encompasses security, defence and foreign policy, while the latter is concerned with welfare and economic policy. This differentiation was designed to show the limits of the neo-functionalist argument that integration was a self-sustaining dynamic. It could not be taken as a foregone conclusion that the Member States would accept integration in areas of "high" politics simply because they were more or less agreed on "low" politics concerns such as single market tariff elimination, and the requisite social regulatory policy implications. In terms of positioning health policy within this division, neither category seems ideal; though perhaps by association with welfare policy, health policy would qualify as a "low" policy area. In accepting this, it still should be pointed out that while health policy may indeed be linked to questions of welfare, the two do not always amount to the same thing. Nevertheless, assuming that health policy is indeed a "low" politics matter for the Community – where intergovernmental co-operation could be expected – why then has there been national resistance to its so-called europeanisation? The reason is that for national governments aspects of health and health care are in fact "high" policy areas. Thus, as Member States decide the pace and direction of integration – and not the European institutions through some sort of momentum of their own – it ought not be surprising that health policy remains predominantly a national-level concern. The exception is those aspects of health and health care policy that fall within the single market context and developed primarily through "spill over" (Mossialos and Permanand, 2000).

Community health and health care competences, therefore, exist where economic priorities are concerned ("low" politics) but do not involve the exercise of executive powers with respect to developing a comprehensive health policy framework at EU-level ("high politics"). As such, a competence division exists where health and some health care matters are currently a shared responsibility between the Community and Member States.

Finally, a third level on which intergovernmentalism is relevant to health policy in the Community is with respect to the more recent liberal intergovernmentalist approach. According to Moravcsik (1995), this perspective takes the emphasis on the Member States one step further and questions the whole validity of supranational decision-making itself. The focus here is on interdependencies between national decision-making and international co-operation. The argument is that although national governments are the main actors and retain control over the integration process, they are motivated (if not in some cases forced) to pursue further integration because of a combination of externalities and particular internal circumstances. In this vein, one can look to the pressures exerted by the global trade liberalisation regimes of the General Agreement on Tariffs and Trade (GATT), and now the World Trade Organization (WTO) as giving rise to further integration in Europe (McKee and Mossialos, 2000). Or else, on a more policy-specific level, it may be in part because of potential negative externalities such as air and water pollution, that Member States have agreed EU environmental standards.

According to theories of liberal intergovernmentalism, Member States in response to these pressures are willing to pool endeavour and effort towards further integration as a manner of consolidating their position relative to others. In relation to health policy, Member States are thus open to persuasion that certain aspects of policy, such as occupational health and safety and those matters relating to the single market (*i.e.* free movement of goods and professionals) are better regulated on their behalf by the EU. Others, which are more sensitive such as health care financing and the pricing of medicines, are guarded jealously. Leaving aside the deficiencies in this wider assessment – for the European institutions have indeed had a major part to play in the integration process – the liberal intergovernmentalist approach (and intergovernmentalism in general) does offer some insight into what motivates the integration process in Europe; and in turn, why certain aspects of health policy have been mandated by the Community and others not. Despite this, it should be noted that neither neo-functionalism nor intergovernmentalism has been shown to generate testable hypotheses regarding the conditions under which supranational institutions exert an independent causal influence on either EU governance or the process of European integration (Pollack, 1997).

III. Perspectives on Process

The duality or competence sharing between the Community and Member States where health policy is concerned is perhaps captured in the understanding of European law as supranational and European policy-making as intergovernmental (Weiler, 1994). More specifically, health-related policy-making is co-operative, as many of the issues remain decided at national level. European legislation meanwhile finds its constitutional basis in the Treaties and, via the ECJ, much of it supersedes that of the Member States. Infringements against Treaty stipulations can result in sanction for the offender, though the development of EU policies/competencies within the framework set down by the Treaties first requires each Member States to agree in the Council of Ministers. Health policy finds itself in the grey area of the middle.

Related to the broader theories of integration and the intergovernmental-supranational dichotomy which, after all, was at the heart of the differences between neo-functionalist and intergovernmental thinking, is the question of process. The original EEC Treaty of Rome (1957) introduced two political dynamics known as "positive" and "negative" integration towards a European common market. These two processes are relevant to our discussion on Community health policy as they support the earlier arguments regarding "spill over" and intergovernmental bargaining over sensitive policy areas. Positive integration involves the establishment of common policies to define the conditions under which European markets operate, whilst negative integration is concerned with the elimination of (national) barriers to the free movement of goods and services within the Community (Scharpf, 1996). The former involves the active harmonisation of national regulations such as in the fields of consumer protection and environmental risks, and goes through the Council of Ministers (intergovernmental). The latter involves the re-scinding of national authority – liberalisation – to the Community through tariff and quota reductions, and is therefore a more straightfor-ward process given the Treaty obligations (supranational).

The two processes were envisaged to run concomitantly towards the implementation of the common market by 1969, but the Luxembourg Compromise of 1966 represented a major setback. The requirement that unanimity be achieved in the Council of Ministers resulted in an awk-ward decision-making process over single market issues – though the Luxembourg Compromise itself was rarely invoked – and meant that negative integration came to the fore.

This hindrance to positive integration accorded the European Court a prominent role in the integration process as arbiter over matters involv-ing the single market. Indeed, through a considerable amount of case law generated between 1970 and 1985, the Court has been credited with giving rise to the Single European Act of 1986 via a process of negative integration (Stone Sweet and Caporaso, 1998). In other areas, however, the Court was successful in generating positive integration. For instance, in the broader field of social policy – as separate from those areas of social regulation related to the single market – a host of legal decisions has granted the Community a greater role than was perhaps envisaged in 1957. A Charter outlining a Community framework for the development and implementation of proposals in social fields has existed since 1989. This is in part because social matters (health and welfare included) have been regarded as "low" politics matters within the Community context. Nonetheless, the Court's role in health has been a combination of posi-tive and negative integration.

Expansive rulings in some cases of social policy have ensured the Court a leading role in issues of gender equity and social protection, and have resulted in national changes that would otherwise have taken considerably longer to occur (Pierson, 1998). Where health matters are concerned, consumer protection issues, food safety and environmental interests fall within this pro-active ECJ mandate; and in many Member

States (particularly those of southern Europe) it has resulted in completely new legislation in the absence of earlier national regimes (Majone, 1996). In areas such as these, therefore, the EU legal system has had a positive (integration) effect on health policy in the Community.

In this vein, it is also relevant to consider the distinction between product regulation and process regulation. Product regulation involves the establishment of common standards on goods and services; where intergovernmental agreement can be expected because differing national product safety and quality requirements would undermine the market harmonisation goals of Articles 30 and 34. Articles 30 and 34 (now Articles 28 and 29 of the Amsterdam Treaty) read: "Quantitative restrictions on imports and all measures having equivalent effect shall be prohibited between Member States" and "Quantitative restrictions on exports and all measures having equivalent effect shall be prohibited between Member States". Thus, despite derogations under Article 30 on the grounds of public health, public policy or national security, amongst others, it is assumed that Member States will reach agreement on product regulation because of their common interest in the single market. Article 36 (now Article 30 of the Amsterdam Treaty) reads in part:

> The provisions of Articles 28 (ex 30) and 29 (ex 34) shall not preclude prohibition or restrictions on imports, exports or goods in transit justified on the grounds of public morality, public policy or public security; the protection of health and life of humans, animals or plants; the protection of national treasures possessing artistic, historic or archaeological value; or the protection of industrial and commercial property. Such prohibitions or restrictions shall not, however, constitute a means of arbitrary discrimination or a disguised restriction on trade between Member States.

This is not the case for process regulations such as environmental and occupational safety requirements. Here, the absence of a "Euro-regime" could in theory mean Member States cutting back on national standards to increase competitiveness (Scharpf, 1996). The incentive for Member States to seek harmonisation in these areas is of course to avoid having to compete on an unequal footing with those countries with more lax standards. But, it was only with the Single European Act that EU-level regulations became possible, if not necessary. And even then – as was mentioned earlier – it was up to the Commission to ensure that a situation of social and ecological dumping did not take place. Positive integration can thus be linked predominantly with progress in the harmonisation of product regulation, though it has had a much weaker impact on harmonising process regulation.

In section II, we have reviewed two of the main interpretations of EU policy-making: neo-functionalism and intergovernmentalism as well as perspectives on process. There are, however, more theoretical approaches such as the regulatory approach, which emphasises the role of the rule-makers and civil society in the decision-making process or theories of consensual or participatory federalism, the theory of integration through the law or new institutionalist approaches (Yataganas, 2001). Nonetheless, there is no all-encompassing theoretical or analytical framework that could explain all aspects of European integration.

As Yataganas (2001) points out:

> While it is true that the Council of Ministers lends itself more to an intergovernmental analysis, it is equally plain that the Commission and in particular the ECJ call for a more constitutionalist approach, while a regulatory approach is also useful for studying complex decision-making procedures, such as the co-decision procedure between Parliament and the Council and in particular what is known as committee procedure or comitology.

We turn now to discuss the role of the European Court of Justice.

IV. The Role of the European Court of Justice

Beyond the social matters mentioned earlier, the ECJ has played a major part in raising health policy issues. This stems from its role in "constitutionalising" the Treaties into something of a European charter, in turn promoting a juridification of the decision-making process (Dehousse, 2000). Along with the Commission, the Parliament and the Council, the Court was one of the original four institutions as established under the Treaty of Rome; Articles 164-168A refer to the ECJ and its powers "[…] to ensure in its interpretation of the Treaty that the law is observed". Its three main purposes can be summarised as: to judge in disputes brought by the Commission or the Member States against the Member States – concerning questions about the legality of action and non-compliance; judicial review of institutions regarding damages, the annulment of actions, and the requirement of action; and to act as preliminary reference procedure *i.e.* a system whereby national courts can refer questions on EC law to the ECJ, which will decide and then pass it back down (this constitutes the majority of its work). In practice, its role often involves filling in the gaps that have developed with respect to the application of the Single European Market.

Before the seminal Van Gend en Loos Case in 1963[1], the Court had a limited role. In this case a private firm sought to invoke EC law against the Dutch customs authority – something that had hitherto not been attempted – and the ECJ decided that individuals did in fact have the right to invoke EC law. It proved a controversial decision in that the ruling was based on the argument that EC law was *sui generis*, as it marked the creation of an entire new legal order, which allowed for individual invocation. More importantly, it resulted in the principle of "direct effect" applying to all primary Treaty Articles. This means that Member States must directly enforce EU law that is clear and precise enough to require no implementing legislation on the part of the Member States, and that such law is relevant and can be invoked by private citizens.

Direct effect had originally only been applied to narrow Treaty provisions, but since the 1970s the idea of horizontal direct effect meant that individuals could take each other to the higher Court. Thus, there are two types of direct effect: horizontal, which is applicable to individuals such that they can defend their rights against other individuals or legal entities *i.e.* companies; and vertical, which enables citizens to defend their rights against the state. However, while Regulations have both effects, the Court ruled in the 1986 Marshall Case[2] that Directives (as the most commonly used instrument) could only be invoked against a state, as they must be transposed into national law, and were thus only vertical. It should, of course, be noted that this decision was taken in the face of much dissent.

To compensate for the lack of horizontal direct effect over Directives, however, the ECJ developed doctrine of "state liability" where the state can be held liable for all national infringements of EU Directives. This was based on the 1991 Francovich Case[3] when the Italian government was held liable to pay redundancy compensation to employees when a firm went bankrupt. This was because the Italian government had failed to transpose a Directive on such "guarantee funds". The decision caused problems as the Italian courts queried the possibility of suing the state for its failure to provide the required institutions. They concluded that it was indeed possible, but only providing that the losses

---

[1] European Court of Justice, C-26/62, Judgement of 05/02/1963, Van Gend en Loos *v.* Nederlandse Administratie der Belastingen.

[2] Marshall *v.* Southampton and South-West Hampshire Area Health Authority, (1986) ECR 723, (1986) 1 CMLR 688.

[3] European Court of Justice, C-6/90, Judgement of 19/11/1991, Francovich and Bonifaci.

were incurred due to state failings. The doctrine of state liability/ responsibility that resulted led to an increase in Member States compliance with Directives, and indeed, direct effect has resulted in a massive increase in the number of cases brought before national courts in the name of European law. Direct effect thus means that European law is more like national than international law, where individuals cannot invoke international law unless it has been transposed into domestic law.

The other major principle established by the Court regarding the *sui generis* status of European law was the "doctrine of supremacy". In the 1964 Costa Case[4], the Court ruled that, in the event of conflict, national law was to cede to European law. This was not accepted quite so easily as direct effect, and the Italian, German and French courts in particular engaged in lengthy negotiations with the ECJ. Human rights protection was a main issue, and the German and Italian constitutional courts retained the right to review Community law against their own human rights standards. The Court, however, went on to include human rights protection as a fundamental principle of European law, and has since built up a considerable volume of case law. Supremacy would appear a logical corollary of direct effect, and has of course ensured that the ECJ plays a major role in the integration process; in particular through single market harmonisation of individual sectors.

Direct effect promotes legal integration amongst the Member States, and as a corollary, political and economic integration *vis-à-vis* specific rulings. Thus, Cases such as Dassonville[5], which rendered impediments to intra-Community trade illegal; and Cassis de Dijon[6] which led to the principle of "mutual recognition" – which itself led to the Single European Market – fostered economic integration. Direct effect also led to an active role for the Court in establishing Community-wide gender equality *i.e.* the Defrenne Case in 1976[7], and Article 119 EC (ex 109h) on "equal pay" was in essence re-interpreted by the Court. The supremacy of EU law also represents a "europeanisation" of national laws and provisions. Together, they represent the underlying legal-constitutionalist doctrines of a federal legal system.

---

[4]   European Court of Justice, C-6/64, Judgement of 03/06/1964, Costa *v*. E.N.E.L.

[5]   European Court of Justice, C- 8/74, Judgement of 11/07/1974, Procureur du Roi Benoît & Dassonville.

[6]   European Court of Justice, C-120/78, Judgement of 20/02/1979, Rewe-Zentral A.G. *v.* Bundesmonopolverwaltung für Branntwein (Cassis de Dijon).

[7]   European Court of Justice, C-43/75, Judgement of 08/04/1976, Defrenne *v.* Sabena (Defrenne II).

Finally the ECJ has the sole power to decide if a rule of Community law is invalid. It is also important to note the extraordinary and unique procedure laid down in Article 226 EC (ex 169), which imposes a responsibility on Member States that is unprecedented in international law and highlights the supranational virtue of the Treaties. Article 226 EC (ex 169) grants the European Commission the right to initiate infringement proceedings against Member States that have failed to fulfil a Treaty obligation.

Consequently, it is not surprising that many analysts have argued that the strong legal dimension has had a major influence on the policy process: policy-makers must take account of the legal meanings of the texts they draw up; policy advocates look for legal rules to achieve their objectives; policy reformers can sometimes employ case law to alter the impact of EU policies; and choosing the right Treaty provision to apply can be key, as the 2000 Tobacco Directive showed (Wallace and Wallace, 2000). That said, one ought equally to recognise that the ECJ's integrationist activism has not been linear (Chalmers, 1997), and that it has often responded to the pace of integration rather than generating it. Nevertheless, we see that the Court has indeed had a considerable, if predominantly indirect, hand in the field of health policy.

There are, for instance, numerous rulings covering health care, medicines, the environment, and workplace health and safety amongst others (Palm *et al.*, 2000). Indeed, the Court has delivered several rulings *vis-à-vis* pharmaceuticals (see Chapter 5) and their distribution in the Community, especially as pertains to the practice of parallel trade (Hancher, 2000). On the other hand, pharmaceutical companies have themselves been successful in many of their lobbying endeavours at both national and EU-level on specific issues; such as being granted extended patent protection on their products (Shechter, 1998), that also contributes to the shape of the Community's health policy mandate. Without looking any further at the Court and its unique position, it is sufficient to note that it has developed as a major contributor to EU health policy.

We now describe a synoptic history of establishing Community health and health care competencies.

V. Establishing Community Health and Health Care Competencies: A Synoptic History

A. The Early Treaties

The rationale behind the foundation of the European Coal and Steel Community (ECSC) indicates that European integration has for the most part been economically driven even though political motivation was the underlying factor (Tsoukalis, 1998). Despite being an outwardly economic enterprise, the ECSC was equally a political undertaking. It was set up as much to present a unified industrial front in the coal and steel industries, as it was to help stabilise post-WWII Western Europe (El-Agraa, 1994). This was in keeping with the federalist and institutional vision of a "United States of Europe" proposed after the First World War (WWI) as a manner of ending the historical cycle of wars in Europe (Mazey, 1996). Originally signed by seven of the current fifteen EU Member States, the 1952 Treaty of Paris establishing the ECSC set the stage for future and further European integration.

The ECSC was an ambitious plan, not only because it established a large free trade area but also because it laid the foundations for what later became the European "common market". This required the setting up of regulatory, overseeing, and standards bodies, which gave the new European organisation its first characteristics of supranationalism. These characteristics have continued to be strengthened and "fine-tuned" through subsequent Treaties. Social concerns, far less specifically health-related ones, were not an integral part of the Paris Treaty's provisions; although in Article 55 it did make allowances for research and co-operation between Member States with respect to the health and safety of workers in the coal and steel industries. The Commission was expected to "promote technical and economic research relating to the production and increased use of coal and steel and to occupational safety in the coal and steel industries". Achieving this involved raising levies on Community coal and steel products, and the use of part of these levies to finance coal and steel research programmes (Mossialos and Permanand, 2000).

In 1957 the Treaty of Rome was signed against the uncertain backdrop of a burgeoning Cold War and the still fresh memories of the Korean War. It sought to build upon the economic successes of the ECSC, as well as readying Europe to face the potential "Communist threat" posed by the geographically proximate and influential Soviet Union. It established two separate contracts, the European Atomic Energy Community (Euratom) and the European Economic Community (EEC). The former includes a chapter on health and safety at work, and led to the early establishment of standards and safety levels for protection against ionising radiation, not only of workers, but also the general population. The latter – which came simply to be known as the European Community – was, however, arguably the more important of the two. More than just consolidating the free trade area initially instituted by the ECSC, it sought to "promote throughout the Community a harmonious development of economic activities, a continuous and balanced expansion, an increase in stability, an accelerated raising of the standard of living and closer relations between the states belonging to it".

This objective obviously implied an expansion (or at least change) in focus, by indicating that the Community would necessarily be better served in its economic undertakings (single market) through an additional commitment to social affairs. It was nevertheless already clear that the free movement of goods and services under a free trade agreement would involve medicines, biotechnology products, health insurance, and have implications for health care; yet these issues were not dealt with specifically (Cadreau, 1991). Health policy (including public health) did not appear as a separate issue within this proposed social agenda, and was instead incorporated within the more general field of health and safety at work.

Between the 1960s and early 1980s there was a relative lapse in interest in the integration process in Europe; a period generally referred to as "eurosclerosis". Nevertheless, during this period several Scientific Committees were established to look at specific Community-relevant issues (some of which were health-related). It was not until 1986 with the Single European Act, however, that the integration process was substantially re-awakened.

The SEA established 1992 as the date for the institution of a true Single European Market for the free movement of capital, goods, services and labour between signatories. To achieve this, the SEA not only recognised, but also emphasised, that greater and closer co-operation in social, economic and environmental affairs between Members would be needed; such that renewed impetus could be injected into the integration process. Nevertheless, as the extension of the Community's interests into social fields (and health specifically) was only undertaken within the context of completing this single market by the 1992 deadline, the SEA was regarded by some as not going far enough (Robertson, 1992; Curwen, 1992), particularly given the earlier, more social implications of the Treaty of Rome.

Thus, despite acknowledgement that the SEA would have an effect on health and health care outcomes in the Community (Altenstetter, 1992a), only those health-related matters that would foster development of the single market were dealt with. Although concrete social matters were given more prominence under the text of the SEA, health policy (including public health) was again not treated as a distinct policy area. Rather, it was once more subsumed within the broader framework of health and safety at work. Nevertheless, the SEA did result in an extension of the Community's scope for action in the field of occupational health and safety, and environmental and consumer protection (relating particularly to foodstuffs, pharmaceuticals and so-called "dangerous substances"), as well as establishing the legal basis for the single market to take consumer health protection requirements into consideration (Mossialos and Permanand, 2000).

B. The Single European Market

Recalling the more theoretical issues raised in section II, we now consider what the direct results of the Single European Market on the EU's health competence has been. One of the most obvious outcomes of the 1986 SEA is that early Community initiatives covering health matters reflect more of an economic and single market priority than they espouse health concerns. It "[...] required the Commission to take, as a base, a high level of protection in its proposals concerning health, safety and environment and consumer protection, as they relate to the working of the Single European Market" (Mossialos and Abel-Smith, 1996). One of its long-standing aims in the health field for instance, has been the establishment of a system for the mutual recognition of professional qualifications in the Community (including doctors, dentists, nursing and paramedical staff) (McKee *et al.*, 1996). With the intention of allowing doctors who have qualified in one Member State to practice in another Member State of their choice, the Community has adopted a series of Directives [two in 1975 (Council of the European Communities, 1975a and b), a third in 1986 (Council of the European Communities, 1986: 26), and a fourth – incorporating the previous three – in 1993 (Council of the European Communities, 1993a)] (see also Chapter 3).

Another example of health decisions being taken within a single market context pertains to medicines in Europe. Despite the creation of a unique body, the European Agency for the Evaluation of Medicinal Products (EMEA) – unique in that it is not simply concerned with the dissemination of information, but is in fact quasi-regulatory – the Community has failed to address key issues concerning the pricing and reimbursement of pharmaceuticals. The focus has instead been on regulating market authorisation requirements, advertising and package-labelling rules, and the information content of inserts for pharmaceutical preparations. While this is partly due to the subsidiarity principle – under which matters pertaining to national health systems are beyond Community competencies, other important issues associated with a medicines industry have not been addressed (Mossialos and Abel-Smith, 1996).

The creation of the single market has, therefore, had a dual role in the development of a EU health policy framework. On the one hand, as it enables the Community to regulate only in some areas, it has not had a fundamental impact on national health policy regimes. Consequently, it has been argued that national health policy frameworks and health care systems will continue to prevail in the EU (Altenstetter, 1992b). On the other hand, the Single European Market (SEM) has served as an important magnet securing intergovernmental agreement on the economic aspects associated with health policy in Europe; although it must be stressed that these do not amount to a coherent strategy.

This trade-off notwithstanding, the single market has nevertheless shown that health policy matters are not the sole purview of national policy-makers. They are now divided between the Community and the Member States, even if the balance is not an equitable one.

C. The "Modern" Treaties

1. The Treaty on European Union (Maastricht)

After the SEA came a series of Intergovernmental Conferences (IGCs) to work out the specifics of achieving the single market on time. These in turn led to the Treaty on European Union (TEU) in 1992. In amending the Treaty of Rome, the TEU (Maastricht Treaty) represented the formalisation of the Community's first real powers with respect to health policy, although it should be pointed out that an earlier impetus for the development of a Community role in cancer came from a 1985 Council of Europe Decision inviting the Commission to propose such a programme (Richards and Smith, 1994). Equally, it is important to note that, prior to the Maastricht negotiations, the Community Charter of the Fundamental Rights of Workers (referred to simply as the Social Charter) was signed in 1989 and had implicit relevance to health matters. Although the Charter may only have been a general articulation of a wider philosophy for the Community rather than addressing specific matters such as health – and was perhaps undermined by the UK's refusal to sign – it did serve to highlight particular areas that were then implemented under the Maastricht Treaty (Ham, 1991).

Specifically, the new Treaty gave the Community concrete legal competencies related to health policy via two new provisions. First, Article 3(o) empowered the Community to "contribute to the attainment of a high level of health protection" for its citizens. Second, and with regard to achieving this objective, Article 129 (since referred to as the "public health Article") delineated a rudimentary framework whereby the Community would meet this obligation. It would do so by "encouraging co-operation between the Member States and, if necessary, lending support to their action". Community action would involve only "the prevention of diseases, in particular the major health scourges, including drug dependence". The promotion of "research into their causes and their transmission, as well as health information and education" were specified as the primary means by which the Community was to achieve its objectives. In terms of rhetoric, perhaps the key phrase in this new provision, at least as regarded the potential wider implications of the Article, was that "health protection requirements shall form a constituent part of the Community's other policies". This seemed to indicate that issues related to health policy and public health would necessarily be taken into consideration in the future development of all other Community policies; something that both the Community institutions and the Member States would have to respect.

Yet, despite this apparently clear statement of intent, it has proven vague both in interpretation and practice. When combined with the other provisions of the Article, particularly the specification of disease prevention and health protection as the Community's two most important priority areas – the new Article failed to provide a comprehensive definition of public health that could be used in Community policy-making. It is also interesting to note that in other areas specified in the Maastricht Treaty, the commitment to such a horizontal approach has been decidedly stronger; most notably in environmental protection, where Article 130(r) includes the provision that "Environmental protection requirements must be integrated into the definition and implementation of other Community polices".

Articles 129 and 3(o) were not the only new provisions to appear under the Maastricht Treaty, and neither are they the only ones impacting on health in the Community (Box 2.1). The TEU also introduced Article 3(b), which is otherwise known as the principle of subsidiarity. Establishing the principle that the EU may act "only if and in so far as the objectives of the proposed action cannot be sufficiently achieved by the Member States and can therefore, by reason of the scale or effects of the proposed action, be better achieved by the Community", subsidiarity empowers the Community to act only in instances where it can be more successful than an individual Member State in achieving a particular objective. In the field of health, subsidiarity applied particularly to health care financing and provision, which were to remain the purview of Member States. While originally developed by then Commission President Jacques Delors as a means of developing a more transparent legislative process, subsidiarity in effect became a "political panacea for the Community's manifest ills" (Dinan, 1994). The subjectivity of interpretation meant that both the Community and Member States could invoke subsidiarity in order to either keep out, or else include, the other in various policy areas.

The subsidiarity principle has been criticised as vague and ineffective. Whilst it has, on the one hand, been interpreted as representing a guiding principle for Community policy, on the other, it appears as a legal restraint on Community activities. As a policy that was decidedly more political than legal in its implementation, subsidiarity has served to further hinder the Community's already limited role in matters relating to health by ensuring that certain matters, specifically those related to health services, remain the responsibility of Member States. Here it is interesting to note an informal remark made by Jacques Delors to then British Prime Minister John Major at the 1995 European Summit meeting in Essen; that, in his view, health was in fact an "inappropriate area" for EU involvement (Brown, 1995). This seems a somewhat ironic comment following years of Commission activity to guarantee the Community a more influential role in EU health matters. Nevertheless, from the framework established by the Maastricht Treaty, several Community-level initiatives and action programmes in the field of public health were developed.

Box 2.1: Articles in the Maastricht Treaty
with an Influence on Health

Article(s)	Provision
3(o)	Stipulates that the Community will contribute to the attainment of a high level of health protection for its citizens
3(s)	Defines that one of the objectives of the Community should be to contribute to the strengthening of consumer protection
30	Prohibits quantitative import restrictions between Member States
34	Prohibits quantitative export restrictions between Member States
36	Permits restrictions on imports and all measures having equivalent effect on grounds of the protection of health and life of humans, animals or plants
43	Agriculture
48-51	Free movement of workers
52-58	Rights of establishment
59-66	Free movement of services including insurance
75(1)	The need to introduce measures to improve transport safety
100-102	The approximation of laws related to the single market
118	Prevention of occupational accidents and diseases and occupational hygiene
129	Health policy and Public health
129a	Consumer protection
130f-130q	Research
130r	(130r-130t of Title XVI) Environment and protection of human health (Environment)
117-125	Related to social provisions and the setting of a Social Fund
130a-	Economic and social cohesion; the Protocol on social policy; and the
130e	Agreement on social policy concluded between the Member States with the exemption of the United Kingdom.
130u	Fostering economic and social development of the developing countries.

Looking at the particulars of Article 129 (Box 2.2), while it may initially have appeared to represent exactly that which the Community was lacking, namely, specific competencies in the field of health policy (including public health) – this proved not to be the case. First, in citing "the prevention of disease" as the Community's main objective, it did not provide a real definition of public health around which wide-ranging competencies could be established. Rather, it led to a framework based almost entirely on specific diseases, despite some Commission officials having expressed their desire for a wider interpretation (Watson, 1994).

Box 2.2: Article 129 of the Maastricht Treaty on European Union

The Community shall contribute towards ensuring a high level of human health protection by encouraging co-operation between the Member States and, if necessary, lending support to their action.

Community action shall be directed towards the prevention of diseases, in particular the major health scourges, including drug dependence, by promoting research into their causes and their transmission, as well as health information and education.

Health protection requirements shall form a constituent part of the Community's other policies.

Member States shall, in liaison with the Commission, co-ordinate among themselves their policies and programmes in the area referred to in paragraph 1. The Commission may, in close contact with other Member States, take any useful initiative to promote such co-ordination.

The Community and the Members shall foster co-operation with third countries and the competent international organisations in the sphere of public health.

In order to contribute to the achievement of the objectives referred to in this Article, the Council:

- Acting in accordance with the procedure referred to in Article 189b, after consulting the Economic and Social Committee and the Committee of the Regions, shall adopt incentive measures, excluding any harmonisation of the laws and regulations of the Member States; and
- Acting by a qualified majority on a proposal from the Commission, shall adopt Recommendations.

Second, a successful (health) policy initiative requires a clear view and statement of aims, priorities, limitations, responsibilities, methods and resource implications; and the new Article contained very little of these (Merkel, 1995). Also, it was unclear what a "high level of human health protection" exactly meant, let alone how this could be measured.

Later, in a 1995 report published by Directorate-General V of the European Commission (Employment, Industrial Relations and Social Affairs), the Community defined "protection" as enabling the Commission to assess proposed policies to ensure that they "do not have an adverse impact on health, or create conditions which undermine the promotion of health" (European Commission, 1995a). Although responsibility for attaining this objective was laid upon the Community as a whole, if the Community could only be involved through the encouragement of "co-operation between Member States" and "lending support" where necessary, the question arose as to who was in fact responsible for carrying out the necessary measures. Furthermore, in establishing that Community intervention was only possible with respect to encouraging national co-operation in the field of disease prevention (specifically the "major health scourges"), and in encouraging collaboration with third countries and international organisations, it was clear that the Commission's role was supplementary rather than pro-active (Lane, 1993).

Equally vague were the measures necessary to undertake these goals. With little more than catch-phrases to the effect of "co-ordinate", "foster", and "contribute", very little was stipulated as to how the provisions could be implemented; especially with harmonisation measures having been ruled out. The term "incentive measures" was also undefined within the provisions. Although a definition was later specified as

> Community measures designed to encourage co-operation between Member States or to support or supplement their action in the areas concerned, including where appropriate through financial support for Community programmes or national or co-operative measures designed to achieve the objective of these Articles (European Council, 1992),

Article 129 did not make this clear at the time.

The Article was just as opaque regarding its identified priority areas for Community action. It did not explain the term "major health scourges"; and even the one that it did name, drug dependency, did not constitute a specific health matter (Merkel and Hübel, 1999). Finally, as Recommendations are not a binding legal instrument within the Community, the Commission's ability to "adopt Recommendations" did not necessarily constitute a significant role in health policy. That said, while Recommendations are legally less potent than Regulations and Directives, they are potentially very influential. One could, for instance, imagine the repercussions if an incident similar to the blood transfusion scandal in France during the 1980s were to arise today, and a Member State had chosen to ignore the recent Council Recommendation on blood and plasma donor suitability (European Commission, 1997b). Hence, the Commission's ability to adopt only Recommendations is not *de facto* representative of a marginal role; though a stronger remit might indeed have had more effect. Thus, although it seemed that the "ideological objective" laid out by the Article "meshed neatly with the fact that the Community had wanted to take and had indeed taken various initiatives in the health field but sometimes with or without any very adequate or specific Treaty base" (Jackson, 1995), the Article proved little more than a general statement of intent couched in vague provisions. What it did do, however, was to set the tone for the future direction of the EU's role in health policy. By laying down a commitment to "the prevention of diseases, in particular the major health scourges", it entrenched the disease-based approach that characterises the present Community approach.

2. The Treaty of Amsterdam

The Treaty of Amsterdam was developed at the 1997 IGC in Amsterdam; though it only came into force on 1 May 1999 following a long ratification process. Although the original agenda for the conference did not feature health, the Treaty of Amsterdam includes a new role for the Community in the field of health policy. It effected a revision of the TEU Article 129 through the addition of several new provisions and changes to parts of the existing text, and renamed it Article 152 (ex 129) in the consolidated text (Box 2.3). Because of the earlier-cited criticisms of Article 129 and the failings they reflected, much was expected of the plans to revise the Community's health policy framework. Expectations for a comprehensive re-evaluation and overhaul of the Article's provisions were not, however, realised in the new Article. Although it does represent a revision of Article 129, in looking beyond the superficial, it seems that Article 152 (ex 129) has not only failed to address several key deficiencies of its predecessor, but may even run counter to other stated Community objectives. The Treaty of Nice, which has yet to be ratified, does not change the provisions that relate to health policy.

Box 2.3: Article 152 of the Treaty of Amsterdam

1. A high level of human health protection shall be ensured in the definition and implementation of all Community policies and activities.

   Community action, which shall complement national policies, shall be directed towards improving public health, preventing human illness and diseases, and obviating scourges of danger to human health. Such action shall cover the fight against the major health scourges, by promoting research into their causes, their transmission and their prevention, as well as health information and education.

   The Community shall complement the Member States' action in reducing drugs-related health damage, including information and prevention.

2. The Community shall encourage co-operation between the Member States in the areas referred to in this Article and, if necessary, lend support to their action.

   Member States shall, in liaison with the Commission, co-ordinate among themselves their policies and programmes in the areas referred to in paragraph 1. The Commission may, in close contact with the Member States, take any useful initiative to promote such co-ordination.

3. The Community and the Member States shall foster co-operation with third countries and the competent international organisations in the sphere of public health.

4. The Council, acting in accordance with the procedure referred to in Article 189b, after consulting the Social and Economic Committee and the Committee of the Regions shall contribute to the achievement of the objectives referred to in this Article through adopting:

   (a) Measures setting high standards of quality and safety of organs and substances of human origin, blood and blood derivatives; these measures shall not prevent any Member States from maintaining or introducing more stringent protective measures;

   (b) By way of derogation from Article 43, measures in the veterinary and phytosanitary fields which have as their direct objective the protection of public health;

   (c) Incentive measures designed to protect and improve human health, excluding any harmonisation of the laws and regulations of the Member States.

   The Council, acting by a qualified majority on a proposal from the Commission, may also adopt Recommendations for the purposes set out in this Article.

Community action in the field of public health shall fully respect the responsibilities of the Member States for the organisation and delivery of health services and medical care. In particular, measures referred to in paragraph 4(a) shall not affect national provisions on the donation or medical use of organs and blood.

First, terms such as the "co-ordination of activities", and "major health scourges" again appear without adequate explanation. What specifically constitute "incentive measures" as regards public health is also not defined. Second, although the new provisions appear to resolve the ambiguities raised under Article 129's loose commitment to "the prevention of disease" – by restating the Community's objective as "improving public health" – closer examination again reveals the lack of an adequate definition of public health incorporating the wider determinants of health. Despite a firm pledge to "ensure a high level of human health protection in the definition and implementation of all Community policies and activities", the provisions fail to specify how this will be done, beyond again referring to the Community's complimentary role in undertaking action with Member States. This can be seen as constricting present Community activities and impeding the initiation of new and innovative proposals by the Commission (Belcher, 1997).

The new provisions also make it clear that Community action must respect the responsibilities of Member States for the organisation and delivery of health services. According to the chair of the European Parliament Committee for the Environment, Public Health and Consumer Protection, the reason for this is that

> the delivery of health care to individual people is better organised nationally and locally than it could ever be from Brussels... [and] the British Department of Health and its equivalents in other Member States would never tolerate interference in the way they run their affairs (Richards and Smith, 1994).

Yet, because of the impact many Community activities have on the provision of health services (both directly and indirectly), this stipulation appears to gainsay other goals (European Commission, 2001b). For instance, the Commission's 1997 Communication on "Modernising and Improving Social Protection" calls for a "European dimension" to health services, specifically regarding the "need to improve efficiency, cost-effectiveness and quality of health systems so that they can meet the growing demands arising from the ageing of the population and other factors" (European Commission, 1997a; ESC, 1998). It is difficult to see how this aim for a "European dimension" to health services can be pursued effectively when health services are not covered under the Treaty. It must, however, be pointed out that the Commission's views are not necessarily representative of those held by the Community, as Member States may not accept an EU role in health services. Nevertheless, excluding health services in this manner may also fuel citizens' perceptions that the EU is not dealing with the practical realities of health, and that the Community is not undertaking those activities which would appear to be most necessary.

With respect to health policy, it is interesting to note the former Social Affairs Commissioner Flynn's statement on a future EU health policy, that "while it is clear that the provision and financing of health care is a matter for Member States, a Community policy on public health which ignored the development and the effectiveness of health systems would be wholly inadequate" (Flynn, 1998). This would support an earlier point made by a British Member of the European Parliament (MEP) who, in 1995, called for the harmonisation of national laws and regulations to ensure minimum Community standards in health care (Bowe, 1995).

Another issue to emerge from Article 152 (ex 129) is the addition of a statement on the health effects of addictive drugs. Traditionally, drug dependency and its health effects are assumed under the remit of national ministers for social affairs and crime, rather than those with responsibilities for health. Illegal drugs, their trafficking and trade (and crime associated with them) have, therefore, generally been deemed matters of "internal affairs" beyond the scope of EU law. Despite the perhaps curious nature of this inclusion, the involvement of the Community in matters pertaining to drugs does represent a positive development as it recognises the health aspects associated with the use of illicit drugs.

Equally noteworthy is the specification of provisions regarding the safety of blood, organs, substances and blood derivatives of human origins, especially given the detail in which they are explained in the text. The addition of these issues to the "health" Article may initially serve to indicate that national arguments over the safety of such products should not hinder their free movement within the single market, but later statements would seem to weaken this. Specifically, subsequent affirmations to the effect that Member States will not be prevented from instituting their own national measures (provided they are more stringent than the Commission's) reflects this lack of clarity.

On the basis of these criticisms the new Article 152 (ex 129) has been deemed a "missed opportunity" for a considered re-evaluation of the Community's health policy role. The primary reason for this is the nature of its revised content, recalling the sudden and specific addition of scope for Community action in phytosanitary and veterinary fields, as well as in the area of blood and human organs. This has led to a widespread view of the Article as a "knee jerk political reaction to the BSE crisis" (Belcher and Mossialos, 1997; Stein, 1997; Randall 2001), and has been attributed to last minute lobbying by the Dutch delegation. In addition, the new Treaty did not address the basic need for institutional reform for the easier development and integration of health considerations into Community policy-making. Even the former Social Affairs Commissioner Flynn was quoted as saying "I must confess to a certain degree of disappointment on the text [...] Yes, the draft Treaty does confer new Community competencies in the field of public health. However [...] in my view, the new Treaty provisions do not provide the Commission with an adequate legal basis to address future concerns"

(Flynn, 1997). This has also been echoed elsewhere (Belcher, 1997; Lahure, 1997). So while the Amsterdam Treaty, and Article 152 (ex 129) specifically, did result in new Community competencies, some blame for the failings outlined above must be directed at the Member States' health ministers who were in office during the IGC. They should have done much more to ensure that health policy concerns were fed into the policy-process, not only in creating the new Treaty, but more so during the preparation period preceding the IGC itself.

In summary, therefore, the Amsterdam Treaty and Article 152 do not outline a clearer and deeper role for the Community in health policy. Yet, this should not come as a surprise given the intergovernmental nature of Community decision-making and, as outlined in the earlier theoretical discussion, the lack of Member State interest in establishing EU authority in the field. Rather than signifying a pro-active Community role, the revision of Article 129 to 152 is a clear result of externalities forcing intergovernmental agreement on health issues. Health policy only came to the IGC table because of the BSE crisis; which in turn prompted both the Treaty change, along with the limited nature of the revision of Article 129.

VI. EU Policy-making: A Synopsis

It is important to recall that the driving force of the European integration process has been the establishment of a single market based on the institutional structures to support this development. Thus, one of the main reasons why health policy competencies are not more developed at EU-level – or at least have evolved in the manner they have done – has to do with the institutional construct of the Community decision-making process. The development of competencies, except where they relate to the requirements of the single market – such as pharmaceuticals, medical devices and the free movement of medical professionals – is framed by a decision-making structure that was originally designed with other purposes in mind. The most recent example is the establishment of the previously mentioned European Medicines Evaluation Agency. As a quasi-regulatory body, the first of its kind in the EU, its mandate covers market authorisation issues for new pharmaceutical products being launched on the European market, but not matters pertaining to pricing and reimbursement. This construct reflects the economic and political imperatives that have driven the Community to-date, and a brief summary of the roles of the institutional actors involved in the EU policy-process elucidates this point quite clearly.

The European Commission, the European Parliament and the Council of Ministers are the principal actors responsible for devising and implementing policy in the EU. The most common mechanisms involves the Commission instigating policy which is then sent to the Parliament and the Council (with the latter voting according to a qualified majority) for co-decision, although less frequent mechanisms, such as a reduced role for the Parliament or a need for unanimity in voting by the Council, in certain circumstances. This seems a straightforward enough configuration, but the procedural aspects assumed within this tripartite structure ensure that the process is a difficult one. Where policies relating to health policy (or other sensitive national issues) are concerned, the process is further complicated because of the principle of subsidiarity.

The Commission's role involves the proposition and adoption of proposals for Regulations, Directives and Decisions, and the issuing of Recommendations and Opinions. The first three are binding, while the latter two are not. A proposal is developed by the Commission services in draft form, with input from relevant experts and national representatives. The Commissioner of the Directorate-General then formally puts it to the Commission for adoption with responsibility for that particular area. Proposals require the collective agreement by the entire "College" of Commissioners before then being presented to the Council. In turn, the Council is required to consult the Parliament for its view before rendering a final decision. Proposals are also sent to the EU's Economic and Social Committee (ECOSOC), which may deliver a non-binding Opinion.

In proposing legislation, beyond the Directorates-General that comprise it, the Commission is reliant on a number of secondary bodies for advice (*via* a system of committees). For health policy matters, it is most often the Health and Consumer Affairs Directorate that is involved in drafting proposals on behalf of the Commission. The Parliament also operates a series of committees, and usually refers health policy questions to its Committee for the Environment, Public Health and Consumer Protection. The Committee drafts a Resolution on the basis of the proposal at hand – seeking additional advice from other Parliamentary Committees – which Parliament then debates before delivering an opinion to the Commission. This (necessary) reliance of the EU decision-making process on a multitude of committees is a structure known as comitology (Christiansen, 1996). This description serves to indicate the complexity of the EU policy-process and goes some way towards explaining the often-lengthy delays involved in implementing policy-decisions. It is likely that provisions in the Amsterdam Treaty relating to the role of committees will increase further the complexity of decision-making (Wessels, 1998).

Although the Parliament has in the past been deemed ineffectual as a legislature (Williams, 1990) – leading to criticisms of the Community's so-called "democratic deficit" (Betten, 1998; Neunreither, 1998) – since the introduction of a procedure known as "co-operation" under the Single European Act, the Parliament's role has been expanded beyond simply recommending amendments to Commission proposals, to veto-ing them. This veto is, however, subject to unanimity in the Council, and only following a failure by the Conciliation Committee (a commit-tee whose aim is to resolve Parliament-Council deadlock in a mutually acceptable manner) to agree a compromise arrangement between the Parliament and the Council over the former's proposed changes.

The Maastricht Treaty through the "co-decision" procedure strength-ened the Parliament's veto. Whilst "co-operation" granted Parliament a second reading of Commission proposals, "co-decision" gave it a third. The Parliament is thereby able to reject Commission proposals outright if, following no result in conciliation, a qualified majority vote is achieved during a third reading. Only in two cases to-date has the "co-decision" procedure failed to render a decision; the first in 1994 pertain-ing to telephony, and the second in 1995 regarding a Commission pro-posal on biotechnology. This latter decision has since been reversed, with Parliament approving the revised proposal on 19 May 1998.

The EU decision-making process is a lengthy and complicated one, although in fairness this is also the case in other situations requiring widespread consensus, as in federal states such as the US, Germany or Belgium. Nowhere is this more the case than with respect to health policy matters. There are two main inter-related reasons for this. The first is that despite the Health and Consumer Protection Directorate having primary responsibility for health matters, Community health policy responsibilities are in fact scattered between the remaining Direc-torates-General (DGs) of the Commission. Second, and the main factor behind this dispersion of responsibility, is that health competencies have primarily been developed with an eye to establishing the single market.

The earlier chronology of the development of EU legislative compe-tencies in health policy served to indicate that the Community's interest in health policy, as a specific policy area of its own, did not feature until the Maastricht Treaty in 1992. Even then, however, it was not clear as to exactly what role Article 129 conferred upon the Community in policy-making terms (Lauridsen and Lund, 1996); especially in light of the Community's focus on the single market. Specific areas in which the single market has impacted on health include increasing competition (Joffe, 1993), the free movement of professionals, the free movement of patients and services, the free movement of medical products, the stan-dardising of liability for medical services and private health insurance

(Leidl, 1991; Busse *et al.*, 2002). The result has been the *ad hoc* development of EU powers alluded to earlier (EHMA, 1994; Randall, 2001). The multitude of individual Community initiatives does not reflect a coherent health policy strategy.

Although few of the other DGs exercise executive powers with respect to health policy per se, the activities in which they engage can, and do, impact on health policy in a variety of ways. As was observed prior to Maastricht, "In sum, health is an EC-policy of minor priority, and selected aspects are scattered in various Directorates-General" (Leidl, 1990). Continuing with this dispersion of health powers, a survey prior to the 1999 reform of the Commission has shown that of the old twenty-four DGs, at least sixteen had a significant involvement in matters related to health policy.

Conclusion

Although this chapter has considered European integration only superficially, it has served to contextualise health policy in a wider European framework. Although neither the theories nor the processes referred to were developed to explain specific policy developments, aspects of both, at each level, are shown to be relevant to the development of EU health policy competencies. In particular, the chapter has shown how the ECJ has played a major role in raising health policy issues and how it has become a major contributor to the development of EU health policy.

This chapter also emphasised that the current system for developing EU health policy (the new DG for Health and Consumer Protection notwithstanding), as it has evolved since the Treaty of Rome in 1957, is no longer appropriate for dealing with contemporary health policy challenges (if, in fact, it ever was). There is no all-encompassing strategic health policy and there is a need for a new Community health policy. It must be one that has at its foundation a new and comprehensive Treaty-based definition of health policy and the EU's role therein, and one that takes into account the wider determinants of health and disease as well as an agreed position among Member States on what they are seeking to achieve through their health care systems.

The attempt by governments of EU Member States to "ring fence" national competence in health matters through Article 152 EC (ex 129) may prove to be unwise. It may be better to recognise that health is an issue where a model of "multi-level governance" applies in the EU context (Cram, 1996; Hervey, 2002). Thus, it may be more appropriate to articulate expressly a "non-market" basis for health care along the lines of social solidarity and universality at both national and EU levels.

Of course, to make such a principle applicable involves the recognition that market models are not desirable, for Europeans at least, in the field of health care. It would seem that broad consensus on this issue is still present within the EU context. However, the accession of new Member States from Central and Eastern Europe could pose significant challenges to the current European social model.

In the next chapters we begin to assess the main implications of EU law for certain key elements of health policies.

CHAPTER 3

Free Movement of Professionals

Introduction

Health professionals have a privileged position. They are entrusted by the state with certain rights denied to others (such as prescribing in the case of physicians and, in some countries, nurses) and they have exclusive rights to be employed in certain positions. Conversely they also have certain responsibilities. As individuals, they must ensure that they continually update their skills and knowledge and they must adhere to certain ethical standards, in particular avoiding situations that might exploit their position in relation to patients. Collectively, health professionals play a major role in determining the scope and nature of professional training, establishing a framework for continuing education, monitoring the quality of clinical practice, and ensuring the application of high ethical standards.

These collective responsibilities are undertaken at the level of the Member State. The mechanisms employed vary considerably, reflecting historical differences in institutions involved (universities, government, professional organisations etc.) and the relationship between health professionals and the state. European law on movement of professionals is essentially blind to these differences, basing its provisions on the principle of mutual recognition. Once educational programmes comply with a basic standard, typically defined in terms of length of training, those completing them are assumed to have reached a level of competence that will enable them to work anywhere in the EU.

There are obvious benefits to be achieved from promoting free movement. The supply of health professionals across Europe is extremely uneven, with surpluses in some countries and shortages in others. The diversity of health care provision, while potentially a problem, also offers many opportunities to exchange examples of good practice. However there are some concerns. First, there are widely held beliefs that qualifications from all countries are not equivalent, often with very different amounts of direct patient contact and resulting practical experience. This can act as a barrier to mobility as, although illegal, indirect forms of discrimination may be employed. Second, the rapid growth in health care knowledge means that someone qualifying even ten years previously will soon be out of date unless they have taken positive steps to keep abreast of developments. This has led some governments to introduce systems of revalidation, in which qualifications only remain valid as long as practitioners can provide evidence that they remain fit to practice. However the whole area of continuing professional development varies enormously across Europe.

The challenge, therefore, is to find ways that promote free movement while at the same time promoting high standards of professional knowledge, both at qualification and throughout the individual's career.

I. The Legal Framework

While the Treaty establishes a general basis for free movement of health professionals, with Article 6 (ex 3c) and Article 47.2 (ex 57.2) allowing for the co-ordination of rules regulating self-employed activities, health professionals have been recognised as requiring special attention. Article 47.3 (ex 57.3) states that "in the case of the medical and allied and pharmaceutical professions, the progressive abolition of restrictions shall be dependent upon co-ordination of the conditions for their exercise in the various Member States". For this reason the medical and other health care professions were among the first to be subject to specific regulations at the EC level (Lonbay, 2000; Richards, 2000).

There are two ways in which professional qualifications can be recognised throughout the EU and two types of Directives that establish the criteria for professional recognition:

- sectoral Directives apply to certain professions such as architects, midwives, pharmacists, doctors, nurses responsible for general care, dentists and veterinary surgeons, and operate on the basis of mutual recognition of diplomas;
- all other professions come under a general system of recognition of professions, which operates on the basis of whether a profession is regulated or not.

In an attempt to facilitate the free movement of health professionals, the so-called "doctors' Directives" 75/362/EEC and 75/363/EEC (Council of the European Communities, 1975a and b) were adopted in 1975 and have been in force since early 1976, well before the establishment of the single market. These entitle doctors to full registration in any EU Member State if they fulfil the following criteria:

- they are citizens of a Member State;

- they have completed primary training in a Member State and hold a recognised qualification.

The first Directive 75/362/EEC (Council of the European Communities, 1975a) deals with the mutual recognition of medical qualifications, which are broken down into three categories:

- diplomas, certificates and other evidence of formal qualifications in general medicine (Articles 2 and 3);
- qualifications relating to specialised medicine common to all Member States (Articles 3 and 4);
- qualifications relating to specialised medicine peculiar to two or more Member States (Articles 6 and 7).

Each Member State is required to recognise the qualifications listed in the Directive by giving those qualifications the same effect in its territory as those that the Member State itself awards. Specialist recognition is more complex than recognition of primary training. If a doctor has completed specialist training in a specialty common to all Member States and which is included in the list in the Directive (Articles 3 and 4), then he/she is entitled to be recognised as a specialist elsewhere in the EU. Specialties common to two or more Member States must also be recognised throughout the EU (Articles 6 and 7). However, these stipulations do not cover all specialties and the process of obtaining recognition for less common specialties can be very slow (Richards, 2000).

Directive 75/363/EEC (Council of the European Communities, 1975b) provides for the co-ordination of medical training courses. Member States are required to provide guarantees that during their training period individuals will acquire:

- adequate knowledge of the sciences on which medicine is based and a good understanding of the scientific methods;
- sufficient understanding of the structure, functions and behaviour of healthy and sick persons, as well as relations between the state of health and the physical and social surroundings of the human being;
- adequate knowledge of clinical disciplines and practices;
- suitable clinical experience in hospitals under appropriate supervision.

Where specialist training is concerned, minimum training periods are specified for each listed specialty.

A further Directive 86/457/EEC (Council of the European Communities, 1986: 26) covers the requirements for general practice, although it did not take full effect until January 1995. Its aim is to correct the considerable imbalance between general practice requirements in different Member States.

II. Key Features of Directive 93/16/EEC

All three of these Directives have now been repealed and consolidated, with various amendments for different specialities, in Council Directive 93/16/EEC (Council of the European Communities, 1993a). The main objective of Directive 93/16/EEC is to establish the minimum training requirements that are necessary and sufficient for the mutual recognition of medical diplomas. Beyond this, the organisation and content of medical training is largely the responsibility of individual Member States [as established in Articles 149-150 of the EC Treaty (ex 126-127)]. The Directive also aims to establish rules regarding the exchange of information between Member States' licensing/disciplinary boards about doctors who have provided substandard treatment due to carelessness, inadequate qualifications, mental health problems including the abuse of alcohol and other addictions.

Article 2 of the Directive requires Member States to recognise the diplomas listed in Article 3 that have been awarded in accordance with Article 23. Article 23 states that medical training should comprise at least a six-year course of 5,500 hours of theoretical instruction at university level. The Directive also deals with specialised medical training (Article 24).

A. General Practitioners

Since January 1990 Member States have been required to institute additional minimum levels of training. Since January 1995 doctors wanting to enter general practice in benefit in kind systems such as the National Health Service in the UK have had to complete a minimum of two years of vocational training, supervised by competent authorities, which is practical (rather than theoretical) in nature. This additional vocational training must include the trainee's participation in professional activities and undertaking responsibilities for the persons with whom he/she works.

B. Specialists

The specialities listed in Article 5 are recognised by all Member States and holders of the relevant diplomas are entitled to automatic recognition whereas specialities listed in Article 7 are common to two or more Member States and are automatically recognised by the Member States listed in this Article. Article 8 requires EU citizens coming from Member States that do not train in a speciality referred to in Articles 4 and 6, who wish to acquire a specialist diploma, to submit to the training required by the host state, subject to recognition of the training he/she has already undertaken.

C. Safeguards

The Directive allows host Member States to request information regarding the good character or reputation of migrant doctors, if these characteristics are required of its own doctors (Article 11). An Advisory Committee of Medical Training (ACMT) was set up by Council Decision 75/364/EEC (Council of the European Communities, 1975c) to ensure that comparably demanding standards were maintained with regard both to basic training and further training. The Committee of Senior Officials on Public Health was also set up to adapt the Directives to changing conditions, but the speed of change has made keeping the Directives up to date a difficult task (Lonbay, 2000).

Directive 93/16/EEC (Council of the European Communities, 1993a) has recently been amended and is now the subject of further amendments. In 1998 the European Commission presented a legislative proposal to update various EU Directives relating to mutual recognition of professional qualifications. The so-called SLIM Directive, part of Simpler Legislation in the Internal Market initiative, aimed to include amendments to the "Doctors' Directive" and those covering diplomas for nurses, midwives, dentists, vets and architects. In May 2001 the European Commission issued a further Directive (2001/19/EC) (European Parliament and Council of the European Union, 2001) amending Directive 93/16/EEC (Council of the European Communities, 1993a) and other Directives concerning the professions of nurse responsible for general care, dental practitioner, veterinary surgeon, midwife, architect, pharmacist and doctor.

III. The Directives in Practice

If the single market provisions on health professionals are to bring tangible benefits to European health systems they must facilitate movement of such a scale as to redress the large inequalities in supply within Europe. There is little evidence that they have succeeded (Jinks *et al.*, 2000). Although health professionals may be better placed than others to transfer their skills from one country to another, the scale of movement within the EU has been extremely limited. Mobility of physicians has been studied most. For example, the United Kingdom, which is traditionally the largest importer of health professionals, in part because of the widespread use of the English language, has attracted relatively few doctors from elsewhere (Brazier *et al.*, 1993; Lonbay, 2000). In 1998,

411 doctors came to the UK from Germany, followed by 291 from Greece, and then Italy and Ireland, from which came with just under 200 doctors each (Lonbay, 2000). In the same year 219 doctors migrated to Greece (156 from Italy and 43 from Germany).

The failure of the doctors' Directives to promote mobility has been attributed to cultural, social and institutional barriers (including the issue of language), and to the persistence of restrictive national policies (Brazier *et al.*, 1993; Hermans, 1998). Not all Member States have implemented the Directive in every area. In 2000 the European Commission referred the Netherlands, Ireland and Portugal to the ECJ for failing to implement Directive 98/21/EC, which amends Directive 93/16/EEC (Council of the European Communities, 1993a) with regard to doctors specialised in occupational medicine. The Commission also sent reasoned opinion to the Netherlands, Ireland, Spain and Portugal for failing to implement Directive 98/63/EC amending Directive 93/16/EEC (Council of the European Communities, 1993a) by modifying the list of specialised doctors' diplomas that are recognised throughout the EU (European Commission, 2000a).

A further problem is that mutual recognition Directives only apply to diplomas obtained in EU Member States and do not cover those from a third country. This poses problems in countries such as the UK, where a significant number of doctors have qualified in non-EU countries (particularly the Indian subcontinent) but have had their qualifications recognised and approved by the GMC (the doctors' regulatory body). Most of these doctors have also obtained further qualifications in the UK. As their qualifications are recognised by the regulatory body in the UK, it is argued that they should be recognised by other Member States as well (Richards, 2000). New legislation is planned to commit registration bodies to take into account the experience acquired elsewhere of doctors registered and practising in the European Economic Area (EEA), so that cases can be considered on an individual basis, although there has been opposition to this in some countries (Richards, 2000).

IV. Implications for Health Care

As noted earlier, the medical Directives simply set minimum training standards. Although these standards are enforceable, the somewhat loose way in which they are defined (Article 31 of Directive 93/16/EEC), based mainly on duration of training without addressing content, means that there is considerable variation in the scope and nature of training required in different Member States. There is currently no harmonisation of the composition, function, or method of working of the National Competent authorities that are responsible for supervising training. There is also no European forum for them to meet to discuss matters of training and quality assurance (Allen, 2001). The issue of specialist medical training has particular implications for health services as trainee doctors are engaged in both training and health care provision roles. Historically, the duration of specialist training has varied considerably, with especially long periods in the UK and Ireland. Both countries have now reduced these periods but this has important implications for hospital staffing, in particular for smaller hospitals, which have long been dependent on a continuing flow of trainees who provide a substantial amount of medical and surgical care, especially at evenings and weekends. A reduction in training periods, accentuated by a shift from the service to the training component, has threatened the viability of some hospitals, with implications for the geographical distribution of facilities. This will be accentuated once the Working Time Directive is applied to junior medical staff (Council of the European Union, 1993). However the most important implication of the Directives is that health professionals meeting the minimum standards set out in the Directives are deemed to be of adequate quality to practice. This view has most recently been endorsed by the ECJ that, in Kohll and Decker[1], asserted its belief that the mutual recognition Directives are sufficient to ensure uniform care across the EU (see Chapter 4). In Decker, the Court famously argued that "the purchase of a pair of spectacles from an optician established in another Member State provides guarantees equivalent to those afforded on the sale of a pair of spectacles by an optician established in the national territory" (Decker, paragraph 43). The Court's basis for this decision has been heavily criticised as being the wrong legal basis on which to assume that there is a similar standard of health care across the EU (Nickless, 2002).

This raises several unresolved issues, the importance of which is growing as more patients are treated in other Member States and, in particular, where health authorities and sickness funds contract with providers in another Member State. Formally, the legal position is clear, in that those contracting with providers cannot impose conditions that are directly or indirectly discriminatory. This means that health professionals in other Member States must comply with any systems of continuing professional development and revalidation that are in place in the first Member State. However, this means that those health professionals engaging in such contracts may have to comply with several

---

[1]   European Court of Justice, C-158/96, Judgement of 28/04/1998, Kohll Union des caisses de maladie and European Court of Justice, C-120/95, Judgement of 28/04/1998, Decker v. Caisse de maladie des employés privés.

different regulatory regimes, with the consequent financial and time costs.

A further issue arises where a health professional who has either failed to be revalidated in his/her own country or has been erased from the relevant professional register. While there are systems, albeit imperfect, in place to address the second issue, it is entirely possible that an individual may be permitted to practice in another Member State but not his/her own.

These issues were explored at a symposium organised by the Dutch Ministry of Health, Welfare and Sport in 1997, which expressed concern at the Directives' implications, particularly with regard to upholding standards and protecting EU citizens from harm caused by substandard medical practice (Segest, 1997). This symposium highlighted the numerous differences between Member States in the areas of education, authorisation and disciplinary and compensatory procedures. It also highlighted the problem some Member States face in keeping records of problematic health professionals and the issue of liability in cases where competent authorities were unable to enforce aspects of Directive 93/16/EEC (Council of the European Communities, 1993a). It concluded the Directive should be more stringent, particularly regarding the description of the content of minimum education, the need for continuous education, the establishment of national databases of doctors with "professional problems" and the necessity of involving patients in the decision-making process.

In summary, the Directives' emphasis on promotion of free movement has been at the expense of consideration of how to ensure the continuing quality of the professionals involved. As Member States move from a model in which qualifying as a health professional entitles one to practice for life to one based on evidence of continuing professional development it will be necessary to incorporate explicitly issues of professional quality.

CHAPTER 4

Free Movement of Patients

Introduction

This chapter reviews recent rulings of the ECJ concerning the free movement of patients within the EU, and discusses the implications of these rulings for health and social care systems in EU Member States.

In theory, national boundaries do not exist for individuals seeking health care in another Member State of the EU, in so far as people are free to move and live anywhere within the territory of the EU. But because authorities responsible for health care usually confine their activities to their own country, statutory health coverage has traditionally been limited to providers established within national boundaries. This is known as the territoriality principle (Cornelissen, 1996).

Since 1958, the EC Treaty provides an exemption to the territoriality principle in order to encourage the free movement of people within the EU. The Community mechanism for the co-ordination of social security systems, based on EEC Regulations 1408/71 and 574/72, has guaranteed migrant workers and their dependant family members moving to or residing in another EU Member State access to health care (Council of the European Union, 1996). These Regulations were subsequently extended to virtually the entire EU population, although nationals from third countries still are excluded from this system, even if they reside in the EU and are affiliated to a national social security system (Fillon, 1999; Van Raepenbusch, 1997).

There are two grounds for eligibility for health care during a temporary stay abroad. They differ as to whether they incorporate the principle of "urgency"; in other words, whether a patient's condition requires immediate and necessary investigation and treatment. Persons who may receive treatment outside their country of residence regardless of whether their condition is urgent include:

- pensioners entitled to a pension and their families;
- employed and self-employed persons not currently in employment and their families who go to another Member State to look for a job;

- employed or self-employed persons exercising their professional activity in another Member State;
- frontier workers (although their families must obtain prior authorisation for non urgent treatment if there is no agreement between the countries concerned);
- students and those undertaking professional training and their families (since October 1997).

For all other persons, the condition of urgency of treatment should be met (under Article 22.1.a of the ECC Regulation 1408/71). Access to health care outside the Member State of residence is therefore essentially limited to urgent health care during a temporary stay in another Member State (certified by form E111). Otherwise, those seeking planned health care in another Member State, under Article 22.1.c of EEC Regulation 1408/71 must obtain prior authorisation from the patient's competent social security institution (certified by form E112).

So far, however, these Regulations have not resulted in widespread movement of patients, largely because Member States have generally taken a restrictive approach to health care provided abroad. In 1978 and 1979, two ECJ judgements relating to the conditions governing the granting of prior authorisation under Article 22.1.c of EEC Regulation 1408/71 established the principle that authorisation must be granted in all cases where it will improve the medical state of the patient, irrespective of any other considerations (the Pierik judgements)[1]. This interpretation forced the Council to restrict the scope of the relevant Regulation (Council of the European Communities, 1981). Under the amended Regulation Member States retain a wide discretion in defining their authorisation policy, as Article 22.2.2 only states when authorisation cannot be refused (Kesteloot *et al.*, 1995):

- when the treatment required by the interested party is part of the health care package covered by the social protection system in the area of health care;
- and this treatment cannot be given to her/him in her/his State of residence within the period that is normally necessary, in view of her/his current state of health and the probable course of her/his disease.

It has been argued that the second condition was put in place in order to prevent patients from bypassing waiting lists by seeking authorisation

---

[1] European Court of Justice, C-117/77, Judgement of 16/03/1978, Bestuur van het algemeen Ziekenfonds Drenthe-Platteland *v.* Pierik I and European Court of Justice, C-182/78, Judgement of 31/05/1979, Pierik II.

for treatment abroad (van der Mei, 2001), although this view could be contested on the grounds that waiting lists were not an issue in 1981. Member States have generally refused to authorise any treatment in another Member State that can be provided on their territory. As table 5.1 shows, even now, a country such as the UK only grants about 600 E112 forms a year, France some 200 and Sweden not more than twenty. Belgium and Luxembourg have been somewhat less restrictive, relative to the size of their populations, issuing about 2,000 and 7,000 E112 authorisations a year respectively (Palm *et al.*, 2000).

Table 5.1: The Number of People Seeking and Obtaining
Prior Authorisation for Treatment Abroad
in Selected EU Member States

Country	Year	No of requests for authorisation	No of authorisations granted
Austria	Each year	Not available	850
Belgium	Each year	Not available	2000
Denmark	Each year	40-50	25-35
France	1996-1999	1240 / 4 years	789 / 4 years
Luxembourg	1998	7130	7082
Sweden	Each year	Not available	20
United Kingdom	Each year	800	600

Source: Palm *et al.*, 2000.

This reluctance on the part of Member States to support greater patient movement partly explains the marginal financial impact of EU cross-border care on public budgets; on average each Member State spends approximately € 2 per inhabitant a year, representing less than 0.5% of public expenditure on health care.

However, other, more natural, obstacles also stand in the way of receiving treatment abroad, such as language, distance, lack of information about the type of health care provided abroad, unfamiliarity with a different health care system, the unwillingness of local doctors to refer patients to other countries, the administrative burden of the procedures involved and travel time and costs (Mountford, 2000). The demand for cross-border health care appears to be concentrated in border areas (or very small states like Luxembourg) and in high technology health care. It generally concerns a limited group of people, in particular those with access to sufficient information (Hermesse, 1999). But even in the cross-border "Euregios", where the potential for cross-border health care is greatest, or between Northern Ireland and the Republic of Ireland, where patient movement is being promoted as part of the Irish peace process (Jamison *et al.*, 2001), there is a lack of adequate information available to potential cross-border patients (Hermans, 2000). The practical and legal obstacles to cross-border care are likely to remain considerable for some time (Coheur, 2001). Nevertheless, the demand for cross-border care will almost certainly increase in future, as the experience of the "Euregios" shows (Coheur, 2001), and as evidenced by the various claims before national Courts and the ECJ, as well as by growing public interest in this issue. Several factors may further stimulate this demand, including: the increased movement of people in general; increasing shortages of human and financial resources creating waiting lists and other access problems; the development of new experimental treatments in some Member States; increased information among patients; growing integration in border areas; the increased ability to compare prices due to monetary union; the possibility of distance selling (see Chapter 8); and the likelihood of further claims before the ECJ, in the light of recent rulings (see below).

Patients are likely to be supported in their efforts to become more active consumers in a European health care market: first, by health care providers, who are better informed about the health services offered in other health care systems and are seeking to stake their own positions in this emerging market; second, by health insurance bodies seeking to offer the best health services to their clients at the lowest cost; third, by politicians and the media, seeking to raise awareness of differences in levels of provision as a means of pressurising low-spending states to increase expenditure. In all this, the European Court of Justice has been playing a central role, through its judgements on claims introduced by patients who were refused reimbursement for medical treatment received outside their home state.

I. The Rulings of the European Court of Justice: A Turning Point?

A. *The Kohll and Decker Rulings of April 1998*

The regulatory framework for access to health care abroad has traditionally been based on the principle of free movement of people within the EU, but in 1998 the ECJ was required to assess these rules in the light of the free movement of goods and services.

The Kohll and Decker rulings of the ECJ concerned two persons insured under the Luxembourg social security system who had obtained orthodontic treatment in Germany (Raymond Kohll) and spectacles that were prescribed by an eye specialist in Luxembourg but were purchased in Belgium (Nicolas Decker). Both wanted to be reimbursed by their health insurance fund in Luxembourg, even though the fund had not previously authorised their treatment abroad[2]. Decker did not ask for prior authorisation to buy spectacles in another Member State, as was required by Luxembourg's regulations, while Kohll requested authorisation but it was refused on the grounds that dental treatment in Germany was not considered to be urgent and therefore could have been provided in Luxembourg. Kohll argued that the prior authorisation procedure restricted him from purchasing services in other EU Member States and therefore contravened Articles 49 (ex 59) and 50 (ex 60) of the EC Treaty. Decker argued that the prior authorisation procedure restricted the free movement of goods within the EU and therefore violated Article 28 (ex 30) of the EC Treaty.

The Luxembourg government, joined in the proceedings by several other governments, initially argued that the rules on the free movement of goods and services did not apply to matters of social security because they were economic rules. After reviewing its case law in this area, the ECJ concluded that although Member States had a wide degree of discretion in organising their social security systems, the rules of those systems were not exempt from the rules on the free movement of goods and services. In his opinion, the Advocate General stated that the Court's consistent view was that "Community law does not detract from the powers of the Member States to organise their social security systems", but that this by no means implied that "the social security sector constitutes an island beyond the reach of Community law and that, as a consequence, all national rules relating to social security fall outside its scope". He thus made it clear that Member States must comply with Community law when exercising their right to decide how to organise their social security systems.

Even if the principle of free movement of goods and services were to be considered applicable, the Luxembourg government justified its reliance on these national rules by arguing that prior authorisation was necessary in order to:

- Ensure the financial balance of the social security system and to enable the government to provide a balanced medical and hospital service open to all insured persons;
- Protect the public health of the population since there would be no way of ensuring the quality of the goods and services provided by orthodontists and opticians in other Member States;

---

[2]   European Court of Justice, C-158/96, Judgement of 28/04/1998, Kohll Union des caisses de maladie and European Court of Justice, C-120/95, Judgement of 28/04/1998, Decker *v.* Caisse de maladie des employés privés.

– Enable the government to provide a balanced medical and hospital service open to all insured persons.

The Court dismissed all of these justifications. Since both Kohll and Decker only requested reimbursement according to national Luxembourg tariffs – instead of the tariff of the country of health care delivery as required by the challenged provisions – the Luxembourg health insurance fund would not have to pay more as a result of the transactions taking place abroad. Therefore there was no adverse impact on the financing of the social security system.

The Court also dismissed the Luxembourg government's second argument concerning the quality of care provided by health practitioners in other Member States. Referring to the mutual recognition of diplomas and efforts made during the 1970s to harmonise training requirements for most medical professions (see, for example, Council of the European Communities, 1993a) which is a consolidation of all mutual recognition legislation for doctors, specialised doctors and general practitioners), the Court claimed that "the purchase of a pair of spectacles from an optician established in another Member State provides guarantees equivalent to those afforded on the sale of a pair of spectacles by an optician established in the national territory" (Decker, paragraph 43). This argument has been heavily criticised on the grounds that it cannot be assumed that there is a similar standard of health care across the EU (Nickless, 2001). In addition, the Court's assumption appears to contradict emerging EU initiatives on accreditation and revalidation (Nickless, 2001). In fact, the rules on mutual recognition were originally introduced to facilitate the freedom of establishment, but have since been used to ensure the free movement of services.

Finally, the Court only would accept the argument for protection of each Member State's own medical infrastructure if it could be shown that otherwise, public health really would be seriously threatened, which the Luxembourg government could not substantiate in this case.

The ECJ concluded that, by requiring prior authorisation, Luxembourg's national rules had created an unjustified impediment to the free movement of goods and services within the EU. In Decker's Case, the Court applied the rules established in the Dassonville ruling[3], finding that Luxembourg's national rules "encouraged insured persons to purchase medical products in Luxembourg rather than in other Member States, and are thus liable to curb the import of spectacles assembled in those states" (paragraph 36). In the Case of Kohll, the Court found that

---

[3] European Court of Justice, C-8/74, Judgement of 11/07/1974, Procureur du Roi Benoit & Dassonville.

"such rules deter insured persons from approaching providers of medical services established in another Member State" (paragraph 35). As in the landmark rulings of Dassonville and Cassis de Dijon in the 1970s, in which the Court established the concept of direct or indirect, effective or potential, barriers to trade and to the freedom to provide services (Bosco, 2000), merely showing that the free movement of goods and services might possibly be prevented was sufficient to be considered incompatible with the EC Treaty.

In refusing to reimburse Kohll and Decker for the treatment they received abroad, the Luxembourg government had relied upon the national rules incorporating EC Regulation 1408/71 into Luxembourg law. However, this Regulation did not and could not take legal precedence over the EC Treaty itself. The Court argued that although EEC Regulation 1408/71 was valid, it did not provide an exhaustive list of the means by which an individual could obtain medical goods and services in another Member State, and should be seen as merely one possible option.

Through the Kohll and Decker rulings, therefore, the ECJ appears to have established a dual system of social protection for non-urgent health care received in another Member State, giving EU citizens a choice of two options for coverage of health care abroad.

On the one hand, the ECJ upheld the classic E112 procedure governed by EEC Regulation 1408/71, in which patients who have received prior authorisation from their social security institution are accepted by the social protection system of the country in which they received the medical treatment "as though [they] were insured with it" (Article 22.1.c). This implies that the patient is subject to the same arrangements and limitations regarding, for example, cost-sharing public or contracted providers and referral for specialist care, and that any health care costs are settled between both social protection systems according to the tariffs of the country in which the treatment was delivered.

On the other hand, the ECJ created an alternative (Kohll and Decker) procedure, based directly on the EC Treaty, by which patients can freely choose a provider abroad without asking for prior authorisation in their home state or appealing to the social security system in the state where they will receive treatment. Instead, they claim reimbursement from their own social protection system 'as if they received the treatment there'. This would mean that reimbursement in the home state is subject to the conditions and according to the tariffs applicable there.

The wider implications of the rulings, at the time they were made, were not clear, and much of the political reaction that followed was fiercely defensive. Some Member States were especially concerned about the possible serious internal implications the rulings might have for the planning of health services and for cost containment policies in health care, should the decisions be generalised. Consequently, most Member States gave a narrow interpretation to the rulings, sometimes even rejecting any implications for their own system. In turn, this caused confusion and legal uncertainty among patients as well as administrators. The legal discussion mainly focussed on two issues. First, whether the ECJ decisions applied to hospital as well as ambulatory care and, secondly, whether they applied to all types of health care systems.

Several official sources argued that in-patient care, having particular characteristics, would not be affected. In fact, in Kohll's Case, the ECJ's Advocate General stated that the provision of orthodontic services did not interfere with the legitimate right of governments to plan their hospital systems, and this was seen to preclude the application of the rulings to hospital services (Palm *et al.*, 2000). The Advocate General noted that

> unlike the benefits provided by individual practitioners, the reality in the case of hospitals is, first, that their location and number is determined by forward planning and, secondly, that the cost of one person's stay in hospital cannot be separated from that of the hospital as a whole. Clearly, if a large number of insured persons chose to avail themselves of hospital facilities located in another Member State, their domestic hospitals would be under-utilised but would have the same staff and equipment overheads as if they were being used to full capacity (paragraph 59 of Advocate General's opinion).

Some Member States also denied that the rulings had any consequences for their health care systems on the grounds that the rulings only applied to systems operating on a reimbursement basis (as with out-patient services in Luxembourg, Belgium and France), whereas their health services were provided in kind through contracted providers via social insurance or a national health system. Arguing that the alternative (Kohll and Decker) option for coverage of health care abroad was not feasible in health care systems where there is no established reimbursement mechanism, they maintained their traditional restrictive policy of authorising non-emergency health care abroad only if medically required.

So, while the Kohll and Decker rulings made it clear that the EC principles concerning the free movement of goods and services could and would be applied to the realm of national social security systems, and that goods and services received by a patient in another Member State could be treated as if they had been delivered in the patient's state of residence, they also led to confusion on two issues. First, whether they applied to hospital as well as ambulatory care and, secondly, whether they applied to all types of health care system, and not just to the reimbursement systems of France, Belgium and Luxembourg. Following the judgements of the ECJ, only Luxembourg, Belgium and Denmark amended their legislation and established administrative procedures for the unconditional reimbursement of certain outpatient services and health care products purchased in another Member State. However, in Austria, even before the Kohll and Decker rulings, socially insured persons were entitled to reimbursement of health care from a non-contracted provider in Austria or abroad at a rate of 80% of the amount paid for the same treatment from a contracted provider (Palm *et al.*, 2000).

Overall, in both Kohll and Decker the ECJ, referring to Community case law, emphasised that Community law does not detract from the powers of the Member States to organise their social security systems[4]. However, in Decker (paragraph 24) the ECJ, referring to Duphar (paragraph 18), has held that measures adopted by Member States in social security matters should also respect Article 28 (ex 30) EC on the free movement of goods.

It had been established, in joined Cases 286/82 and 26/83 Luisi and Carbone[5], that the freedom to provide services includes the freedom, for the recipients of services, to go to another Member State in order to receive a service there, without being obstructed by restrictions, even in relation to payments and that tourists, persons receiving medical treatment and persons travelling for the purpose of education or business are to be regarded as recipients of services (paragraph 16). The Luisi and Carbone ruling was confirmed by the Grogan ruling, in which the Court clarified the economic nature of medical activities and found that medical termination of pregnancy constituted a service within the meaning of Article 60 (ex 73g) of the EC Treaty[6]. Furthermore, in Sodemare[7] the ECJ found that Articles 43 and 58 (ex 52 and 73d) of the EC Treaty do not preclude a Member State from allowing only non-profit-making private contractors to participate in the running of its social welfare system. This measure created a restriction on the freedom of establishment but "in view of the powers [the State] retains to organise its social

---

[4] European Court of Justice, C-238/82, Duphar and Others *v.* Netherlands (1984) ECR 523, paragraph 16 and European Court of Justice, C-70/95, Sodemare and Others *v.* Regione Lombardia (1997), ECR I-3395, paragraph 27.

[5] European Court of Justice, Joined Cases C-286/82 and C-26/83, Luisi and Carbone *v.* Ministero del Tesoro, ECR I-377.

[6] European Court of Justice, C-159/90, Judgement of 04/10/1991, Society for the Protection of Unborn Children Ireland *v.* Grogan and others.

[7] European Court of Justice, C-70/95, Judgement of 17 June 1997, Sodemare and others *v.* Regione Lombardia Sodemare and others.

security system", the Court upheld it merely because it did not discriminate on the basis of place of operators' establishment. (Hatzopoulos, 2002).

Therefore, it could be argued that the Kohll and Decker rulings are the logical transposition, to the field of services, of the Duphar Case law, in accordance with the ECJ's findings in Luisi and Carbone, Grogan and Sodemare.

B. The Smits-Peerbooms and Vanbraekel Rulings of July 2001

It is against this background that subsequent cases brought before the ECJ in July 2001 allowed further clarification of the ambit of the Kohll and Decker rulings. Mrs. Smits and Mr. Peerbooms[8] were both insured under the benefits in kind system of the social health insurance scheme in the Netherlands, where permission to obtain treatment from non contracted providers abroad is only granted if:

- the required treatment falls within the scope of what is regarded as "usual in the professional circles concerned";
- the required treatment is necessary and is not available without undue delay in the Netherlands.

Mrs. Geraets-Smits received multidisciplinary treatment for Parkinson's disease from a specialised clinic in Germany without obtaining prior authorisation from her Dutch sickness fund, paid the clinic directly and then requested reimbursement from the fund according to the procedure set in place by Kohll and Decker. The Dutch sickness fund refused to reimburse her on the grounds that the treatment she had obtained was not "usual", that satisfactory and adequate treatment for her symptoms was available in the Netherlands from a contracted provider and that the treatment provided in Germany conferred no additional advantage.

Mr. Peerbooms went into a coma after a car accident at the age of 36. At the request of his consultant neurologist, he was moved to a university hospital in Austria where he received intensive neuro-stimulation therapy and recovered full consciousness. In the Netherlands this therapy was only available on an experimental basis in two institutions and only to people less than 25 years old, whereas it was fully covered by the social health insurance scheme in Austria. Mr. Peerbooms' consultant requested reimbursement for the cost of the treatment but was refused on the grounds that appropriate care could have been obtained from a contracted provider in the Netherlands.

---

[8] European Court of Justice, C-157/99, Judgement of 12/07/2001, Smits and Peerbooms.

Mrs. Smits and Mr. Peerbooms initiated Court action, claiming that they were entitled to a refund of the costs of their treatment under the EC rules on the free movement of services. The ECJ had to decide whether (Nickless, 2002):

- the EC Treaty provisions on the free movement of services applied to health care provided in hospitals;
- the requirement of prior authorisation for hospital treatment abroad violated these Treaty provisions;
- if so, whether the Dutch system of authorisation could be justified.

In Smits-Peerbooms and Vanbraekel (see below) the Court began by reiterating its consistent view, according to its own case law[9], that while Community law does not detract from the power of Member States to organise their social security systems, Member States must comply with Community law (and in particular with the principle of freedom to provide services) when exercising that power.

The Court then dismissed the argument advanced by several Member States that had joined in the action, that hospital services should not be regarded as services in the sense of Article 50 (ex 60) of the EC Treaty (that is, as an economic activity that is provided for remuneration), especially when they are provided in kind and free of charge (as opposed to through a system of reimbursement). By regarding them not to be "services" they would be exempt from many aspects of EU law. The Member States argued that:

- there was no remuneration within the meaning of Article 50 (ex 60) when the patient received treatment without paying for it (as a benefit in kind) or where all or part of the amount paid was reimbursed;
- in order to constitute an economic activity within the meaning of Article 50 (ex 60) the person providing the service must do so with a view to making a profit;
- Social security systems could not come within the sphere of the fundamental economic freedoms guaranteed by the Treaty because the persons concerned are unable to decide for themselves the content, type and extent of a service and the price they will pay.

---

[9] European Court of Justice, C-158/96, Judgement of 28/04/1998, Kohll, Union des caisses de maladie and European Court of Justice, C-70/95, Judgement of 17/06/1997, Sodemare and others *v.* Regione Lombardia Sodemare and others.

The Court did not uphold any of these arguments. Instead, it reaffirmed its view, on the basis of previous case law, that medical activities do fall within the scope of the rules on the freedom to provide services, and that there is "no need to distinguish in that regard between care provided in a hospital environment and care provided outside such an environment" (Smits-Peerbooms, paragraph 53). The Court went on to note that Mrs. Geraets-Smits and Mr. Peerbooms did actually pay the hospitals that treated them directly, even though they subsequently applied for reimbursement, although the ECJ also noted that a service did not necessarily have to be paid for by the person receiving it, in order for it to be classified as a service. Because hospitals are paid for the services they provide, the ECJ concluded that treatment in a contracted or foreign hospital was a service in the sense given in the EC Treaty. Thus the Court confirmed that the alternative Kohll and Decker procedure, in principle, applies to all health care systems, whether based on reimbursement or on in kind benefits, and to all health services, in-patient and out-patient.

The ECJ found that the need to apply for prior authorisation for treatment abroad would deter – if not prevent – insured persons from applying to providers of medical services established in another Member State and thus constituted, for insured persons and service providers, a barrier to the freedom to provide services.

However, under Articles 46 (ex 56) and 55 (ex 66) of the EC Treaty, Member States may enact legislation that restricts freedom granted under Articles 49 (ex 59) and 50 (ex 60) on the "grounds of public policy, public security and public health". The freedom to provide services can only be limited by "overriding reasons relating to the public interest"[10]. In Smits-Peerbooms, the Court stated that such a barrier could be justified in the light of overriding reasons in the general interest, such as:

- where there is a risk of seriously undermining a social security system's financial balance;
- where the objective of maintaining a balanced medical and hospital service open to all is jeopardised;
- where the maintenance of treatment capacity or medical competence on national territory is essential for the public health, and even the survival of, the population.

---

[10] European Court of Justice, C-353/89, Commission v. Netherlands (1991) ECR I-4069.

In Smits-Peerbooms the Court, referring itself to the four-tier test expressed in the Gebhard case[11], made clear that an exemption to the principle of the free movement of services was only acceptable if the system of prior authorisation proved to be necessary and proportional and was based on objective criteria that did not discriminate against providers established in another Member State. The Court found that, in such cases as they related to medical services provided within hospital infrastructure, prior authorisation could indeed be justified as a necessary and reasonable measure for guaranteeing a rational, stable, balanced and accessible supply of hospital services by means of planning and contracting. The Court recognised that

> medical services provided in a hospital take place within an infrastructure with, undoubtedly, certain very distinct characteristics. It is thus well known that the number of hospitals, their geographical distribution, the mode of their organisation and the equipment with which they are provided, and even the nature of the medical services which they are able to offer, are all matters for which planning must be possible (Smits-Peerbooms, paragraph 76).

It explained that planning and contracting were also necessary to avoid wasting financial, technical and human resources and to control costs. The Court therefore concluded that

> if insured persons were at liberty, regardless of the circumstances, to use the services of hospitals with which their sickness insurance fund had no contractual arrangements, whether they were situated in the Netherlands or in another Member State, all the planning which goes into the contractual system in an effort to guarantee a rationalised, stable, balanced and accessible supply of hospital services would be jeopardised at a stroke (Smits-Peerbooms, paragraph 81).

The Court did not give any guidance as to what could be considered to be necessary and proportional. Schilling (1995) points out that the facts in the Grogan case demonstrate the difficulties in applying the public policy approach which uses the free provision of services as the yardstick for checking how national measures to protect the foetus relate to the legality of or access to abortion. Schilling also argues that

> the proportionality test does not allow to take into account the size of the restriction of the yardstick provision, *i.e.*, in Grogan, the free provision of services. Subject matter of the test is the question whether the national measure restrictive of the yardstick provision is proportional to the target it aims at. Subject matter is not the relationship between the target and the size of the restriction of the internal market liberty.

---

[11]   European Court of Justice, C-55/94, Gebhard (1995) ECR I-191-236.

Even if the measure were to be considered necessary and proportional, for the Court such an exemption to the principle of free movement of services would only be acceptable if the applied criteria to grant the authorisation were objective and non-discriminatory *vis-à-vis* providers established in another Member State. In that respect, it found the Dutch authorisation conditions were not compatible with the principle of equal treatment, because they actually favour Dutch providers.

As to the first condition, that the foreign medical service should be held to be "usual" treatment, the Court noted that this condition also applies to medical services provided in the Netherlands. The ECJ noted that a Member State can define the scope of its own social security system and, consequently, can establish limited lists excluding certain products or services from reimbursement under its social security system, in order to contain costs. Community law cannot in principle require Member States to extend the list of medical services that are paid for by their social security systems (regardless of whether a particular type of treatment is covered by the social insurance schemes of other Member States). However, the package of benefits covered by social security must be defined in accordance with Article 30 (ex 36) of the EC Treaty; that is, defined according to "objective criteria, without reference to the origin of the products" (Smits-Peerbooms, paragraph 89, based on Duphar and Others, paragraph 21).

Similarly, in order for a prior authorisation scheme to be justified, it must be based on "objective, non discriminatory criteria that are known in advance, in such a way as to circumscribe the exercise of the national authorities' discretion, so that it is not used arbitrarily" (Smits-Peerbooms, paragraph 90). In addition to being based on fair, objective and transparent criteria, decisions to grant or refuse prior authorisation must be made within a "reasonable time" and "be capable of being challenged in judicial or quasi-judicial proceedings" (Smits-Peerbooms, paragraph 90).

Therefore, decisions about what is considered "usual" within professional circles must be based on what is "sufficiently tried and tested by international medical science" rather than just what is considered usual in Dutch professional circles (Smits-Peerbooms, paragraph 108). The Court added that "to allow only treatment habitually carried out on national territory and scientific views prevailing in national medical circles to determine what is or is not normal will not offer those guarantees and will make it likely that Dutch providers will always be preferred in practice" (Smits-Peerbooms, paragraph 96).

Secondly, concerning the authorisation condition that the foreign treatment is necessary for the insured person, the Court noted that this condition also applies to non-contracted providers in the Netherlands: if equally effective treatment cannot be obtained without undue delay from a contracted establishment, the patient can be treated by a provider who is not contracted with his or her sickness fund. The Court went on to state that this condition should be implemented in the same way for foreign providers as for non-contracted Dutch providers. In other words, Dutch sickness funds cannot favour non-contracted providers in the Netherlands over providers established in another Member State (Smits-Peerbooms, paragraph 107). In order to determine whether equally effective treatment can be obtained without undue delay from a contracted provider, national authorities are required to "have regard to all the circumstances of each specific case and to take due account not only of the patient's medical condition at the time when authorisation is sought but also of his past record" (Smits-Peerbooms, paragraph 104). The Roermond county court, taking into account the judgements of the ECJ in the Smits-Peerbooms Cases, has now issued its final judgement and ruled that the Dutch sickness funds were correct in refusing to pay for treatment abroad in both cases (EHMA, 2001). In the Smits Case the Dutch county court ruled that the treatment could be obtained locally without "undue delay" and that the Dutch treatment was equally effective to that offered in Germany despite the fact that its nature may differ. In the Peerbooms Case the Roermond county court ruled that the treatment provided in Austria was not considered common practice by international medical standards.

Whereas in its Kohll and Decker rulings, the ECJ and their sequels established an alternative procedure for the coverage of health care received in another Member State, in its Vanbraekel ruling it directly linked the procedure based on the co-ordination of social security systems (EEC Regulation 1408/71) with the principle of free movement of services. Ms Descamps (Vanbraekel), a Belgian national insured under the Belgium social security system, requested authorisation from her sickness insurance fund to undergo orthopaedic surgery in France[12]. Under Belgian law, treatment abroad, which is reimbursed according to Belgian tariffs, is to be authorised if:

- treatment abroad can be provided under better medical conditions,
- and has been considered (prior to the treatment) indispensable for the patient (to be certified by a medical expert from a Belgian university hospital).

---

[12] European Court of Justice, C-368/98, Judgement of 12/07/2001, Vanbraekel and others.

Even if a circular letter issued by the national institute of health insurance (RIZIV/INAMI), made clear that this alternative procedure would not apply to Community cases, the Belgian judge did not take into account the stricter authorisation criteria designed for the procedure established by Article 22.1.c of EC Regulation 1408/71 (E112).

The Belgian authorities refused Ms. Descamps' request for authorisation because she had not obtained the opinion of an expert in a national university hospital. After obtaining treatment in France (without authorisation) Ms. Descamps returned to Belgium and launched a successful appeal in the Belgian courts. Based upon an expert report, the courts agreed that she should have been given authorisation, because the restoration of her health did require surgery that could be performed under better medical conditions in France. However, they could not decide whether she should be reimbursed according to the Belgian or the French tariffs. Under the E112 system she would have been reimbursed according to the French tariff (FF 38,608.99), whereas under the Kohll and Decker procedure she should have been reimbursed according to the Belgian tariff (FF 49,935.44). Consequently, they asked the ECJ to advise on which course should be adopted.

Since Article 22.1.c of EEC Regulation 1408/71 does not define the criteria for prior authorisation, the ECJ considered that those provided under the Belgian alternative procedure should also be considered to apply to the Community procedure. Therefore, if an insured person was incorrectly refused authorisation to receive hospital treatment in another Member State, he or she should be guaranteed reimbursement according to the rules applicable in the Member State of treatment (as indicated in Article 22.1.c of EEC Regulation 1408/71). Citing Kohll, the Court found that EEC Regulation 1408/71 does not prevent the insuring state from reimbursing according to its own tariffs when they would appear to be more favourable (Vanbraekel, paragraph 36). The Court then went on to investigate whether such a "top up arrangement" would be necessary for the free movement of services. It concluded that, if a patient would be guaranteed a lower reimbursement than if treated in his home state, this would deter, if not prevent him from looking to foreign health care providers (Vanbraekel, paragraph 45). Therefore, the Belgian authorities were required to grant the patient an additional reimbursement to compensate for the difference, as this could not be justified by any risk of jeopardising the fundamental objectives of the national health system.

II. Issues Raised by the ECJ's Rulings

The Kohll and Decker rulings established clearly, for the first time, that the economic rules regarding the free movement of goods and services within the EU could be applied to social security systems. The Court of Justice, in Smits-Peerbooms and Vanbraekel, also successfully answered the two questions raised by Kohll and Decker. First, that hospital services are considered services in the sense of Article 50 (ex 60) of the EC Treaty and are not, therefore, exempt from the rules on the freedom to provide services. Secondly, that the Kohll and Decker rulings apply to all types of health care system, including systems that provide benefits in kind, and not just to reimbursement systems.

However, the recent rulings raise further issues, and we may have to wait for the conclusion of cases still pending to shed light on them. First there is the issue of definitions. Even if Member States retain the right to define the package of treatment that they will cover, the evolving case law clearly indicates an expectation of a European-wide consensus on what should be covered and what is deemed to be evidence-based. In the Case of Smits-Peerbooms, the ECJ did not define what it meant by criteria based on "international medical science" (rather than what is considered normal treatment in Dutch professional circles), presumably on the assumption that there is a common medical paradigm in Europe (and the rest of the world) (Mossialos and McKee, 2001). But this disregards evidence concerning the diversity of national health beliefs and treatment patterns (Payer, 1989).

The ECJ also failed to define "undue delay", a vague term which might have very different meanings in different health care systems. In Smits-Peerbooms the ECJ stated that prior authorisation could only be refused if "the same or equally effective treatment can be obtained without undue delay" from a contracted provider. It could be argued that the Court's ruling in this instance goes beyond the minimum preconditions for treatment abroad set out in the Regulation (Article 22.2.2.), and that "undue delay" can now be interpreted in the patient's favour (as opposed to the national authority's). According to Smits-Peerbooms, national authorities must now "have regard to all the circumstances of each specific case and to take due account not only of the patient's medical condition at the time when authorisation is sought but also of his past record". The Court does not specify what it means by taking due account of a patient's "past record", but giving citizens the right to challenge prior authorisation decisions in judicial or quasi-judicial proceedings seems to suggest that the Court is unwilling to tolerate blanket refusals on the part of national authorities.

In this respect, the pending Van Riet Case, in which a Dutch citizen received an arthroscopic intervention in a Belgian hospital instead of waiting for six months for the same treatment in the Netherlands, might enable the Court to clarify how far national discretion can go in limiting access to health care through delay mechanisms. Because of the highly topical issue of waiting lists, pertinent in several Member States[13] this case may attract significant attention.

The Smits-Peerbooms Case confirmed a Member State's competence to define the scope of medical services covered under a statutory health care system, but the Court warned that boundaries must be fair, objective, transparent and open to challenge (Nickless, 2002). National rules that explicitly exclude providers from other Member States will be outlawed and any rules that make it more difficult for providers from other Member States to participate in another Member State's health care system will need to be justified, perhaps on the basis of providing sustainable health care for all or maintaining the financial balance of the health care system (Nickless, 2002). The Court also noted a Member State's capacity to draw up limited lists of treatment, which exclude certain products or services from reimbursement under its social security system, in order to contain costs. Nickless (2001) explains what effect this might have in practice. For example, allowing patients to attend any doctor in the country could be interpreted as allowing them to attend any doctor in the EU. Offering to reimburse emergency treatment provided by non-contracted hospitals in one country, when the patient's condition prevents them from being taken to a contracted hospital, may also apply to non-contracted hospitals in other countries. When emergency treatment is provided under the E111 system, patients are treated as though they are insured in the state of treatment, which means that they would be taken to contracted hospitals and would have to pay any co-payments. The pending Case of Müller-Fauré, in which a Dutch citizen deliberately requested dental care during her holiday in Germany, could reveal whether the priority given to contracted providers would also be upheld for ambulatory medical services. This case is not only important because of an increasing perception that provisions for emergency care (certified by E111) are actually being used to by-pass the restrictive policies on non-emergency health care (Mountford, 2000). It is all the more important because, by deciding whether the justification upheld in Smits-Peerbooms would also count for outpatient care, the Court will

---

[13] European Court of Justice, C-385/99, Pending Case, Müller-Fauré and van Riet.

decide upon the tenability of the in-kind-benefit system, based on selective contracting with providers.

A further change brought about by the Vanbraekel ruling concerns the additional reimbursement that Member States seem to be obliged to pay now if their system would have provided a higher level of reimbursement than the country in which the patient received treatment. Nickless points out that this ruling goes beyond EEC Regulation 1408/71; as with the Kohll and Decker rulings, the Court has considered the system established by the Regulation to be merely suggestive or non-exhaustive, thereby perpetuating the legal uncertainty (Nickless, 2002). In this way, the ECJ is likely to have upset rules of coverage under the E111 and E112 procedures by instituting a double guarantee of the most favourable coverage: the principle of equal treatment thus applies differently according to the respective levels of reimbursement in the home state and the treatment state. The ECJ, in the Ferlini Case, had already established the principle of equal treatment on the basis of nationality for the application of medical tariffs[14]. It remains to be seen whether this could be considered to be an attempt to integrate both procedures; the standard procedures provided under EEC Regulation 1408/71 and the Kohll and Decker procedure.

Finally, there are equity considerations, such as travel time and costs, making direct payments for treatment and proximity to borders. Under the Kohll and Decker procedure, travel and treatment costs must be paid directly by the patient, which raises the scenario of a two tier system in which wealthier patients are able to obtain unauthorised treatment abroad, while poorer patients or those living furthest from neighbouring countries, will have to use the existing system of prior authorisation (certified by E112) (Hermans, 2000). While the ruling sought to change the effect of the E112 procedure that prevented patients getting treatment abroad, this could continue where reimbursement is according to tariffs of one's home state under the Kohll and Decker procedure where individuals live in countries with low medical tariffs. If governments are to make the most of these rulings by using them to ease waiting lists in their own country, this may be most likely to benefit patients living in relatively close proximity to the borders of another Member State, and governments would have to avoid creating a "postcode lottery".

---

[14]   European Court of Justice, C-411/98, Judgement of 3/10/2000, Ferlini.

Conclusions

It would appear from these latest judgements that the ECJ has not only radically restricted Member States' discretion to determine their own authorisation policies. It also seems to have changed rules of coverage under the classic social security co-ordination system. Consequently it seems that a revision of the legal framework regulating access to health care across the EU will be necessary.

The impact of the ECJ's rulings extends beyond the sole scope of access to cross-border care. From the outset, the national authorities involved generally showed greater concern about the possible "internal effects" on the organisation, operation and management of their health care systems, than about a massive outflow of patients (Palm *et al.*, 2000). Besides the issue of waiting lists, they mentioned the risk of undermining measures aimed at containing costs and ensuring quality of care. National providers might consider national regulations being imposed upon them as distortions in comparison with foreign competitors. It should be noted that since the Kohll and Decker rulings were made, the Luxembourg authorities have not succeeded in concluding a new agreement with the Luxembourg medical profession.

The case law of the ECJ indirectly pits the possibility of extended choice for patients (at an EU level) against the principle of territoriality and Member States' control over their social security systems (Bosco, 2000). However, while Member States have raised concerns about the impact of the ECJ rulings on "medical tourism" and governmental capacity for budgetary planning, expectations of significant numbers of patients crossing borders for treatment have not materialised (Sussex, 2001). As yet the flow of patients across borders is relatively limited, and the demand for cross-border care continues to be constrained both by legal uncertainties and extra-legal factors.

As the ECJ rulings examined in this chapter have clearly prohibited any unjustifiable discrimination against health care providers established in other Member States, as a "side-effect" they could force national contracting mechanisms to be opened to all health care providers in the EU. In this respect it is important to recall that the ECJ previously declared European public procurement rules applicable to social security institutions contracting with service providers[15].

While awaiting further clarification from the European institutions, Member States should now develop a more proactive policy concerning

---

[15]   European Court of Justice, C-76/97, Judgement of 24/09/1998, Tögel *v.* Niederösterreichische Gebietskrankenkasse.

cross-border access, integrating foreign supply into national health care planning and procurement. At a grass-roots level, some actors in the field of health care and social protection are already turning towards a European strategy and looking for less bureaucratic solutions that are better adapted to meet their needs and those of European patients. Instead of the emergence of what many see as a worst case scenario, with unregulated free movement of patients, European cross-border contracting could become an attractive means to improve access to health care while maintaining control over the cost and quality of care (Pieters, 1999: 80). This is not necessarily limited to border areas, where contracting across the border could complement a limited regional supply of medical services (during the last decade, initiatives and pilot projects have been developed in so-called Euregios to improve access to cross-border care in certain border areas essentially for the benefit of local residents, especially through promoting complementarity for existing medical services on either side of the border, in particular through the conclusion of bilateral agreements). Some countries seeking to ease existing waiting lists arising because of shortage of staff or other resources are also currently exploring it. It could also be used in tourist areas, where seasonal concentration of foreigners might justify contracting with a local provider that can offer culturally and linguistically appropriate facilities.

As rapid technological development seems to be leading towards more concentration and specialisation, European-wide planning of internationally renowned centres of excellence could offer a more cost-effective way of ensuring highly technical care in a few specialised areas. This necessary complementarity between people seeking treatment and facilities capable of treating them is an important part of the European integration process, in particular for achieving the EU goal of a minimum level of social cohesion. The process of enlargement highlights the efforts that must be made to bridge the gap in health status of Europe's citizens. In this respect, it should be reminded that the Charter of Fundamental Rights of the European Union, declared at the recent Nice Summit, contains a right to medical treatment "under the conditions established by national laws and practices" (Article 35).

The creation of an internal health care market and the further development of cross-border purchasing of care, will undoubtedly bring about the need for a kind of European reference framework providing benchmarks as to quality standards, equivalence of medical practice, licensing and accreditation, and patient rights. The ECJ was criticised on this point when it stated in Kohll and Decker that comparable levels of quality of care are sufficiently guaranteed through the system of mutual recognition of diplomas in the medical professions (Nickless, 2001).

A note of caution is required. It will be necessary to ensure that further health care integration does not increase social inequalities in access to care. Wealthier and better-informed citizens will be most likely to benefit from the extended rights to health care abroad. It is thus important that the creation of a European health care market does not weaken national health policy goals on equity. This is anyway a general obligation for all Community policies.

These issues can only be addressed adequately at the European level. In this context, the latest Community strategies on concerted action in the fields of social protection (European Commission, 1999a; Council of the European Union, 1999) and public health (European Commission, 2000b) could provide for the necessary instruments.

CHAPTER 5

Pharmaceuticals and Medical Devices

Introduction

Over the last ten years the general approach through which both pharmaceuticals and medical devices have been regulated in the EU has been changing. The requirements of the Single European Market (SEM) have prompted much action to harmonise national requirements and systems. The European Commission and, to a degree the two industries involved, have played the role of "policy entrepreneur" in pushing this agenda. But the ECJ has also been involved, helping clarify outstanding issues and technical matters where necessary. Further, the move towards the international harmonisation of regulatory requirements in both industries is beginning to affect the manner in which products are developed, marketed and sold. International rules for medical devices via the Global Harmonisation Task Force (GHTF) and, for medicines, through the International Conference on Harmonisation of Technical Requirements of Pharmaceuticals for Human Use (ICH), are becoming more encompassing and streamlined. There is also a concerted Europe-wide effort to reduce the duplication of effort and delays in market authorisation. Member States and supranational policy-makers alike have to reshape current regulations and devise new ones that conform to the changing environment. This push towards homogeneity of guidelines under international regimes is, of course, a pattern mirrored in other non-EU countries as well.

The expanding role of the Community in the two sectors, and the increasing Europeanisation of the markets and their regulation, are the result of two complementary processes that contribute to the wider European integration dynamic. The first is the growing regulatory function of the Community, and the second is the expanding scope of European law. The former, which has been widely acknowledged by analysts seeking to explain its role in policy setting, has evolved predominately from the single market programme (Mossialos and Permanand, 2002). Meanwhile, the latter is mainly the result of gaps that have developed with respect to the application of the SEM in practice. Though both are therefore relevant to understanding how European law for pharmaceuticals and medical devices affects national health care systems, the discussion here concentrates on the latter.

This chapter examines the part played by European law and the European Court (both the Court of First Instance and European Court of Justice) specifically, in terms of "Europeanising" policy for pharmaceuticals and medical devices. In so doing, it considers the implications of this process for national decision-makers *vis-à-vis* their health care systems, particularly in terms of the effect on the national policy environment. Nonetheless, as the two go hand-in-hand, a brief look at both is first necessary.

We first briefly examine Community law relating to pharmaceuticals and medical devices. We then discuss in some detail issues related to market authorisation (including the European Agency for the Evaluation of Medicinal Products and the Medical Device Directive) and examine questions on pricing and reimbursement, parallel trade, intellectual property, product/producer liability, electronic commerce and pharmaceutical advertising.

I. Community Regulation and European Law –
Some Initial Remarks

In academic circles, the concept of the Community as a "regulatory state", one that makes rules and regulations to create a level playing field for the fifteen Member States, has been proposed. This involves "creeping" European competencies and implies a re-shaping of the national context. It generally represents a voluntary rescinding of powers by the Member States and the transfer of regulatory responsibilities upwards to the European level. In other words, it is an intentional de-regulation at the national level. The expansion of the Community's regulatory function is thus partly the result of instances where national governments either feel the European arena is the more appropriate one in which decisions should be made or where the EU may be better placed to regulate, as well as reflecting concerns about which governments are willing to co-operate. Despite the explicit exclusion of health care systems matters from the Community's competencies under the Amsterdam Treaty, the single market's regulatory function has spilled into health care and other social policy areas (Majone, 1993). The Community regulatory function in respect of medicines product authorisation first appeared in 1965 (Council of the European Communities, 1965) but the process has subsequently deepened reflecting the development of the single market.

European law, meanwhile, also affects national rules and policy in a variety of ways, particularly through rulings delivered by the ECJ. By insisting that national legal systems comply with European dictates, the development of European law complements the regulatory function of the Community. It impacts on Member States' health (care) policy and systems, from simply taking away some responsibility from national decision-makers, to being integrated in full into national legislation.

As noted in Chapter 2, the ECJ's "constitutional" role in establishing European law as a *sui generis* system has thus had a major role in advancing integration in Europe generally (Wincott, 1996), and promoting the evolution of a European health care policy more specifically (Mossialos and McKee, 2001). And while the Court has at times been accused of undue judicial activism, ECJ decisions are sometimes said to impinge on the decision-making sovereignty of the Member States by underlining both the principle of "direct effect" and the "doctrine of supremacy" of European law, it essentially plugs the holes left where national and EU legislation are discordant (see Chapter 2). In addition, it clarifies any outstanding issues relating to the completion of the single market. In the case of pharmaceuticals and medical devices, these gaps have to do with the clash between the principles of subsidiarity and the free movement of goods and services as enshrined under Article 28 (ex 30) of the Treaty. As the Court also fills in the gaps where the harmonisation of national provisions is concerned, it has undoubtedly helped establish the working rules of the Single European Market framework. Much of this legislation and the Court's interpretations are therefore as relevant to health care as other areas (Mossialos and Permanand, 2002).

Together, the continuing development of Community regulatory competencies and European law are promoting the "europeanisation" of policy on medicines and medical devices in the EU. In practice, there are two main dimensions to the process. The first is the issue of market authorisation and the Community's attempts to harmonise and standardise, at EU-level, guidelines and approval procedures that fulfil health and safety criteria while meeting the interests of the main stakeholders in an equitable manner. These stakeholders are the Member States, the European Commission, consumers (patients) and the relevant industries. The second is the question of facilitating the free movement of products within the internal market, especially in terms of competition and industrial property rights issues. The two are unquestionably bound together. Although they represent different elements of the pursuit of harmonisation, they are both tied to the Single European Market programme. As the influence of European law is, of course, not limited to these areas, the chapter also looks at other relevant questions such as the pricing and reimbursement of pharmaceuticals – most notably the divisive matter of parallel trade – and intellectual property rights, where the ECJ has had an especially prominent role and continues to set precedents.

II. "Europeanising" Medical Devices and Pharmaceuticals

Both industrial policy and regulation of the Community's pharmaceutical and medical devices sectors remain shared competences between the Community and the Member States. The reasons are widely documented and are too extensive to be detailed here. Briefly, the level at which regulation is carried out depends on whether one adopts an industrial or health policy perspective. Industrial policy is underpinned by wider harmonisation powers than health policy, but they both exist concurrently. What should be noted, however, is that despite this potential conflict, the continuing development of European competencies in both fields means that policy is increasingly being decided at the supranational level.

The EU regulatory frameworks for medicines and medical devices are vastly different. The former has a relatively long history dating back to 1965 when the first piece of Community pharmaceutical policy, Directive 65/65/EEC (Council of the European Communities, 1965) was passed in the wake of the thalidomide tragedy. Its development has been driven largely by the requirements of the single market, though numerous pieces of Community legislation did in fact precede 1992. The latter framework is younger by some twenty-five years, having begun formally in 1990 with the Active Implantable Medical Devices Directive (AIMDD), as the first legislative measure in the field. Indeed, until the late 1980s there had been very little discussion about device regulation at EU-level (Council of the European Communities, 1990). It was only with the prospect of the Single European Market that national policymakers first came to recognise the need for a European framework. Since then the development of a politically and economically acceptable regulatory approach has followed relatively quickly. It has been driven primarily by the French, German and British ministries of health, with the support of the industry; the leading individual companies (European and American) and the trade organisations (Altenstetter, 1999). Thus, unlike medicines, the initial push for a Community medical device framework originated in pressure to enhance cross-border trade, rather than as the result of a specific public health concern. That said, health protection concerns have featured more prominently in subsequent years (Altenstetter, 1999).

The Community's pharmaceutical framework consists of some twenty pieces of EU legislation, both Directives and Regulations (which are binding measures). Its development has been somewhat *ad hoc*, reflecting the lack of a long-standing pan-European strategy for regulating the sector (Permanand and Mossialos, 2001). This is largely due to the clash between the principle of subsidiarity on the one hand (political and tied to health care), and the requirements of the single market on the other (legal and pertaining to free movement). It is compounded by the European Commission's interest in maintaining a strong and successful industry (particularly *vis-à-vis* the US and to a lesser degree Japan), and its push for greater harmonisation of national systems. The result is that, despite a host of competencies relating to industrial policy and promoting the single market, the market remains incomplete because pricing and reimbursement of medicines remain national concerns.

In comparison, the medical devices framework consists of only three Directives: the earlier-mentioned Active Implantable Medical Devices Directive (AIMDD); the broader "catch-all" Medical Devices Directive (MDD) (Council of the European Communities, 1993b) and the In Vitro Diagnostics Directive (European Parliament and the Council of the European Union, 1998). Between them they establish the rules of the European regulatory system. In so doing they also define the specific roles of the Commission, the Member State governments and the so-called "notified bodies", which are the public or private groups that act as the review and approval organisations for new devices. The system places public health protection at its heart, but it has unquestionably been designed to promote internal market goals in the first instance (Chai, 2000).

One reason as to why medical devices legislation and policy have trailed pharmaceuticals is that the term "medical device" covers a huge range of treatments from simple tongue depressors and orthotics to more complex implantable equipment such as cardiac pacemakers. In addition, the terminology also differs among Member States. Medicines are a more straightforward product in terms of what they are designed to do, and were defined in a Directive as long ago as 1965. Another point of differentiation from pharmaceuticals – notwithstanding differences between the ethical, generic and over-the-counter sub-markets – is that there is no single medical device industry. According to Altenstetter (2001a), "Instead, there is a cluster of producers that can be subdivided roughly into four sectors: (i) medical-electrical devices; (ii) non-electrical products; (iii) implantables; and (iv) diagnostic products". The companies producing these goods are often not especially health-focussed. With the MDD, however, the EU has been able to establish a working definition of a medical device, which will allow for increased harmonisation of national standards and regulatory regimes in the future.

Part of this regime involves post-marketing surveillance mechanisms to enhance product safety. For medical devices these can be divided into two categories: performance tracking or "vigilance", which is the duty of the manufacturer, and "product field performance", which is a EU function. The two are separate but concurrent, and ideally, mutually reinforcing processes. Manufacturers are obliged to report all adverse events associated with their products to their competent national authority (in the US this reporting is to the Federal Drug Administration). The Member States are themselves required to institute measures to gather and assess information derived from such reporting. On the basis of the information collated, the national authorities may then act to withdraw or simply restrict the (further) marketing of any devices found to have such adverse effects. Thus, going beyond pharmacovigilance for drugs, responsibility for medical devices lies not just with the manufacturer, but extends to national health care professionals and health care systems (Altenstetter, 2001a). In turn, the Member States must pass on the details of their actions to the European Commission, which reviews the action, ultimately sanctioning or overturning it. An important difference between the American and European regimes should be noted. While American reporting includes serious injury attributable to the device, EU reporting is limited to events involving death (Chai, 2000).

It should also be added that where medicines are concerned, the principles for product approval were also laid down in the original Directive, and that these have been at the heart of all EU pharmaceutical policy ever since. In comparison with medical devices, therefore, pharmaceuticals are a far more consolidated area of Community competence, even if a single medicines market does not yet exist. The device regime is still evolving and is subject to a much greater reliance on national regulation.

III. Market Authorisation

The Single Market programme is the basis upon which the Community has been able to act, and indeed take over aspects of medicines and medical device market authorisation in the EU. The pursuit of market integration and the harmonisation of national rules and regulations have seen the EU develop a host of competencies. For pharmaceuticals this includes policy on labelling and packaging (Directive 92/27/EEC) (Council of the European Communities, 1992b), advertising and sales promotion (Directive 92/26/EEC) (Council of the European Communities, 1992c), and wholesale distribution (Directive 92/25/EEC) (Council of the European Communities, 1992d), all of which reflect priorities of the single market. With a centralised European medicines office since

1995, the European Agency for the Evaluation of Medicinal Products (EMEA), even some elements of market approval have been taken out of the hands of national regulators.

This is not the case for medical devices where a so-called "Euro agency" does not exist, and where market authorisation is not as strictly regulated. Rather than having to pass the so-called "public health test" and meet the "three hurdles" of quality, safety and efficacy to which medicines are subject before being granted market approval, medical devices are instead simply required to carry the CE Mark (Conformité européenne) signifying their conformity with the standards requisite for sale in the EU.

Following much negotiation amongst the Member States and the industry, the CE Mark was established by means of the Medical Devices Directive (MDD). The idea was to create (harmonise) common technical guidelines that would be recognised by all Member States. This also involved device certification and an inspection process for manufacturers, so as to ensure safety and product quality. All new medical devices must now carry this seal of approval in order to comply with European law.

The CE Mark became operational in 1998 with all fifteen countries having enacted it into national law. There are, however, remaining problems with the system as the transposition of the CE Mark legislation differs among Member States. Some have simply written it into their own law books virtually verbatim, whilst others, generally those with expansive systems of their own, have instead adapted their own rules to accommodate the European legislation. Such differences mean that the new regime is still somewhat incomplete. This is compounded by the fact that the European Free Trade Area (EFTA) countries are also part of the CE Mark regime, and their legislation in matters pertaining to the single market is of course even more diverse than that of fifteen EU Members.

Unlike the strict independent regulatory approval procedures for medicines, the CE Mark for medical devices serves to indicate the manufacturer's own judgement that the product meets certain minimum standards. These are the "essential requirements" laid down for the specific category of product. The list of essential requirements for each category covers a multitude of areas, including: "[…] safe design and construction, clinical efficacy, disclosure of residual risks, protective packaging, infection control, compatibility with other devices, calibration and stability, radiation protection, electrical safety, labelling and instruction manuals" (Epstein *et al.*, 1996). Furthermore, the CE Mark indicates that the product is fit for its intended purpose and can, therefore, be freely marketed in the European Economic Area. In emphasising product standards and self-regulation, rather than involving government regulators (as is the case for medicines), the CE Mark regime is thus designed to facilitate the single market. Its aim has clearly been to facilitate intra-Community trade in medical devices, perhaps reflecting lessons learned from the difficulties encountered with the medicines system.

According to some analysts, this has meant that, without compromising safety, approval of new medical devices in Europe takes approximately half the time required in the US market, where the Food and Drug Administration (FDA), as for medicines, is the regulatory authority (Miller, 2000). The United State General Accounting Office (GAO) put the difference between the American and EU systems down to different regulatory requirements: "Devices marketed in the EU are reviewed for safety and performing as the manufacturer intended; devices marketed in the United States are reviewed for safety and effectiveness. Effectiveness includes the additional standard of providing a benefit to patients" (GAO, 1996). The impetus for the GAO report came primarily from the American device industry and its perception that the then-emerging European system was more efficient (Chai, 2000).

The manufacturers asked whether the FDA should therefore adopt aspects of the EU regime. Although the GAO's findings were that it was premature to change, it does seem that time to market is indeed quicker in Europe. The CE Mark system has thus helped to promote the European industry in a high-technology sector where the US is otherwise dominant.

Undoubtedly the most important development was the establishment in 1995 of the EMEA. Created under Regulation 2309/93/EEC, the agency occupies a unique place in the EU framework (Council of the European Communities, 1993c). It is the first, and as yet only, independent Community office exercising a real regulatory mandate. Rather than simply gathering and disseminating information, the EMEA proposes decisions that, if endorsed by the Commission, create Community policy and are binding on Member States. By means of its centralised and decentralised procedures, it proposes to the Commission decisions on market approval for new medicines, including those derived from biotechnology. Its assessments are based on the Community's safety, efficacy and quality criteria, first established under Directive 65/65/EEC (Council of the European Communities, 1965).

The impact of the EMEA cannot be overstated. Greeted as "a real European milestone" by at least one analyst (Albedo, 1995), the European Commission regards it as "[...] an important part of the overall strategy of the creation of a single market for pharmaceuticals" (European Commission, 1995b). The reason for such applause is that, unlike previous attempts to create a unified approval procedure for new medicines, the authorisations issued by the EMEA, once endorsed by the Commission, are binding and valid throughout the EU. Obviously, the purpose of single authorisation process is to avoid the duplication of effort by fifteen different national regulatory procedures, a review process that is considerably more specialised and expensive than for traditional industrial products (including medical devices), thereby easing bureaucratic and administrative pressures on manufacturers and national administrations alike. It also speeds the time required to bring new products to market; again a process that is unique to pharmaceuticals in terms of the time and detail required. However, a EU-wide system also has the effect of removing a great deal of responsibility from the Member States (Mossialos and Permanand, 2000).

As far as the authorisation process itself is concerned, on the basis of work carried out by national authorities acting as rapporteurs for each drug applications, the EMEA makes recommendations to the European Commission which then delivers the decision. The national agencies thus have little say over what drugs are being approved for their market; the EMEA procedure simply makes use of the existing Member State machinery. The Member States are entitled to question and even reject an authorisation issued by the EMEA, though such disputes rarely occur. In the event that they do, they are referred back the agency via its Committee for Proprietary Medicinal Products (CPMP) to be resolved.

As the body responsible for deciding on behalf of the EMEA, the probity of the CPMP must be ensured. Consequently, it is comprised of scientific experts from each of the Member States who are nominated by their national administrations, and these individuals are required to put aside any national or other interests they may have. By seeking to exclude vested interests, the intention is to guarantee scientific decision-making of the highest quality. Indeed, both manufacturers and Commission officials have been at pains to stress their considerable satisfaction with the agency and its work so far.

There are, however, some criticisms of the agency, relating primarily to the nature of the system and the resultant abrogation of social responsibility at national level. One criticism, from some analysts and commentators, has to do with a perceived lack of transparency in the agency's work (Dukes, 1996; Abraham and Lewis, 1998; Garattini and Bertele, 2001), which may lead to undue influence by industry. As a corollary perhaps, the second critique asks whether the agency's work to date (and perhaps even its remit) is therefore geared more towards the needs and interests of industry (*i.e.* the applicant) than it is to the consumer. Thus, it is claimed that the agency's emphasis on improving time-to-market (TTM) for new drugs is given precedence over protecting public health.

The first charge is one that the agency has fought since its inception, with some degree of success. Primarily through the maintenance of an updated and relatively user-friendly website (www.eudra.org), the EMEA has sought to make its activities accessible. The site posts a considerable array of information and material, ranging from the usual "Who we are/what we do" and "Frequently-Asked Questions" summaries, through to a listing of all legislation pertinent to medicines in the Community. It also includes contact details for all staff involved in the agency's work, including those at the national level. More importantly, it publishes the Summary of Product Characteristics (SPCs) for new drugs and the detailed assessments of new applications, known as European Public Assessment Reports (EPARs), for all positive opinions granted under the centralised procedure. Although much of this material is very specialised, it confirms the agency's self-declared open approach (Mossialos and Permanand, 2002).

The nature of this information has, nevertheless, been questioned, and the charge of secrecy has not gone away. It is one that reverberates especially sharply with those interested in the public health dimension of medicines regulation in the Community, particularly as the "public health test" is now a supranational rather than Member State responsibility. Thus, the International Society of Drug Bulletins (ISDB) has argued that the information on the EMEA website is opaque, inconsistent, and unhelpful. It has characterised the EPARs as "increasingly hazy and irrelevant". It accuses the agency of employing obscure and coded language in the presentation of these reports that diminishes the value of their content (ISDB, 2001). Consequently, the ISDB has long sought improved access to EMEA information. While issues of commercial and industrial secrecy must be respected, exclusion of the general public from even basic information does not inspire confidence where public health is concerned.

SPCs have also been criticised. These are supposed to provide detail about individual drugs in order that interested parties, primarily physicians and national regulatory officials, can obtain objective information about the drugs, thereby allowing them to better understand how they work. First, unlike many national agencies that distribute their findings to physicians, physicians must look for information from the EMEA themselves. It has thus been suggested that national regulatory agencies should be able to distribute SPCs (Garattini and Bertele, 2001). Next, the SPCs describe drugs without reference to similar preparations, let alone those designed to treat similar conditions. Furthermore, the manufacturers are themselves involved in writing both SPCs and the EPARs, leading to some variation in the quality of these documents (ISDB, 2001). This prevails despite a process of harmonisation of summaries under a centralised process; the majority of medicines circulating in Europe do, however, predate this process, and thus carry often widely differing summaries (Mossialos and Permanand, 2002).

Such shortcomings have led to the second line of criticism; namely, wider questions about the agency's true function. While established to regulate the safety, quality and efficacy of new medicines in Europe, the EMEA is viewed as serving primarily the interests of industry. Both the agency and the Commission (and the industry) have consistently stressed public health as the EMEA's first priority but many commentators remain unconvinced. They ask why, for instance, the applicant companies are privy to the CPMP's consultation documentation (that includes preliminary votes by the committee's Members) prior to the final decision (Garattini and Bertele, 2001). This gives manufacturers an initial "feel" with regard to how the authorisation is going, and allows them to either withdraw the product before assessment or else accept a preliminary negative decision at an early stage in order to have time to prepare an appeal (Mossialos and Permanand, 2002).

In addition, details of negative decisions or those in progress before a company's withdrawal of the proposed product are not published on the agency's website alongside positive decisions. A comparison between "acceptable" and "not acceptable" judgements would offer interested parties, particularly doctors and national regulators, the chance to see the EMEA's criteria in practice. Instead, only the industry is privy to this comparative information. Withholding such information does not seem to serve patient interests. In fairness, however, prior to 1995, when there was neither a centralised European agency nor a website, information about the review process and applications under consideration, such as EPARs or SPCs, was even less available than it is now (Mossialos and Permanand, 2002).

A further concern is that the industry is able to choose one of the two CPMP officials that act a rapporteur in the application. This does not imply that public health is compromised – clearly, more lax EU standards than those applied by some Member States could not be countenanced by European or national policy-makers – but it is to question the industry's role in the EMEA's work and to ask about the lack of transparency as perceived by some analysts.

What is the prospect of a European Agency for Medical Devices?
As previously noted, there is no equivalent to the EMEA for medical devices. This is despite forceful arguments during the late 1990s by the

French government for a European regulatory office. Unlike medicines, there was insufficient support from Member States. More importantly, the industry was not interested (Altenstetter, 1999). The idea has, however, recently resurfaced in the context of changes to the EU regulatory environment for devices. With the continuing globalisation of the sector, and the implementation of a system of Mutual Recognition Agreements (MRA) with the United States, there have been calls to re-assess the current framework. A discussion of the Mutual Recognition Agreements between the EU and the United States is beyond the scope of this chapter, though it should be mentioned that their general purpose is to improve each party's access to the others markets (Johnson, 2001). Specifically, the French and British governments have asked for a review of the Medical Devices Directive (MDD), and this has rekindled the idea of a centralised European office. They seem to feel that the current system represents the lowest common denominator rather than a functioning Europe-wide regime, and they are seeking to retain their own stricter national requirements.

The UK Medical Devices Agency (MDA) put the UK's call for a review of the MDD to the European Commission at the end of 2000. The MDA's position was that:

> overall, we believe that the MDD has worked reasonably well since its introduction in 1994, but several factors led us to call for this review. These included the adequacy of safety controls in some areas, rapid changes in the device industry and the technology which underpins its, and the proposed enlargement of the European Union (MDA, 2000).

Concerns about particular groups of devices and some system-wide concerns were also cited as problem areas. These were said to require either improved "guidance" from the EU or else major amendments to the current legislation. One of the problems identified, as with the EMEA, was a question about the transparency of the framework, though more with regard to clarifying the device manufacturer's position, rather than commenting on the process itself. Another concern was the need for improved clarity as to who bears responsibility for placing medical devices on the market. The Commission has taken the UK's submissions into consideration, along with those of other Member States, and is expected to deliver its conclusions soon.

IV. Pricing and Reimbursement Issues

The Community has no specific competence with regard to the pricing and reimbursement of medicines and medical devices under national health care systems. Pricing regulations are the responsibility of Member States. The mechanism employed may reflect a variety of factors and usually requires a balance between affordability and a reasonable reward for innovation. Thus, the UK operates a system of profit controls on manufacturers (the Pharmaceutical Price Regulation Scheme, PPRS), while in Germany prices of off-patent products reflect the availability of alternative products. This involves "reference-pricing" in relation to the lowest-priced equivalent. Decisions are made by the Bundesausschuss der Ärzte und Krankenkassen (BÄK), the Federal Standing Committee of Physicians and Sickness Funds, allowing the Sickness Funds to make considerable cost savings (Busse, 2001a).

Recently, however, this system has been challenged under both German constitutional law and European competition law (Kaesbach, 2001). The question is whether the German reference price system, given the BÄK's role, infringes European competition law. In 1999 a German Court ruled that the Sickness Funds' price-setting responsibility represented a violation of the EU's regulation of cartel practices, and on 3 July 2001 the German Federal Supreme Court decided to refer this to the ECJ for a preliminary ruling. The German Court asked the ECJ to clarify whether or not the representative organisations of social health insurance funds constitute company cartels under Article 81.1 (ex 85.1), and if so, could they be exempted from anti-cartel regulations (Article 86.2 – ex 90.2) on the grounds that they provide services fulfilling the public interest and do not interfere with the operation of the common market.

In addition to this request to the ECJ, the Federal Social Law Court had submitted a question to the Federal Constitutional Court in 1995. The question centred on whether or not price setting by non-state actors is deemed compatible with the principles of freedom of occupation and entrepreneurial activity within the pharmaceutical industry, pursuant to Article 12 of the German Basic Law. In Germany, strong limitations on basic rights are normally expected to be set only by state actors. However, the Constitutional Court has not yet produced a decision. Furthermore, the Federal Anti-Cartel Agency in 2001 warned the sickness funds that it would welcome a change in the system with regard to EU anti-cartel regulations (Richter, 2001). The Ministry of Health responded by introducing the Reference Price Adjustment Act, 2001 (forming a new section, §35a, of the Social Law Code Book V) which allows the Ministry of Health to issue a new reference price list.

In the UK two recent rulings of the Office of Fair Trading and the Competition Commission questioned whether the PPRS (under which pharmaceutical companies can freely set the prices of patented medicines and branded generics provided that they do not exceed a limit on the rate of return that a company can earn on its sales of prescription medicines to the NHS) offers immunity to companies' pricing policies.

In May 2001 the Office of Fair Trading's ruling that Napp Pharmaceuticals abused a dominant market position (a breach of the 1998 Competition Act) last year has been upheld by the Competition Commission Appeal Tribunal on appeal[1]. Napp was found to have abused a dominant position by charging patients in the community excessively high prices for its MST Continus sustained-release morphine tablets while offering them to hospitals at a highly discounted rate, thus blocking competition. The Director General of Fair Trading argued that "Napp charges excessively low and/or discriminatory prices in the hospital segment and thereby sustains very high prices and market share in the community segment of the market. These two markets are interlinked". Napp argued that, under the UK Pharmaceutical Price Regulation Scheme (PPRS), the company had not charged excessive prices and that for many years the company has been within the limits of return on capital invested permitted by the PPRS.

Rejecting Napp's argument, the Tribunal found that the PPRS was irrelevant to this case as it is not concerned with the control of anti-competitive practices, including charging of a higher price by reason of conduct excluding competitors. In its judgement the Tribunal made extensive reference to the case law of the ECJ. The Tribunal reviewed several ECJ rulings including Case 85/76 Hoffman-La Roche *v.* Commission[2] which concerned a system of loyalty rebates operated by the dominant firm which made it difficult for competitors to enter the market, Case C-62/86 AKZO Chemie *v.* Commission[3] where the dominant firm offered prices discounted below cost in order to force a competitor out of business and Cases T-83/91 Tetra Pak *v.* Commission[4] and 333/94 Tetra Pak *v.* Commission[5] where the Court of First Instance, applying the criteria set out in AKZO, found certain of Tetra Pak's prices were below direct variable costs and had no other economic rationale other than ousting Tetra Pak's principal competitor.

Although the Community does not have a role in the pricing of drugs per se, it does have an indirect effect. For instance, in 1984 the ECJ

---

[1]   Competition Commission. Appeal Tribunal Napp Pharmaceutical Holdings Limited and Subsidiaries and The Director General of Fair Trading, Case No.1000/1/1/01 (IR) (www.competition-commission.org.uk/appeals/judge01.pdf).

[2]   European Court of Justice, C-85/76 Judgement of 13/02/1979, Hoffmann-La Roche *v.* Commission.

[3]   European Court of Justice, C-62/86 Judgement of 03/07/1991, AKZO *v.* Commission.

[4]   Court of First Instance, T-83/91, Judgement of 06/10/1994, Tetra Pak *v.* Commission.

[5]   European Court of Justice, C-333/94 Judgement of 14/11/1996, Tetra Pak *v.* Commission.

delivered a ruling in the Duphar Case[6], which enabled Member States to organise their health social security systems in a way that sustained financial stability. The case involved Dutch law, which excluded certain drugs from the compulsory health care scheme on the basis that there were other medicines with the same therapeutic effect available, but which were less expensive. Although seemingly running against the free movement of goods provisions of Article 28 (ex 30), the Court in fact ruled that such restrictions were permissible, but only if they promoted the financial security of the health insurance schemes. While not representing a formal restriction on the free movement of medicines in the Community, the ruling did provide for a potential indirect restriction on imports, depending on how the decision was applied. Thus, for the legislation to be consistent with Article 28 (ex 30), the Court stressed that the choice of medicines excluded from reimbursement must meet certain objective criteria. Furthermore, these criteria had to apply regardless of the origin of the medicines. Where this criterion was fulfilled, any medicine could be imported into the Netherlands (and thus any Member State) providing that it had the same therapeutic effect at lower cost than products already available.

Another by-product of the ruling was that national controls on doctors' prescribing behaviour, in terms of only certain products being reimbursable under social security systems, was deemed consistent with the Treaty of Rome. The legal basis for the national implementation of so-called "negative" and "positive" lists was endorsed by the ECJ ruling. Since then the Duphar Case has been widely invoked to underline the case that Community law does not detract from the powers of the Member States to organise their social security systems (Mossialos and Permanand, 2002).

Similarly, the European Commission recently decided to pursue infringement proceedings against Greece for introducing national practices with regard to the reimbursement of medical devices, which, it was argued, violated free movement principles. The Commission issued a formal request ("reasoned opinion") to the Greek government to alter its reimbursement rules as they discriminated against products imported from other Member States (European Commission, 2001). Specifically, a 1999 government document stated that, in order to qualify for reimbursement, certain orthopaedic devices were required to carry the "serial number" of the insured. Furthermore, the product invoice was to refer to the professional licence of a special technician for such products. Not only was this viewed as a potential limitation on imports, but as the

---

[6]   European Court of Justice, C-238/82, Judgement of 07/02/1984, Duphar and Others.

document also stipulated that imported products that were more expensive that Greek ones would not be reimbursed, the Commission took the view that this was clearly against Article 28 (ex 30).

The initial push for a "European" dimension to pricing methodologies, not in terms of a standardising prices, but with regard to making pricing policies objective and clear, came with Directive 89/105/EEC (Council of the European Communities, 1989a). The so-called "Transparency Directive", which came into force in early 1990, was designed to assure open and verifiable criteria in national pricing and reimbursement decisions. This was to ensure that national policies did not inhibit the trade in medicines in the Community; in other words, to ensure the functioning of the single market. The final Directive was a thinner version of the first draft issued by the Council in 1986, in which the Commission had proposed measures that would have promoted price harmonisation. As this was not realistic in light of Member States' opposition, the Directive's preamble refers simply to "further progress towards convergence", and the Commission acknowledged that it was only an initial move in a step-by-step approach towards eventual price harmonisation (Mossialos and Abel-Smith, 1996).

Where medicines are included in a positive list for full or partial reimbursement, Article 6 of the "Transparency Directive" provides for a detailed procedure to be followed by any marketing authorisation holder. The evaluation process is accompanied by procedural guarantees (European Parliament, 2001). A decision on an application submitted has to be adopted and communicated to the applicant within strict and rather short deadlines. Furthermore, periods of time laid down in the Directive are mandatory and decisions not to include a medicinal product in the positive list have to contain a statement of reasons based upon objective and verifiable criteria (including, if appropriate, any expert opinions or recommendation on which the decision is based). In addition, the applicant must be informed of the remedies available to him in terms of national procedural law (European Parliament, 2001).

In 1999 the Commission launched legal proceedings against Austria, pursuant to Article 226 (ex 169) of the EC Treaty, for, amongst other issues, not complying with the "Transparency Directive" regarding the legal remedies available to companies when their applications for inclusion of medicines to the registry of reimbursed products are rejected.

In Austria medicinal products proposed for inclusion in the register of reimbursed products are examined by the bureau of the Federation. The result of the examination is submitted, by way of a proposal for a recommendation, to the small technical advisory board and communicated to the relevant pharmaceutical company. This board then examines the proposals and issues a recommendation. If the pharmaceutical company does not accept the rejection of its proposal it may lodge a written complaint with the Federation[7]. If its recommendation is not in favour of the applicant, it must submit the complaint, accompanied by any new information and its observations, to the main technical advisory board. That board considers whether the recommendation of the small technical advisory board is reasonable and may alter it. The Commission claimed that the Austrian legislation does not provide for any genuine judicial protection, contrary to the requirements of Article 6(2) of the "Transparency Directive". In the Commission's view, neither the complaint against the first recommendation of the small technical advisory board, nor, where the opinion of that board is again negative, the application for inclusion which may be submitted to the main technical advisory board, can be described as appeals since that remedy lies not before the Courts but before the administrative authorities[8].

The ECJ ruled that appeals to independent experts cannot be equated with the remedies mentioned in the Directive and that the applicant concerned must be able to avail himself of remedies ensuring effective legal protection. Moreover, since both the small technical advisory board and the main one can only issue recommendations they have no decision-making power, which rests with the Federation[9].

The requirement of judicial review reflects a general principle of Community law stemming from the constitutional traditions common to the Member States and enshrined in Articles 6 and 13 of the European Convention for the Protection of Human Rights and Fundamental Freedoms[10].

Although it is only possible to speculate at present, it may be that this ruling has implications for the way in which health authorities implement systems that seek to ration particular treatments.

The Commission did seek to launch a second Transparency Directive, but this failed, as the other stakeholders were unwilling to address the issue in the terms the Commission wanted. First, the industry voiced

---

[7] European Court of Justice, C-424/99 Judgement of 27/11/2001, Commission of the European Communities *v.* Republic of Austria.

[8] *Ibidem.*

[9] *Ibidem.*

[10] European Court of Justice, C-224/84 Judgement of 15/05/1986, Johnston *v.* Chief Constable of the Royal Ulster Constabulary; European Court of Justice, C-97/91 Judgement of 03/12/1992, Oleificio Borelli *v.* Commission; European Court of Justice, C-1/99 Judgement of 11/01/2001, Kofisa Italia and European Court of Justice, C-226/99 Judgement of 11/01/2001, Siples.

its concerns about direct Commission involvement in Member State pricing policies as potentially harmful to business. And the Member States, at least those who responded to a Commission questionnaire in 1992 as a follow-up to the original Transparency Directive, generally emphasised that they would not accept any Community infringement on their sovereignty where health was concerned. The then Commission Vice-President, Leon Brittan, attributed this to Member States exercising the principle of subsidiarity, which he saw as representing a formal limitation on the further development of Community competence in the area of pricing (Brittan, 1992). The price differentials that the Commission sought to overcome in the Transparency Directive discussions, and which continue today, have led to the practice of parallel trade in medicines in Europe since the 1970s.

Parallel trade is one of the most vexing issues concerning pharmaceuticals in the single market. It involves the purchase of branded medicines in one Member State, and their sale at below the market price pertaining in another, more expensive Member State. Specifically, this entails a distributor buying drugs from wholesalers in cheaper countries and then exporting them to more expensive countries where they are then sold on to local wholesalers (often directly to pharmacies as well) at prices lower than the manufacturer is itself offering them in that market.

As this has considerable cost-saving implications for national health care systems, it is not surprising that several Member States have effectively endorsed it as a means of reducing health care spending. In the UK alone the number of prescriptions filled by parallel imported products rose from one in ten in 1997 to one in eight by 1998, and, in 1997, applications to the Medicines Control Agency (MCA) for parallel licence imports increased by 18% compared with the previous year (House of Commons, 1999). It should be noted that the MCA grants a product licence to import a drug only after it has been shown that it is therapeutically equivalent to the domestic version. Nonetheless, as this parallel importation impinges on the profit-making abilities of the manufacturers whose medicines are being "parallel traded", they tend to oppose the practice.

The main reason for the development of parallel trade in prescription medicines is that considerable price differentials exist amongst the Member States. In the UK, for example, the retail price for an identical product often exceeds that in France or Spain by up to 100% (Kanavos, 2000). Because medicine pricing and reimbursement is tied to national health and social security systems, and are thus subject to the jurisdiction of Member States, such differentials are permissible within the single market. This is not the case for other commodities such as automobiles where the European Commission has taken steps to harmonise national pricing regimes. As these price differentials for medicines cannot be "legislated out", parallel trade has developed as an acceptable manner of ensuring relatively equal access to the same drugs throughout the Community, whilst at the same time fulfilling the free movement requirements of the SEM. This has been the view of the ECJ in several important cases so far (Mossialos and Permanand, 2002).

Another reason for the consolidation of this practice, although more difficult to substantiate, is that parallel trade can help check what many view as excessive industry profits. As industry is often accused of actively exploiting the differences between national regulatory systems, hence its reluctance to endorse a true single market in medicines, parallel trade evens the playing field somewhat. Both factors have unquestionably had a role to play in fostering the practice and, according to Hancher. It is probably fair to say that the truth of the matter lies somewhere in between these two poles: the industry must continue to live with a scatter gram of national policies on pricing and profit control, but is of course able to react to this situation in a number of ways, even it cannot necessarily control it. Currency movements have further fuelled price divergences (Hancher, 2000).

It seems, therefore, that there are both benefits and disadvantages to the practice. Concerning the disadvantages, the industry claims that parallel trade gives an unfair competitive advantage to distributors and thereby undermines their ability to undertake costly research and development; or that lower profits mean less innovation. The result, in practice, is that companies may, potentially, withdraw products from the market on non-health-related grounds; something that they are not permitted to do. This has lead to bitter complaints from several groups, most notably the European Generics Association (EGA), that by such withdrawals the large manufacturers compromise public health (EGA, 2000).

Turning to the benefits, parallel importers argue that parallel trade promotes competition. More players could potentially lead to greater choice for the purchaser. The wider availability of lower-priced, though still innovative and efficacious medicines, might also, eventually, bring about some degree of price convergence. Thus, the European Commission has traditionally seen removal of price differentials as central to completing the single market (Bangemann, 1997). Ultimately, parallel trade could help bring about closer market integration; something that the ECJ has recognised in several rulings it has delivered in favour of the practice.

It should, however, be recognised that the empirical evidence on the effects of parallel trade (both good and bad) is limited. Based on data from Sweden, the authors of a recent study have concluded that

> [...] the prices of drugs subject to competition from parallel imports increased less than other drugs during the period 1995-1998. Approximately ¾ of this effect can be attributed to lower prices for parallel imports and ¼ to lower prices charged by the manufacturing firm (Ganslandt and Maskus, 2001).

This would seem to bring benefits in terms of health spending. However, the authors go on to say that "Econometric analysis finds that rents to parallel importers (or resource costs in parallel trade) could be more than the gain to consumers from lower prices". There are, therefore, mitigating factors. While the jury is still out concerning the long-term impact of parallel trade, manufacturers have nonetheless tried to limit the practice where possible. For the most part they have attempted to do so through European Courts on the basis of intellectual property infringement, an issue explored later.

V. Questions of Free Movement

The 1957 Treaty of Rome established the earliest rules regarding the free movement of goods. It also laid down provisions on competition, a field in which the ECJ has been extensively involved. Both sets of provision affect the movement of medicines and medical devices in the Community.

In European competition law there is an immediate tension, stemming from its dual role. In addition to fulfilling the classical requirement of ensuring the lowest (fair) price for goods and services, along with the best allocation of resources, European competition law is designed to promote, or at least facilitate, the single market. It seeks to ensure that private enterprise does not treat the fifteen different Member States as independent markets. Accordingly, European competition law is enforced not just at the supranational level, but also equally in the Member States through its integration into national legislation. This dual function, and the tension which results, has accorded the ECJ a prominent role where competition issues are concerned, and particularly so over matters of intellectual property (Mossialos and Permanand, 2002).

Intellectual property rights are central to all high technology industries, such as pharmaceuticals and medical devices given the investment required in new products. The need to recover massive research and development costs (both in time and financial terms) and to remain competitive in a tight global marketplace has driven many drug manufacturers to seek extensive European-level intellectual property rights.

They have done so primarily through direct action; either by unilaterally lobbying their home governments on the need to recoup costs or, jointly, through, their EU trade organisation, the European Federation of Pharmaceutical Industry Associations (EFPIA), lobbying the Commission on patent durations. Another approach has been to bring a variety of cases before the ECJ to seek clarification, most notably on intellectual property issues (Mossialos and Permanand, 2002).

The pharmaceutical industry's lobbying on intellectual property rights has been successful (Shechter, 1998). During the 1980s its pressure on national governments resulted in some countries – France, Italy and the United Kingdom – either establishing, or seeking to do so, extended patent protection periods for pharmaceuticals. The desire of these governments to both ensure the profitability (and hence the economic contribution) of local industry and the procurement of efficacious medicines, saw them side with industry and, unilaterally, invoke national derogations from the standard provisions of the European Patent Convention. Such pressure at the national level inevitably emerged in the European arena and, given mounting pressure from EFPIA, ultimately required European Commission action. Following much political negotiation, this took the form of Regulation 1786/92, otherwise known as the Supplementary Protection Certificate (Council of the European Communities, 1992e).

Notwithstanding the fact that, as with other industrial products, pharmaceuticals fall under the auspices of the 1973 European Patent Convention (EPC), in 1992 the Commission introduced the Supplementary Protection Certificate (SPC) legislation in order to extend patent protection times. Manufacturers were granted fifteen years protection for their products from the date of first market authorisation in the Community; the EPC provided twenty years from first patent application. The passing of the new Regulation was not an easy affair as the Commission was subject to intense lobbying by the major stakeholders. Several drafts were thus prepared over a two-year period before the final text was adopted (Mossialos and Permanand, 2002).

The reasons for this lengthy process stem from the, at times, vastly different interests of the stakeholders. The research-based industry argued that, as the number of new chemical entities (NCEs) being discovered was diminishing, the length of the discovery and approval processes (and hence their own costs) were increasing (EFPIA, 1999). Lengthier patent protection would allow them to recoup their costs and reinvest them in research and development. The European generics industry was not in favour of more protection as longer patent times lessened their ability to compete; at the same time as their own research and development costs were rising. Consumer and patient groups also opposed the legislation, arguing that it represented a setback to the patient who would not only have to wait longer for (generic) medicines, but would also and have less choice (Mossialos and Permanand, 2002).

The Member States also expressed concerns with the SPC proposals. Their primary interest was in controlling health care costs and it was felt that patent extensions could delay the introduction of cheaper generics, thereby keeping drug prices high (Mossialos and Le Grand, 1999). There were, however, differences within this broad position. Countries such as the United Kingdom and Germany, which have major research-based industries, were initially reluctant to see patent times extended because of the effects any changes might have on pharmaceutical prices. Others Members such as Greece and Spain, with generic industries, simply opposed the proposals outright (Mossialos and Permanand, 2002).

The reasons for the development of a parallel trade market in medicines in the Community were outlined above. So too was the industry's displeasure with the practice, with the consequence that the ECJ has played an important role. In the subsequent section we look at how manufacturers have sought to limit parallel trade, and what the ECJ's role has been.

The industry's unhappiness has been manifest by some of the large research-based firms taking parallel importers to the ECJ on several occasions, on the formal grounds that parallel importation represents an infringement of their copyright and trademark rights. Informally, industry representatives also claim that the practice undermines innovation by undercutting the amount of money they can put into the research and development process for new drugs, as well as reducing their (and hence Europe's) competitiveness in the global marketplace. The implications of this position are that: (i) companies benefit from the current divergence in national prices and comparative lack of competition in the market; and (ii) that profit drives innovation. Neither can be adequately sustained. Nevertheless, as the costs of bringing a new drug to market have risen over the past few years – some industry estimates are now as high as € 500 million (EFPIA, 1999) – there has been a growing tension between the major stakeholders over the practice of parallel trade in medicines, bringing the ECJ into play. It should however, be noted that such cost data are supplied by the industry and include many factors that do not apply specifically to the generation of any single product. It is therefore advisable to treat these estimates with a degree of caution.

In its many rulings in this area, the ECJ has had to address several issues. First is the extent to which the practice is in keeping with internal market priorities. Second is the issue of intellectual property rights and the doctrine of European and international exhaustion of rights. Exhaustion of rights applies where a company chooses to market a product in two or more Member States. In doing so, it takes advantage of opportunities for international trade, and so exhausts its rights to control subsequent trade in the product in question by others between the States concerned. This raises wider issues relating to competition, particularly as manufacturers have been accused of trying to limit wholesalers' ability to sell to parallel distributors. The final question is how to ensure public health. Commentators have often sought to underline the value of parallel trade in enabling national health care systems to afford the (high quality) branded medicines and so benefit public health. A brief summary of several of the Court's more important rulings shows how one or more of these often over-lapping issues have been addressed.

As mentioned previously, European law according to Article 28 (ex 30), prohibits restrictions on imports or other measures "having equivalent effect". But Article 30 (ex 36) does permit certain derogations, including where the protection of industrial and commercial property is concerned. This derogation is permitted insofar as it does not constitute a "means of arbitrary discrimination or restriction on trade between Member States". Pharmaceutical companies have invoked this exception on several occasions as a means of limiting parallel trade although their attempts have been unsuccessful. The ECJ has generally ruled that once a medicine is made available in any two national markets with the manufacturer's consent, the manufacturer cannot then employ the intellectual property derogation of Article 30 to prevent any subsequent trade of the product between the two countries. For this reason, ECJ rulings have addressed copyrights, trademarks and patents (Hancher, 2000).

The Court's decisions have often centred on the "exhaustion of rights" principle. For instance, in 1974 the ECJ ruled that, once a company sells its product in a second market, it has recovered its so-called "motivation reward" and cannot then seek to influence any further Community distribution of that product[11]. The Court held that allowing the patent holder to restrict distribution – as a means of preventing parallel imports – was tantamount to sanctioning the continued partition of national markets, thus violating Article 28 (ex 30). This interpretation of the exhaustion of rights doctrine has been re-affirmed and widened in subsequent cases.

---

[11]   European Court of Justice, C-15/74 Judgement of 31/10/1974, Centrafarm B.V. and others *v*. Sterling Drug.

In the Stephar Case brought by Merck & Co. Inc. (hereafter, Merck) in 1981 to prevent the parallel trade of its anti-hypertensive drug, Moduretic, between Italy and the Netherlands, the ECJ went even further[12]. It did not simply uphold the principle that the patent owner's rights were "exhausted" once sale of the relevant product had occurred with their consent, but held that this applied even where there were differing intellectual property rights between the countries involved. In this case Merck had patents for the drug in all Member States except Italy and Luxembourg, and for its manufacturing process in all the Member States except Denmark, the Federal Republic of Germany, Italy and Luxembourg. The Court ruled that arbitrage between the Netherlands and Italy could not be hindered even if patents were not held in the country where this sale took place (Italy). The "exhaustion of rights" doctrine applied even when the second Member State did not provide patent protection; even if this meant reducing the return on investment of patent holder. The argument was that, by releasing the product in a country where national law does not provide intellectual property protection, companies must accept the consequences of further distribution within the EU and that withholding sales to avoid exhaustion could be left to the patent owner's discretion. This ruling set a precedent in reversing an earlier decision that there was no such exhaustion of rights if there was no patent in the country of first sale.

More recently, in 1996, the Court delivered its judgement in the Primecrown joined Cases, which had also been brought by Merck[13]. Here the issue was the parallel importation of certain medicines from Spain and Portugal that were, prior to their accession to the Community in 1986, not patented in either. Merck's concern was that, with accession, the effect of existing EU case law on intellectual property rights exhaustion would have permitted generic products from Spain and Portugal to be exported to other Member States where the products were protected. The Court permitted the patent owners to continue using their patents for a "limited period" to prevent importation from Spain and Portugal. However, questions arose with regard to the duration of this "limited period", and whether law on parallel importing should in fact be up-dated in its entirety.

Merck argued for a complete review of existing law, given both the increase in parallel importing since the Stephar ruling, and because the

---

[12] European Court of Justice, C-187/80 Judgement of 14/07/1981, Merck *v*. Stephar and Exler Merck & Co. Inc.

[13] European Court of Justice, C-267/95, Judgement of 05/12/1996. Merck *v*. Primecrown and Beecham *v*. Europharm.

Supplementary Protection Certificate, which had in part been designed to overcome this, would lose its meaning if parallel imports from the Iberian countries were to be permitted. It was argued that the research and development context had changed, as had the price differential between Spain and Portugal and the rest of the EU since the Stephar ruling. Merck claimed that pharmaceutical manufacturers generally have no choice other than to market their products, and that the idea of exhaustion at the time of sale should not therefore apply; how could they exhaust patent rights they did not in fact have? The Advocate General's recommendation was that the patent holders should be able to prevent parallel imports from Spain and Portugal and that Article 28 (ex 30) should not disadvantage the patentees when they did not previously enjoy patent protection in a country from which products are later exported. Nevertheless, despite the Advocate General's recommendation, the Court maintained its view on exhaustion line in previous rulings. These cases have since been the subject of extensive analysis and it has become clear that intellectual property rights are not a barrier to parallel trade in medicines within the Community. Nevertheless, there are potential problems because intellectual property rights continue to differ among countries (Mossialos and Permanand, 2002).

The most recent case concerning parallel trade and the pharmaceutical industry was the appeal (5 February 2001) to the ECJ by the European Commission against the Court of First Instance's decision of 26 October 2000 to quash a € 3 million fine levied on the German drugs company Bayer[14]. The fine had been awarded by the Commission on 10 January 1996 for what was viewed as uncompetitive practices by the company. Specifically, Bayer was said to have attempted to prevent the parallel trade of its cardiovascular drug, Adalat to the UK market from France. At the time, Adalat was available for approximately half the UK price in France (Hancher, 2001a). Given the rulings discussed above, Bayer had not sought to exercise intellectual property rights to reduce trade. Bayer was instead accused of limiting deliveries of the drug to wholesalers in France and Spain (as supplier countries to the UK). Through collusion with its own wholesalers in those countries, Bayer was accused of trying to prevent the drug being sold to distributors who might re-sell it to the UK.

The Commission's case was based on Article 81.1 (ex 85.1), which prohibits agreements between companies that amount to restrictions on competition (cartel practices). Bayer claimed that it had acted unilater-

---

[14] Court of First Instance. T-41/96, Judgement of 26/10/2000, Bayer *v.* Commission of the European Communities.

ally and not in collusion with its wholesalers, and launched an appeal which was upheld by the Court of First Instance in 1999. The Court did not find sufficient evidence of the Commission's claim of bilateral collaboration between Bayer and its wholesalers, and supported Bayer's argument that it had not imposed what the Commission had claimed in essence amounted to an export ban. The Court's decision was based on its finding that Bayer had no ability to control subsequent distribution of its products (that is, beyond distributing to its wholesalers). Furthermore, the company had no policy to ensure that the wholesalers did not export, nor one to sanction those that did. The Court thus quashed the fine and ordered the Commission to pay Bayer's costs. However, the ECJ did not question that contractually agreed obstacles to parallel trade fall foul of Article 81 (ex 85) but concluded that the Commission had not proven its case against Bayer.

In appealing this reversal to the ECJ, the Commission has stressed that the ruling does not call into question the principle by which obstacles to parallel imports or exports are banned. Put quite simply, the Commission "wants to continue its policy under Article 81.1 (ex 85.1) of challenging agreements between a manufacturer and his distributors, *e.g.* supply quota arrangements, which partition the common market along national lines" (Macarthur, 2001). This was a sentiment also expressed in the Commission's earlier Decision of 8 May 2001 to prohibit Glaxo Wellcome from operating a dual-pricing scheme (European Commission, 2001d). Glaxo Wellcome was charging its Spanish wholesalers higher prices for those medicines it was planning to export, than those intended for the domestic market. Although neither the Bayer nor Glaxo Wellcome Decisions are intellectual property cases per se, they are further indication of the drug companies' displeasure with the practice and their various attempts to limit it; not to mention the Commission's ongoing push for a single medicines market.

So what is the future of parallel trade? Beyond taking the parallel importers to Court, the industry has other tactics that it employs to limit the practice. As well as claiming that the safety and quality of the parallel imported products can be undermined in attempts to repackage the drugs, these include:

> [...] Making products available only in small batch sizes; supplying direct to pharmacy outlets at reduced prices; applying for licences in different strengths of drug dosage (for example, 10 mg strength in Spain but 20 mg in Germany) [...] different pack sizes [and] making tablets of different colours, shapes or with different packaging (House of Commons, 1999).

It remains to be seen, however, whether these tactics can be legislated against effectively, *i.e.* are they "police-able" in the future? If not, how they can be properly regulated within the single market.

All the Court cases so far outlined contain a tension between support for intellectual property rights and promotion of the single market (and not just for medicines), which continues even today. According to a study commissioned by the European Commission in 1994:

> The European Community's policy for intellectual property is twofold: on the one hand it wants to ensure that "products" are adequately protected both internally and externally, while on the other, it seeks to harmonise national legislation on intellectual property rights so as to remove any trade restrictions between Member States. In particular, the Community seeks to establish greater protection of intellectual property rights [...] and efficient control over illegal and counterfeit goods (Coopers & Lybrand, 1994: 80).

Furthermore, Competition Commissioner Monti in a recent speech argued (2001a): "Leaving aside the details, we take the view that the industry is wrong first and foremost – in contending that parallel trade in medicines even harms consumers and secondly in arguing that the Commission's policy brings no benefits at all for consumers in the high price countries".

The Commission has recently supported the implementation of a global tiered pricing system, to enable access of medicines in developing countries. A prerequisite for the implementation of a tiered system is to prohibit parallel trade from third countries into the Community. The industry has, however, argued that attempts to block parallel imports may contravene Article 81 (ex 85) EC Treaty. According to Commissioner Monti "measures against parallel trade within the Community are one thing, and those against parallel trade into the Community another". Monti argues that companies are free to take measures to stop parallel trade at the external Community borders (Monti, 2001b).

The most likely result of this tension is that parallel trade will continue for the foreseeable future. Any ECJ ruling that seeks to abolish it would, in essence, be undermining the free trade principle that lies at the heart of the single market. While the Court has toned down its apparent support for "integration through free movement", as change would also require the approval of both the Commission and the Council, any compromise on what many regard as the fundamental basis of the European Union, seems highly unlikely (Mossialos and Permanand, 2002).

VI. Product/Producer Liability, Electronic Commerce and Pharmaceutical Advertising

As the Community consolidates the regulatory regimes for medicines and medical devices, European law is likely to continue to play a major role, which will extend to other areas. This will require further changes to national health care systems, with implications for Member States' decision-making power.

One is product and producer liability. For both medicines and medical devices, the Community is continuing to develop a Euro-regime in the field of product liability. Disparate national laws on the right of consumers to seek redress from the manufacturer for any loss or injury incurred through the use of a product have been harmonised by a 1985 Directive (Council of the European Communities, 1985). These diverse national systems were seen as hampering both the free movement of products and the development of a common market for consumers. Thus, the Directive established a stringent liability protocol requiring litigants to demonstrate not simply that the product was defective, but that injury occurred as a direct result. Until then, national rules had generally required the litigant to prove that the manufacturer had been negligent and that it had therefore been aware of the problem.

There has been much recent discussion about amending the Directive and, on 28 July 1999 the Commission issued a Green Paper on Producer Liability (European Commission, 1999b). In doing so, it set out two aims: first, "to enable practical and factual information to be collected from those concerned (in particular industry and consumers), in order to assess how the Directive is applied 'in the field', and to establish definitively whether it is achieving its objectives"; and second "to 'gauge' reactions to a possible revision as regards the most sensitive points of this legislation". EUCOMED, the EU medical device manufacturers' umbrella organisation issued a response which, amongst other things, served to stress the differences between medical devices and other products where producer liability is potentially an issue (EUCOMED, 1999). They also stressed that the current (predominantly national self-regulation) rules were more than adequate to assure safety and efficacy, and that there was little need for any substantive adjustments for medical devices.

Another area in which the Community will soon be required to take a stance is with regard to "e-commerce" and the role of the Internet *vis-à-vis* medicines and medical devices. The implications of the World Wide Web as both a source of information and a vehicle for purchases has been recognised by the Commission as having specific implications for pharmaceuticals and it featured heavily in the 1996-1998 Commission "roundtable" discussions with the industry on measures towards completing the single market. Beginning with the information issue, there are innumerable disease and health-dedicated websites. Health-related sites are not only the most numerous, but among the most frequently visited. There is an enormous amount of information 'out there'. The complexity of the information and the challenge of judging its applicability in different circumstances mean that few people have the specialised knowledge needed to interpret the information on offer. Worryingly, it also widely recognised that much of the information available on the Web is out-dated, misleading, untested and often wholly incorrect. There is a further question as to who is providing the information, why, and how responsible they are. At present, many sites are sponsored by the large pharmaceutical firms, which immediately suggests a potential conflict of interest with regard to presentation of the material as it opens the door for manufacturers to promote their own medicines on these sites, an action that is contrary to the ban on direct-to-consumer advertising in Europe (see below). This poses problems for European policy-makers on several levels. While the possibility of independent regulation of these sites to ensure their accuracy and quality might seem an answer, in the short- to medium-term at least, the practical implications of implementing such a system are not immediately apparent.

As well as having instant access to reams of unregulated information, the continuing growth of the Internet in Europe, though still well behind the United States, has brought with it the possibility to buy medicines on-line. Thus, the Internet is proving a major contributor to the growing practice of mail-order trade in medicines. Given the continuing price differentials between Member States, it is clear that the EU will have to develop an explicit policy. E-Pharmacy and mail order is resisted in most EU countries. It is encouraged in the Netherlands while in the UK there is no legal restriction per se and it is only the pharmacy bodies that attempt to restrain such practices. The first UK online pharmacy started operations in 2000 and, at the same time the Royal Pharmaceutical Society issued guidelines for Internet pharmacies. The British government's view is that, if proper safeguards and professional standards are in place, there is no reason in principle why medicines should not be dispensed electronically. The government plans that, by 2004, every NHS general practitioner will have the ability to transmit prescriptions electronically to pharmacist (NHS, 2000). In Denmark fifty pharmacies have recently started to sell over the counter (OTC) medicines on-line and the government is considering the introduction of on-line sales of prescription medicines.

Countries such as Germany, that have made mail order trade in medicines illegal (since 1998), are finding that distributors and pharmacists in other Member States are shipping to their markets, defending their right to do so on the principle of free movement (Kaesbach, 2001). Germany has in fact banned the sale of all prescription and OTC drugs outside of pharmacies, and pharmacists themselves have expressed reluctance to move to e-commerce. In 2000, DocMorris.com, a Dutch e-pharmacy, was involved in a number of cases before German regional Courts. The Hamburg, Stuttgart and Frankfurt Courts have all granted temporary injunctions prohibiting the supply of mail order pharmaceuticals to German patients. The last of these courts ruled that the right to import for personal use (allowed under German law) did not cover mail order activity as there was a commercial element involved (Simmons & Simmons, 2001). The DocMorris.com Case is being discussed before the ECJ[15]. Currently three EU Directives deal with regulatory issues related to online pharmacies. Directive 2000/31/EC on electronic commerce (European Parliament and the Council of the European Union, 2000) may enable e-pharmacies to supply consumers in EU Member States. Mail orders and delivery could be made possible under Directive 97/7/EC on distance selling (European Parliament and the Council of the European Union, 1997a). However, Member States could refuse to apply e-commerce in pharmaceuticals on the basis of public health and consumer protection considerations. Moreover, Directive 95/46/EC on data protection sets constraints on the use of patients or consumers databases by e-pharmacies (European Parliament and the Council of the European Union, 1995).

In France, meanwhile, the Internet has not yet permeated the mundane to the same degree; largely because of the prevalence of the so-called "Minitel" service which all homes have access to. France is, however, slowly catching up, though it remains to be seen whether e-commerce will take off as it has in Sweden or Switzerland for example. In the former, all pharmacies fall under the state umbrella organisation, Apoteket – which has its own website – and which could therefore potentially act as a catalyst for medicines e-commerce. This is especially likely as Sweden is one of the most 'wired' countries in the EU. Switzerland, although not a EU Member, has already embraced the Internet as a way to buy medicines. In 2000 some 16% of all prescription and over the counter medicines (OTC) sales in Switzerland were acquired via mail order or online (Starnes, 2000). Effective regulation at the European level must take account of this diversity.

The expansion of the Internet also has ramifications for the divisive issue of drug advertising. As a result, the European Commission is

---

[15]   European Court of Justice, C-322/01, Pending Case, Deutscher Apothekerverband.

slowly starting to re-assess the European position on banning direct-to-consumer marketing in the face of a strengthening US market, which permits it.

The provisions governing the advertising of medicines in the Community are another example of how European law impacts on matters affecting national health care systems. In 1992 the Community set out to harmonise Member State rules on advertising medicines for human use as part of the singe market programme. Directive 92/28/EEC (Council of the European Communities, 1992f) differentiated between advertising to health professionals (doctors and pharmacists) and that aimed at the general public. The former pertains to prescription medicines (and those containing narcotics or psychotropic substances), and the latter to OTC preparations. Advertising for non-prescribed pharmaceuticals is first subject to the need for market authorisation of the relevant product.

National advertising rules differ substantially between the Member States (European Commission, 1996a). For instance, while Belgium and Denmark have traditionally banned the advertising of OTC medicines on all audio-visual media, Sweden, Italy and France have insisted on pre-notification for OTC advertising. Belgium and France meanwhile, have outlawed all sales promotions for OTC. Even among those countries that do have similar advertising regulations, the specific requirements can also be quite different. For example, with regard to television advertising, some countries require that very stringent warning messages accompany the advertisement, or that the advertisement be only of a particular length. Another problem for advertisers has been that the same products are not available in all Member States, either in terms of those on positive lists or reimbursed via national social security systems.

In laying down the Community rules, the pharmaceutical advertising Directive has tried to overcome these differentials. Key amongst its provisions is a reference to an earlier piece of legislation, Directive 84/450/EEC of 1984 (Council of the European Communities, 1984) on advertising in general. This prohibits "misleading advertising" which, where drugs are concerned, takes on an added significance. Accordingly, pharmaceutical advertising must not simply meet the criteria of the Summary of Product Characteristics, but it must also be undertaken such that recognition of the product as a medicine, and the advertising medium itself as a form of market promotion, is easy and immediate. There are minimum information requirements that product leaflets must contain, including the name of the medicine, potential side effects, and instructions for correct use and application. Where the general public is concerned, product advertising must make it clear that taking the medicine does not guarantee the effects it is designed to offer. Where health professionals are targeted, the Directive forbids advertising that involves inducing doctors to prescribe specific products *i.e.* companies are prohibited from offering gifts or other inducements. The Directive also permits Member States to disallow advertising outright, though only of prescription medicines eligible for reimbursement under the national health care system.

As mentioned previously, the pharmaceutical advertising Directive was adopted to foster the free movement of products within Europe. To facilitate this, so that at least all Member States would apply similar conditions, harmonised advertising standards were deemed essential. This need is becoming even clearer as the Internet continues to change not simply the way people shop and the (unregulated) information they have access to, but also the nature of health care and its provision. The Commission has long recognised the issues arising from electronic commerce and online advertising of medicinal products. On 21 March 2000 the Commission hosted a meeting dedicated to this specific question with several interested parties; though it remains unclear on what basis those attending were invited. What has resulted is a shift in the Commission's thinking with regard to pharmaceutical advertising in general, and direct-to-consumer advertising (DTC) more specifically.

DTC for medicines has long been permissible in the United States where it is viewed as cost-effective, given that medical costs are covered by private rather than state-funded health insurance (Dewulf, 2000). DTC advertising spending in the US is growing rapidly. It increased from US$ 1.53 billion for the twelve months up to March 1999 (Sullivan, 2000) to $ 2.6 billion in 2001 (IMS Health, 2002). This growth is in large part due to the Internet, and the advertising generally takes the form of companies setting up websites to explain the relevance of their medicines as well as providing detailed information on the specific diseases they are designed to treat. In addition, the companies are increasingly sponsoring a variety of other health care and disease-oriented websites to get their product messages across. Such activities are illegal in Europe and opposition to the idea remains widespread. The reasons for this are several fold, and are voiced not simply by patient and consumer groups, but more importantly, by doctors, medical associations and regulatory authorities.

The reasons for such opposition stem from uncertainty about any benefits DTC might bring, while there are numerous studies indicating its many problems. The industry points to advantages in "empowering the consumer through information", resulting in a higher degree of autonomy and an ability to assist the doctor, as well as speedier access to medicines. This is to be weighed against the often-dubious nature of the information provided on the Web, as mentioned earlier. There is no guarantee that industry websites are necessarily better at providing higher-quality information. This is apparent from evidence that, in the United States, even over-the-counter advertisements – which the FDA regulates – often make inaccurate statements and neglect to mention potential side-effects (Sansgiry *et al.*, 1999). The dividing-line between information and advertising is therefore tenuous.

More worrisome still are other concerns about the impact of DTC advertising. According to Hoffman and Wilkes: "Extending the scope of already ubiquitous promotions about 'post-nasal drip', 'unsightly rashes' or 'cures' for baldness has little to do with educating the patients or relieving suffering" (Hoffman and Wilkes, 1999). DTC has thus been seen as an industry tool, not for the promotion of information as they argue, but rather to make further profit. In providing information in this way, especially through the Internet, the industry can link the ability to buy on-line or via mail order as mentioned earlier. This eliminates pharmacists and even doctors as the "middlemen", and potentially leads to the consumer relying more on medication than on advice from health professionals. In turn, this raises the prospect of more inappropriate use of medicines.

It is therefore not surprising that doctors have been amongst the most vociferous opponents to DTC advertising, and still are in the United States. Many claim that their ability to practice evidence-based medicine is being undermined (Goldstein, 1998). In addition, doctors have expressed their frustration with growing numbers of patients who come to them with demands for specific medicines or courses of treatment, based on industry promotions, and promising to go elsewhere should the doctor be unwilling to prescribe them. A survey carried out in 1999 among primary care doctors in Ohio and Pennsylvania found that most felt under pressure to prescribe drugs so marketed; and that between 30-36% admitted giving in to this pressure (Spurgeon, 1999). The results of an earlier study carried out in 1997 by the North-Western Medical School in Chicago found that physicians across America expressed generally negative views about DTC: 80% felt that it was not a good idea and 84% were unhappy with current television and radio advertising (Lipsky and Taylor, 1997).

There are other fears associated with DTC. Companies may shift their advertising budgets further towards new drugs. These are generally more expensive than existing medicines or generics, and do not necessarily bring an improved health benefit. There are other cost implications. DTC advertising in the US has been linked with both rising numbers of prescriptions issued and choice of more costly medicines, putting pressure on health insurers (Finley, 2001). These are all issues that any future liberalisation of the DTC rules in Europe will have to accommodate. Nevertheless, despite such evidence, the prevailing view on DTC is changing as European companies complain about their inability to compete effectively with American firms.

In the UK for instance, despite disagreeing about allowing DTC advertising, a joint government-industry Task Force (established in March 2000) agreed on the need for companies to be able to provide more information about medicines (Gopal, 2001). This reflects the danger, as acknowledged by Enterprise Commissioner Erkki Liikanen, that European consumers are accessing a great deal of information from American company websites (Liikanen, 2001). The implication is that if European patients are going to get their information from somewhere, it might as well be from Europe. The industry's view is that the continuing prohibition of DTC in Europe is therefore unsustainable, and legislation needs to be changed in order that accurate information can be made available to the public. This type of pressure, exerted by powerful national stakeholders such as the Association of British Pharmaceutical Industries (ABPI), is something which the national governments, and in turn the European Commission, will not be able to ignore indefinitely. Changes to the legal environment thus appear almost inevitable if Europe is to keep pace with the US.

Some national medical organisations, such as the British Medical Association (BMA) seem to have already accepted the inevitability of change. At a meeting between the BMA and the ABPI, Dr. George Rae, Chairman of the Prescribing Subcommittee of the BMA's General Practice Committee, said: "We believe that what is happening in the United States now could be happening in Europe within the next five to ten years. We want to shape what happens rather than just oppose it"[16]. In stressing specific requirements, this is a sentiment echoed by the Association of the European Self-Medication Industry (AEGSP):

> consumer-friendly information through leaflets and labels as well as the possibility to advertise in all media are important to make the public aware of a newly introduced OTC medicine. In this context, it should be kept in mind that the successful self-control instruments introduced in many countries around the globe are also competent for the clearing of switched products. We remain convinced that the best way to inform the public through OTC advertising is to mention only the name of the product, the indication and an express invitation to read the label or the leaflet (Kranz, 1999).

Despite re-iterating that the benefits of DTC are not (yet) accepted in the EU, the European Commission has nevertheless indicated its willingness to pursue some deregulation of advertising.

---

[16]   *News. Pharmaceutical Journal* 2000; 265(7107): 151.

As part of its review of community pharmaceutical legislation, a five-year pilot programme has been proposed by the Commission for specific disease areas – AIDS, diabetes and asthma – whereby pharmaceutical companies could make available drug information on request from a patient or consumer group. Termed disease-awareness campaigns, the companies will be permitted to provide information about their medicines either via the Internet or in specialised publications. A code of conduct on the type, content and presentation of information is still to be drawn up, and it is expected that the EMEA will be asked to review this. As an aside, the choice of AIDS, diabetes and asthma for the trial still requires some clarification. While Commissioner Liikanen said that: "These diseases are long-term and chronic, there is strong patient demand for information, and the results of the 5-year pilot should be relatively easy to monitor. This will be coupled with strict control measures", on that basis a case could equally be made for cancer or even multiple sclerosis awareness campaigns. The Commission has yet to offer any real justification for its choice. In any event, the idea has also met with criticism from several consumer groups who equate it as an endorsement of DTC, and the negative effects this can bring (as outlined earlier), and who thus fear the effects on state health care funding.

For example, Health Action International (HAI), a non-governmental organisation dedicated to "working for a more rational use of medicinal drugs" was amongst the first to respond to the Commission's announcement: "HAI Europe deeply regrets the recent decision by the European Commission to recommend that pharmaceutical companies be allowed to mount disease awareness campaigns. This is the thin end of the wedge to open the door to Direct-to-consumer Advertising" (HAI Europe, 2001). The statement cited specific examples of where DTC has had negative effects, including promotions of AIDS drugs in San Francisco that were being considered for withdrawal for having provided misleading and unrealistic imagery about what sort of lifestyles AIDS-infected individuals could enjoy. HAI thus questions the self-regulatory nature of the Commission proposal and asks what guarantees the Commission has that European firms will behave any more responsibly.

At the national level too there has been criticism, and the United Kingdom Consumer's Association also released a "briefing paper" in response to the announcement. It accepts that there is a strong consumer push for more information but it claims that the US experience with DTC has caused considerable harm. Specifically, the paper points to the distortion of prescribing behaviour in favour of newer, more expensive medicines; a clear relationship between advertising and a "huge increase" in the drugs bill; that much of the DTC information provided does not in fact enable patients to make informed choices – it is often incomplete and misleading; and that advertising is actually being used by US companies to enforce brand loyalty and increase profits (UK Consumers Association, 2001).

Of course it remains to be seen what the Commission is actually proposing. On the one side is the view expressed by those who favour (or fear) that the proposal is a clear indication of the Commission's plan to introduce DTC in the medium-term, perhaps within the next ten years. On the other is the perception, voiced most notably by European policymakers themselves, that this is intended only as a trial in providing patients with more information on the drugs that are available to treat the three specific diseases cited (Glass, 2001). If it offers any clarity, in announcing the launch of the pilot scheme, Commissioner Liikanen stressed that "This is not direct-to-consumer advertising. We are not introducing advertising for prescription drugs. I am against direct marketing as massive advertising could place a lot of pressure on the health costs that are covered by public authorities" (Watson, 2001). While this may be the Commissioner's own position, it should be borne in mind that the disease awareness proposal was made within the scope of the review of pharmaceutical legislation more generally. Other provisions included: a fast track registration procedure for products of "major therapeutic interest"; reform of the EMEA mandate to perhaps include a role in providing scientific advice to the drugs companies (*i.e.* with respect to market approval); and the idea of a Europe-wide system of pre-authorisation availability for certain medicines on grounds of so-called "compassionate use".

The basis for these accompanying proposals seems quite clear. While they may, in the Commission's words, aim to guarantee the highest possible level of health protection for European citizens via the safety, quality and efficacy criteria, they are undoubtedly designed to speed the authorisation process. And while the Commissioner himself admitted as much "We want to increase the availability of new and innovative medicines on the European market" the review of advertising is undoubtedly part of an effort to keep pace with the US, albeit on the basis of anecdotal evidence rather than through any detailed examination of the evidence (on either the potential benefits or problems) associated with the practice.

The evidence cited by HAI, the UK Consumer's Association, and the other DTC studies mentioned earlier, all question the Commission's real motivation. The advertising announcement appears to have taken none of these into account. Indeed, we are unaware of any study commissioned by the Commission either on the effects of DTC in the United States or New Zealand, or its potential impact in Europe. The Commission's announcement appears a first step towards the liberalisation of pharmaceutical advertising regulations in Europe. This would, after all, be in keeping with previous initiatives to speed the market authorisation process. It seems likely then, that the direct-to-consumer advertising of medicines may be developed in Europe in tandem with other measures favoured by industry; perhaps coming sooner than may have previously been anticipated.

Conclusion

Pharmaceutical and medical device policy in the EU clearly have an enormous impact on the Member States, both with regard to shaping domestic policy decision-making, and in terms of re-adjusting the operation and structure of their health care systems. And yet the EU frameworks for both fields remain incomplete. There are still a host of issues to be dealt with at the European level, promising further impact at national level.

For instance, the pricing and reimbursement of pharmaceuticals conundrum has still not been solved at EU level. There is doubt as to whether it can be. But as our discussion has suggested, the Member States appear in general more willing to countenance European intervention in health care matters than previously. Not only that, but as the European industry continues to put pressure on national governments and the EU with regard to loss of competitiveness *vis-à-vis* their US counterparts, both of which appear to be listening to these complaints, this may offer the Commission a renewed chance to address the matter.

The recent findings that institutional and regulatory factors might serve to protect and insulate the European industry from competition as opposed to forming barriers to the further expansion of what it usually viewed as one of Europe's most competitive sectors may well offer the Commission a new point of departure from which to tackle the vexed issue of price regulation (Hancher, 2001b).

It remains to be seen what form the Commission's new approach might take, though one suggestion from industry is that price controls should be instituted for those medicines which are reimbursed by national social security systems (Viehbacher and Benbow, 2001). A common approach to the pricing of branded medicines would undoubtedly help promote the internal market, and has the added benefit of not impacting too heavily on health sovereignty. Member States would still be able to decide their positive and negative lists, and would continue to regulate prices of all other medicines, including those subsidised by the state. It also gives the research-based industry enough room to manoeuvre in terms of rewarding innovation. As an industry suggestion, it should of course be borne in mind that the underlying rationale is to enhance competitiveness and protect intellectual property, particularly in a changing European landscape with regard to the first wave of new Member States from Eastern Europe. Consequently, such an intervention could be regarded as a first step, though not as the "end of the story".

Indeed, the accession of these countries and their effect on the existing pharmaceutical sector is playing heavily on industry minds at the moment (and indeed European policy-makers generally). Major reforms of these health systems are going to be required, and this includes their medicine and medical device sectors (Kanavos, 1999). Currently the Central and East European Countries (CEEC) have lower intellectual property standards and comparatively poor patent coverage, and are considerable manufacturers of generics. Perhaps, therefore, it is the prospect for increased parallel importation, coupled with moves in these countries towards permitting pre-patent expiry manufacturing of branded medicines (introduction of the so-called "Roche-Bolar" type provisions), which is contributing to the European pharmaceutical industry's apparent mood of flexibility. They seem to be actively seeking dialogue with the Commission, the Member States and even groups representing patient interests, something neither they nor the Commission have always done in the past (Mossialos and Permanand, 2002).

We have seen, therefore, Commissioner Liikanen call together the so-called "High Level Group on Innovation and the Provision of Medicines" (otherwise known as the "G10") to discuss the future of the sector. It should of course be borne in mind that the industry's interest in such collaborative effort is equally to make the case for enhancing their global competitiveness (Lawson, 2001); and the membership of the G10 again reflects this, as patient interests are not prioritised. The G10 was established in March 2001 and brings together the Enterprise and Health and Consumer Protection Commissioners, with selected Member State health ministers, selected industry representatives (including members of the European self-medication and generic trade groups), the Association Internationale de la Mutualité (AIM) which represents health insurance and social protection bodies, and the Picker Institute, an organisation which specialises in measuring patient satisfaction with health care. Indeed, the idea of the G10 itself was born from a report commissioned by the Commission (DG Enterprise) into the competitiveness of Europe's pharmaceutical industry, which was published in June 2000 (Gambardella *et al.*, 2000).

It is important in the present climate of health care cost-containment, especially given the Commission's focus on promoting the competitiveness of the industry, to consider the question of generic competition and the place of the generics industry in the current system. According to Hancher (2001b), not just "'intra-brand' (parallel trade) but so too 'inter-brand' (generics) competition [is] considered by the European Commission, particularly the Directorate-General for Competition, as essential for the eventual realisation of a single market across the EU". That said, the Community exercises no competence in this area, as the requisite measures such as generic substitution and influencing doctors' prescribing patterns are matters of health care policy. These remain firmly in the hands of national governments.

The problem of a lack of industrial competitiveness in the EU was recognised in the recent report commissioned by the European Commission (Gambardella *et al.*, 2000). But the reasons for this lack of competitiveness, what this means in practice, and indeed the possible solutions, are very different depending whether one asks the research or generic companies. According to the research-based industries, the report cites three reasons as to why the European industry is becoming less competitive:

- US multinationals appear to be more successful than their European counterparts in producing innovative medicines;
- The US also benefits enormously from the immense creative potential of its biotech sector;
- Demand has grown much faster in the US than Europe over a comparative period, both in quality and quantity (Lawson, 2001).

The report's suggested solutions include: the implementation of effective intellectual property protection; governments to support basic bio-medical research; and the pursuit of market-based competition and customer choice.

The generics industry has a different perspective. According to Andrew Kay, President of the EGA, the problems identified in the report and their solutions lie not so much with the lack of appropriate enabling conditions for innovative research, but rather the lack of support received by the generics industry:

> [...] the EU lacks the triggers for generic competition which exist in the US. The EU grants longer periods of special market protection for branded pharmaceuticals, provides no encouragement for early development of generics, and has created a regulatory system which failed to ensure the registration of generic medicines quickly and efficiently [...]. Unless competitive generic mechanisms are put in place in the EU, the pharmaceutical sector will remain over protected and under competitive (Kay, 2000).

From this perspective, it is not simply a question of decreasing competitiveness *vis-à-vis* the US, but rather a lack of competition in the market. The Commission will need to address this, and quickly if the research-industry's veiled threats about moving research and development capacity to the United States are to be avoided. But the question is how? Given the lack of a health care policy role, the Commission will have to convince the Member States to pursue appropriate policies. Hancher has suggested the possibility of copying the US "experiment" and moving more prescription drugs into the over-the-counter market (Hancher, 2001b). With governments keen to protect local industry, this will – as with so much in the pharmaceutical industry – prove problematic and require the striking of a delicate balance between industrial and health care policy requirements.

With regard to medical devices, further adjustments to national regulatory regimes will also be required. For example, although the new Euro-system includes the post-market monitoring protocol outlined earlier, this is not to say that it is either final or flawless in practice let alone theory. The system may appear stringent and multi-layered, but a word of caution has been expressed by at least one commentator with respect to the vigilance or self-regulation aspect; Altenstetter writes that:

> [...] One weakness remains which will make a difference for the operation of an effective vigilance system in the medical device field. It is the absence of strong traditions in market surveillance in most Member States not only in regard to healthcare products and pharmaceuticals but also in regard to consumer goods in general [...]. Who is responsible for the operation of a vigilance system is hardly perceived as a responsibility (Altenstetter, 2001b).

This suggests national differences in both reporting and implementation. The question is how to merge these without compromising the health and safety of patients in countries with stricter provisions *i.e.* avoiding regulating downwards to the lowest common denominator, while meeting industrial policy goals. Such national differences will ensure that the post-marketing surveillance of medical devices in the EU proves a complicated and difficult process.

From our admittedly selective summary of the still-evolving EU regulatory regimes for pharmaceuticals and medical devices, it is obvious that national health care systems are not as free from European legislation as Article 152 (ex 129) might suggest. First, EU policy in these fields is aimed at achieving several concurrent goals ranging from health protection and convergence of national standards, to consolidation of the internal market and promotion of successful industries. Second, through many of its recent decisions, the ECJ in particular has made it clear that the Member States are required to apply and respect European law when organising their health and social security systems.

Together these two processes, growing European regulation *via* the "regulatory state" and the development of European law, are putting pressure on the Member States' systems. Recent manifestations of this includes the British Minister of Health's announcement on cross-border care, and what appears to be the Commission's interest in phasing in direct-to-consumer advertising of medicines under the review of pharmaceutical legislation. When the as yet "unknown ingredient" of Eastern enlargement is added, with all that it brings, it promises interesting times for health care (and wider social policy) at both the supranational and national levels in the European Union.

CHAPTER 6

Voluntary Health Insurance

Introduction

The types of Voluntary Health Insurance (VHI) on offer in a particular Member State reflect both the historical development and the current rules and arrangements of that Member State's statutory health care system. Public policy in EU Member States has aimed to preserve the principle of health care funded by the state or social insurance and made available to all citizens, regardless of ability to pay. As a result, statutory health care systems in the European Union are broadly characterised by near universal coverage, mandatory participation, the provision of comprehensive benefits and high levels of public expenditure.

These characteristics have been important determinants of the scope and size of VHI markets in the European Union, and the voluntary nature of such markets means that they generally operate in areas that the state does not cover. In the EU context, therefore, VHI can be classified according to whether it:

- substitutes for cover that would otherwise be available from the state (substitutive VHI);
- provides complementary cover for services excluded or not fully covered by the state, including cover for co-payments imposed by the statutory health care system (complementary VHI);
- provides supplementary cover for faster access and increased consumer choice (supplementary VHI).

Complementary and supplementary VHI are open to the whole population and some form of complementary and/or supplementary VHI is available in every Member State. In contrast, substitutive VHI is limited to specific population groups in a handful of Member States. It is usually purchased by:

- those who are excluded from participating in some or all aspects of the statutory health insurance scheme (high-earners in the Netherlands and self-employed people in Belgium and Germany);

-   those who are exempt from contributing to the statutory health insurance scheme because they are allowed to opt out of it (high-earning employees in Germany and some self-employed people in Austria).

The proportion of the population covered by VHI varies between Member States. Levels of substitutive VHI cover range from 0.2% of the population in Austria to 24.7% in the Netherlands. Data on levels of complementary and supplementary VHI coverage are less comparable, partly because they do not always distinguish between the two types of coverage and partly due to variation in the quality of coverage. In Member States where complementary VHI predominates, levels of coverage range from about 20 to 70%. Since the introduction of free complementary VHI cover for people on low incomes in France in 2000, coverage has risen from 85% to 94%. Where supplementary VHI predominates, it generally covers around 10% of the population (Mossialos and Thomson, 2001 and 2002).

VHI does not play a significant role in funding health care in the European Union. Spending on VHI as a proportion of total expenditure on health care is low. In 1998 it accounted for less than 10% of total expenditure in every Member State except France (12.2%) and the Netherlands (17.7%) and well under 5% of total expenditure in Belgium, Denmark, Finland, Greece, Italy, Luxembourg, Portugal, Spain, Sweden and the United Kingdom (UK). Although the last twenty years have seen some growth in levels of private expenditure as a proportion of total expenditure on health care, this growth has been influenced more by increases in cost-sharing through user charges than by rising demand for VHI. However, sustained economic growth and cutbacks in public expenditure on health care during the 1980s did increase demand for VHI in many Member States. Demand for VHI continued to grow throughout the 1990s in some Member States, but the pace of growth was much slower (Mossialos and Thomson, 2001). The fact that levels of VHI coverage in many Member States have remained fairly stable for some time now suggests that the market for VHI may have reached saturation point (within current health care system structures).

For largely historical reasons, some of the most extensive VHI markets in the European Union are currently dominated by non-profit mutual or provident associations. Many (but not all) of these non-profit insurers adhere to solidarity principles in their provision of VHI. In recent years their share of the VHI market has declined in some Member States and in future they may lose further market share to for-profit commercial insurers (Mossialos and Thomson, 2002).

Although social protection systems remain primarily within the remit of Member States, this is not so for voluntary health insurance. As with medical services, which are increasingly compatible with EU law[1], voluntary health insurance is considered mainly as an economic activity, and so subject to the application of European law on the single market. Even where the Community regulatory framework recognises the specific nature and social importance of private health insurance, it is far from clear how far Member States can determine the method of operation of health insurers operating on their territory. This chapter outlines recent regulatory developments at the EU level and considers the way in which they affect the market for VHI.

I. The Non-Life Insurance Directives

Consumer protection in the field of insurance generally depends on a range of national regulations. These include measures to secure a stable and transparent market, supervising the financial basis of insurers and their state of solvency.

In the past there were two main models by which insurance operations were supervised in EU Member States: contract control and prudential control (Freeman, 1994). Contract control is based on the premise that if insurers are sufficiently controlled in the type of contracts they offer and the level of premiums charged, there should be no question of insolvency. This model applied in Germany, where the supervisory body scrutinised policies before they were offered for sale, restricted price competition by enforcing compulsory tariffs and only permitted insurers who specialised in health care to operate in the field of voluntary health insurance. Prudential control, as practised in the United Kingdom, is concerned with the general ability of the insurance company to meet its obligations; the regulatory body's role is restricted to examining detailed financial returns on business. Since the 1970s, however, supervision and regulation of insurance companies has been progressively harmonised, so as to promote a single market for life and non-life insurance in the EU. The European legislative framework has aimed to provide the necessary legal framework to ensure the development of private insurance in an integrated European market, while stimulating competition, increasing choice for consumers and protecting them against financial loss. The focus of this Community regulation has consequently moved from contract to prudential control. The only distinction made is that

---

[1] European Court of Justice, C-157/99, Judgement of 12/07/2001, Smits and Peerbooms.

between life and non-life insurance, for which rather different frameworks have been agreed.

It took nearly twenty years and three generations of Directives to harmonise insurance regulation with the intention of liberalising the direct non-life insurance market. The first generation (Directive 73/239/EEC) (Council of the European Communities, 1973) allowed insurance companies to establish a branch office or an agency in another Member State. By co-ordinating legal and financial conditions, an authorisation could be obtained more easily. The second generation (Directive 88/357/EEC) (Council of the European Communities, 1988) realised the principle of free provision of services, allowing insurance companies to cover a risk located on the territory of another Member State without having to set up a branch or agency in that Member State. However, the application was limited to policyholders whose status, size or the nature of the risk to be insured did not require special protection. Hence, health insurance was excluded from the right freely to provide services. The third non-life insurance Directive (Directive 92/49/EEC) (Council of the European Communities, 1992g) completed the harmonised framework for regulation of insurance services by extending the principle of free movement of insurance services to all risks and all policyholders (Mabbet, 2000; Nemeth, 2001).

The single market for voluntary health insurance, as a part of the non-life insurance branch, came into effect in the second half of 1994. Henceforth, private insurers were in principle allowed to:

- establish a branch office or agency in another Member State, without the need to receive authorisation by the competent national authorities of that State;
- provide insurance services in another Member State without the need to establish a branch office or agency.

This was realised through:

- the introduction of a single licensing and financial control system with responsibility residing with the Member State where the head office is situated (home country control);
- the mutual recognition of authorisation and prudential control systems on the state of solvency, the establishment of technical provisions and coverage of those provisions by matching assets;
- the abolition of control by the risk based Member States or prior notification of policy tariffs and contractual conditions. For some groups the right to systematic – but not prior – notification may remain.

II. Implementing the Internal Voluntary Health Insurance Market

Despite the fact that the third non-life insurance Directive concluded a long process that started more than twenty years earlier, its relevance to the field of voluntary health insurance is not self-evident, mainly because it has to confront a complex and diverse situation in the Member States.

A. The Intersection between Social Security and Voluntary Health Insurance

First and foremost, private health insurance in the EU works alongside public protection systems. Health insurance "forming part of a statutory system of social security" is explicitly excluded from the scope of the insurance Directives (Article 2(1)(d) Directive 73/239/EEC) (Council of the European Communities, 1973). Since different definitions of social security exist, there is room for confusion.

From the case law of the ECJ, it can be inferred that compulsory affiliation is a decisive criterion for defining non-economic, solidarity-based activities performed by social security bodies. Referring to the Poucet-Pistre rulings[2], the ECJ recalled in Garcia and others[3] that social security schemes require compulsory contributions in order to ensure that the principle of solidarity is applied and that their financial equilibrium is maintained. Furthermore, in a recent judgement the ECJ specified that the exclusion of social security schemes from the insurance Directives only applies to for public social security institutions[4]. If a compulsory statutory social security scheme is administered by private insurance undertakings operating at their own risk with a view to profit – as is the case for the Belgian social security scheme for accidents at work – it is subject to the third non-life insurance Directive. This case is specifically provided for in Article 55 (ex 66), which allows Member States by way of exception to require compliance with specific national provisions, except for provisions concerning financial supervision, from private insurance companies offering compulsory insurance against accidents at work and operating at their own risk.

---

[2] European Court of Justice, C-159/91, Judgement of 17/02/1993, Poucet and Pistre AGF and Cancava. Joined Case with C-160/91.

[3] European Court of Justice, C-238/94, Judgement of 26/03/1996, Garcia and others *v.* Mutuelle de Prévoyance sociale d'Aquitaine and others.

[4] European Court of Justice, C-206/98 Judgement of 18/05/2000, Commission *v.* Belgium.

The question remains whether the same reasoning could apply to compulsory health insurance, especially if public or non-profit social security institutions are operating in a more market-oriented context, as instituted by different social security reforms in several Member States, or if they would compete directly with private commercial insurers offering substitute forms of protection to categories authorised to opt out of social security.

This issue directly influences the current debate on the future reform of the Dutch health insurance system. The goal of reform is a more efficient and demand-driven health care system in which accessibility and solidarity prevails. On the insurance side, the idea is to integrate the different schemes into one compulsory basic scheme, based on mandatory acceptance by the insurer and premium uniformity. In previous advice, the Dutch social-economic council (SER), a tripartite advisory body, promoted the idea of a private health insurance with social safeguards and administered by private insurance companies. However, the Dutch reform plan (Ministerie van Volksgezondheid, Welzijn en Sport, 2001) finally chose a public framework of health insurance. This was inspired by more recent opinion from a special government commission, which warned against a private model as it would entail application of the European insurance Directives (ICER, 2001).

B. The General Good Exception

The existence of statutory health protection and the way it is organised also influences the demand for private voluntary health insurance. For this reason the form of voluntary health insurance, as well as the way in which it is regulated, is very different from one country to another, since it is essentially filling the gaps left by public health care protection in terms of personal and material scope of application as well as in terms of option choices.

The need for regulation in voluntary health insurance has traditionally been strongest for substitutive systems, providing private cover for persons excluded or exempted from statutory protection. This kind of voluntary health insurance is offered in Germany and the Netherlands, where some professional categories earning high incomes use private insurance. Given its importance, governments have traditionally intervened in this area to ensure that no one would stay without any coverage.

When establishing the rules for integrating insurance markets, the Member States agreed in the non-life Directive to make explicit provision for the particular nature and social consequences of health insurance contracts that partially or completely substitute for health cover provided by the social security system. Therefore, under Article 54 of the third non-life insurance Directive, Member States are authorised to adopt or maintain specific national requirements imposed on insurers in order to protect the general good (Withers, 1996). As reminded by Recitals 22-24, such provisions must, if they aim to ensure access to private health cover irrespective of age or risk profile, be shown to be necessary and proportional to this aim as well as being non-discriminatory. Measures that might be justifiable on this basis include open enrolment, community rating, lifetime cover, legally fixed standard policies as well as participation in loss compensation schemes. In the German context, Article 54 (2) allows a Member State to require substitutive health insurance to be operated on a technical basis similar to life assurance, implying specific provisions related to premium calculation, establishing age reserves, contract cancellation. In that case, the home Member State shall receive all relevant statistical data to calculate the basis of premiums (Article 54 (2) 2).

The question as to what extent Member States can rely upon this provision of Article 54 to justify national regulation in the field of voluntary health insurance is far from clear. It can be hard to predict how the jurisprudence of the ECJ might apply in any given circumstances. The interpretative Communication issued by the European Commission on the concept of general good in insurance business (European Commission, 2000c) did not add much in this respect.

It seems quite obvious that national regulation of substitutive health insurance, where it partially or completely substitutes health cover provided by the statutory social security system, could fit these criteria. The Dutch Medical Insurance Access Act (WTZ), introducing a publicly designed private substitutive insurance with a legally defined scope of benefits (comparable to statutory cover) and a legally fixed maximum premium, could benefit from this exception. Also the German regulation, requiring health insurers to offer standard tariff policies to persons over 55 who have been privately insured for at least ten years, covering the same range of benefits under the statutory health insurance system, at a price comparable to the average statutory health insurance contribution could be justified under Article 54. However, as was stated explicitly in Recital 25, the German speciality clause, prohibiting the simultaneous transaction of health insurance and other insurance branches, can no longer be justified by the general good principle, even if it was tolerated for many years.

Traditionally, the German supervisory body has only allowed insurers specialising in health to sell VHI, in order to protect policy holders from insolvency arising from other business (Bundesaufsichtsamt für das Versicherungswesen, 2001). The legislation transposing the third non-life insurance Directive into German law formally abolished this rule (Article 5 of the Directive), but the German government added a new provision to German social law, prohibiting employees from benefiting from employer-paid contributions if the insurer combined health with other types of insurance (Busse, 2001b). The European Commission considered this to be an indirect infringement of the Directive and sent a so-called "reasoned opinion" to Germany in 1996 (European Commission, 1996b). In the absence of a satisfactory response from the German government, the European Commission has referred Germany to the ECJ[5]. The principle of separation of VHI from other types of insurance does not apply to foreign insurers.

The challenge of sustainability is especially great when leaving the scope of substitutive health insurance and entering the field of complementary or supplementary health insurance, which covers services or providers excluded fully or partially from the scope of social protection. In order to preserve the principles of its former open system of complementary health insurance in the face of EU market liberalisation, Ireland relied upon the general good exemption to establish a regulatory framework and a level playing field for all voluntary health insurers. The 1994 Health Insurance Act sets out three main principles for voluntary health insurance to be respected by all insurers: community rating, open enrolment, life time cover. In support of these principles, the Irish government announced proposals for a risk equalisation scheme based on age, gender and prior utilisation, intended to compensate for the possible effect of risk selection. The legality of this scheme is being questioned by the first competitor in the newly liberalised market (Kinsella and Cully, 2001; see also Light, 1998).

The issue of legality does not appear to concern the government, however, who state that the third non-life insurance Directive permits risk equalisation or loss compensation schemes in the interest of the general good. The Department of Health and Children note that "the changes now in train in relation to the framework for risk equalisation under the 2001 (Health Insurance Amendment) Act have particular regard to the need for proportionality in legislating to protect the common good". It is the Department's view that the Directive

> should continue to recognise the basis for adopting specific legal provisions to protect the common (general) good where the conduct of health insurance business is concerned. It is important that it should be open to Member States to adopt such measures in relation to the organisation of their health care systems, while also taking account of the fundamental principles of EU

---

[5]   European Court of Justice, C-298/01 Pending Case, Commission *v*. Germany.

law. It is considered that any future change to the EU regulatory framework should retain the basis for the reasonable exercise of discretion of this nature by Member States (Department of Health and Children, 2001).

The concept of the general good is based on the case law of the ECJ, which has never actually defined the general good, preferring to maintain its evolving nature (European Commission, 2000c). For this reason, the concept is not defined by the third non-life insurance Directive. The absence of a clear definition has led to confusion and tension between the European Commission, Member States and insurance companies (CEA, 1997; Mossialos and Le Grand, 1999).

In 2000 the European Commission issued an interpretive communication regarding the general good (European Commission, 2000c). The communication analyses the concept of the general good as developed by the case law of the ECJ and systemises this doctrine and the ways in which it is applied to the freedom of establishment and the freedom to provide services. It also maps out the framework within which a host Member State can invoke the concept of the general good in order to enforce compliance with its own rules by an insurance undertaking wishing to conduct insurance business within its territory, either through a branch or through the freedom to provide services. An insurance undertaking operating through a branch or under the freedom to provide services that is required by a host Member State to comply with a national rule that, in its view, constitutes a restriction, may challenge the application of that measure if it considers that one of the following six criteria is not met. In order to be justified on grounds of the general good, a national measure (European Commission, 2000c):

– must not have been the subject of prior Community harmonisation;
– must not be discriminatory;
– must be justified for imperative reasons relating to the general good (such as consumer protection, prevention of fraud, cohesion of the tax system and worker protection);
– must be objectively necessary;
– must not duplicate home country rules;
– must be proportionate to the objective pursued.

The communication notes that the Directive does not define the general good so as to make it possible to assess the conformity with Community law of a national measure that is taken in a non-harmonised area at Community level and hinders freedom of establishment and freedom to provide services. In non-harmonised areas the level of what is regarded as the general good depends first on the assessment made by the

Member States and can vary substantially from one country to another according to national traditions and the objectives of the Member States. It is necessary, therefore, to refer to the relevant case law of the Court of Justice.

III. Commercial Insurers *v.* Mutual Health Funds

A. The Specificity of Mutuality

Besides the differing material scope of the insurance Directives, there are also uncertainties about the types of operators to whom they might apply. It seems that neither the legal status of the operator, nor the non-profit or profit orientation, are relevant in deciding the application of the Directives. Every undertaking developing an economic activity of insurance, "normally provided for remuneration" (Article 50, EC Treaty – ex 60), is presumed to be within the internal market for insurance services. However, the activity of insurance is not further defined. All this is likely to lend uncertainty to the application of the insurance Directives, especially for mutual health funds.

Mutual health funds have traditionally played a vital part in the field of health care cover, even before the existence of social security (Dreyfus and Gibaud, 1995; Vand der Linden, 1996; Duranton *et al.*, 2001). However, their role extends beyond the scope of insurance, which distinguishes them from private commercial insurers. Generally, mutual benefit societies can be characterised as personal non-profit associations, based on individual affiliation (membership), providing social services and protection, democratically defined by the members and financed in solidarity, with a view of mutually improving social conditions. Accordingly, they are typically committed to guarantee open enrolment, lifelong affiliation and non-selection of risks. As personal societies, mutual health funds operate essentially according to the principle of self-governance, where stakeholders or their representatives participate in defining the funds' policy. This feature is regarded important for creating a specific dynamic essentially driven by patients' interests, adapting the services to actual needs.

Although mutual health funds and for-profit insurers traditionally operated in different segments of the market, the emerging need for complementary or alternative cover as well as the possibility of a Single European Market for voluntary health insurance increasingly risks to creating conflicts. The open unregulated confrontation of these different approaches of protection certainly is detrimental for solidarity-based insurance, as so-called good risks may be drained from this pool by risk rating insurers and would therefore lead to premium increases for the remaining higher risks. By being put on the same footing as "classic" commercial insurers, a real threat exists of "cannibalisation" of mutual health funds and a forced drifting towards lowest-common-denominator market practices (Light, 1996). This could have serious consequences for patients, especially those presenting higher health risks.

B. The Maladjustment of the Insurance Directives for Mutual Benefit Societies

The difficulty of integrating mutual health activities into the narrow concept of insurance, while preserving the specific nature of mutuality, has been demonstrated by the troublesome transposition of the insurance Directives in the French "Code de la mutualité". In 1992 the French government took the initiative of inserting the "mutualité" as one of the French legal forms an insurance undertaking can adopt to be authorised to provide insurance services throughout the European Union[6].

Besides the more general problem for individual mutual health funds of meeting the financial requirements, several other factors seem likely to put the specific character of French mutual health funds at risk.

- The contractual relation between insurer and insured quite profoundly differs from the membership in, democratically structured personal society;
- The obligation to "limit its objects to the business of insurance and operations directly arising there from, to the exclusion of all other commercial business" would prohibit the French mutual health funds from managing within the same legal structure own social and health care facilities, through which they provide services in kind to their members;
- The prudential obligations combined with the freedom of insurance services, would not allow restriction of reinsurance or transfer of portfolios solely to other mutual health funds, unless this could be justified by reasons of general interest. This could seriously affect the autonomy of mutual health funds in defining guarantees and preserving their specific principles of mutuality.

The incomplete transposition of the third non-life insurance Directive into French law during the period defined by the Directive finally led to France being condemned by the European Court of Justice[7].

---

[6] Article 8 (1) a Directive 73/239/EEC as modified by Article 6 Council Directive 92/49/EEC (Council of the European Communities, 1973 and 1992g).

[7] European Court of Justice, C-239/98, Judgement of 16/12/1999, Commission *v.* Republic of France.

Based upon moves to resolve the deadlock, entrusted to former Prime Minister Michel Rocard (1999), the French government ultimately enacted a revised Mutuality Code, which incorporates the Community Directives while respecting and modernising mutuality principles[8]. To link the legally separated insurance activities with health care benefits in kind, the concept of "twinning organisations" (mutuelles et unions soeurs) was instituted, with partially overlapping boards of administrations and limited financial commitments towards each other. To preserve the specific mutuality character, the general assemblies are entrusted with decisions on transfer of portfolio and reinsurance. The specific (contractual) relationship between the member and his or her mutual health fund is evidenced by the signature of an affiliation booklet. Also the status (rights and duties) of the elected administrator is clarified. Finally, the specific mutuality principles are instituted in law: absence of medical selection, non-individualisation of premiums according to health status and lifetime cover.

C. Unfair Competition?

In recognition of their social mission and their specific commitments towards their members, mutual health funds are often granted a specific status by law. These national laws explicitly refer to their more comprehensive role, including their involvement in activities related to prevention and health education, social cohesion, solidarity and reducing social inequalities in health. From a EU law perspective, however, any practice or preferential treatment, likely to distort competition and affecting trade between Member States, is in principle outlawed (Articles 81-89 EC Treaty – ex 85-94). Anti-competitive behaviour can however be justified if it serves a higher cause (Articles 81.3 – ex 85.3 – and 87.2-3 – ex 92.2-3 – EC Treaty). Thus, Article 87.2 (a) (ex 92.2) permits aid having a social character, granted to individual consumers, provided that such aid is granted without discrimination related to the origin of the products concerned and Article 87.3 (e) (ex 92.3) permits such other categories of aid as may be specified by Decision of the Council acting by a qualified majority on a proposal from the Commission. Otherwise it may be permitted if it is deemed to be necessary for achieving a specific task of general economic interest entrusted to public undertakings and undertakings to which Member States grant special or exclusive rights (Article 86.1-2 EC Treaty – ex 90.1-2). The latter exception is

---

[8]   Ordonnance de réforme du Code de la Mutualité, *Journal Officiel*, Paris, 22 April 2001.

particularly relevant to certain activities performed by sickness funds (Kapteyn and Verloren van Themat, 1995).

Differential treatment, especially with respect to taxation, is more and increasingly challenged as market distortion or unfair competition. This different fiscal treatment is increasingly challenged by private for profit insurers as market distortions and unfair competition. Member States are under pressure to justify the advantages they permit.

Tax incentives in Belgium, France, Italy and Luxembourg favour mutual or provident associations over commercial insurers. The exemption from insurance premium tax for mutual and provident associations in France has been valued at FF 3 billion (€ 457.35 million) a year (Sandier and Ulmann, 2001). In March 1993 the French Federation of Insurance Associations (FFSA) lodged a complaint against the French government with the European Commission (Sandier and Ulmann, 2001). In November 2001 the European Commission (2001e) urged the French government to abolish these advantages, since it considered them disproportionate to the need to compensate for the real burden related to services of a general good, which would only represent a minor fraction of activities. This confirms the Commission's practice to tie down services of general economic interest within clearly circumscribed limits.

In Luxembourg, the existence of a "gentleman's agreement" between mutual associations and commercial insurers has prevented the latter from lodging a complaint with the European Commission. This informal agreement rests on the understanding that mutual associations will not encroach on commercial insurers' dominance of the market for pensions and other types of insurance (Mossialos and Thomson, 2001).

But mutual health funds are also accused of abuse arising from the dominant position they take in compulsory insurance[9]. In Belgium, one of the leading mutual health funds, administering compulsory health insurance for 10% of the population, was sued for providing a complementary hospital insurance service to all its members, guaranteeing full cover of patient payments in excess of fixed amount. This service is based on principles of solidarity: all affiliated members are automatically enrolled; no medical or age-related exclusions are applied. According to the Belgian Arbitrage Court, the service fits within the mutual health funds' statutory mission: providing complementary service in the field of health, while administering compulsory health insurance, all aimed at promoting health and well-being of its members (Palm, 2002).

---

[9] European Court of Justice, C-244/94, Judgement of 16/11/1995, FFSA and others *v.* Ministère de l'Agriculture et de la Pêche.

It is however very likely that this case will end up before the European Court of Justice.

The question as to what activities in the field of health care protection must be considered as economic and to which Community competition rules therefore apply, cannot be answered unambiguously. It would be an oversimplification to refer only to the distinction between social security provisions and other arrangements. The question is not only whether the operator acts as an undertaking, but also in which circumstances and for what objective the activity is pursued. Traditionally the European Court of Justice applies a quite extensive concept of "undertaking", irrespective of the organisation's legal status and the way in which it is financed[10]. Only the management of a compulsory social security scheme, based on solidarity principles such as income-related contributions, pay-as-you-go funding, cross subsidies between schemes and benefit entitlements that are not proportional to the contributions paid[11] is exempt. However, this would not mean that all other activities are automatically subject to the competition rules contained in the EC Treaty. Other Treaty objectives could counterbalance the rules on competition. This was confirmed by the ECJ, when it ruled that mandatory membership of a pension fund[12] or a substitutive health insurance[13] established by collective agreement between the social partners in a sector of industry, even if the activity was considered economic, is not covered by EC competition law. Indeed, the ECJ recognised the particular social task of general interest which that fund had been charged with, which may justify the awarding of exclusive rights if the application of competition rules would seriously undermine the social policy objectives.

Conclusion

The strategy of European economic integration is essentially based on the assumption that the market economy is the ideal instrument for ensuring best quality services and goods at the best price. However, this assumption is not always compatible with the specific features of a

---

[10] European Court of Justice, C-41/90, Judgement of 23/04/1991, Höfner and Elser *v.* Macrotron.

[11] European Court of Justice, C-159/91, Judgement of 17/02/1993, Poucet and Pistre AGF and Cancava, Joined Case with C-160/91.

[12] European Court of Justice, C-67/96, Judgement of 21/09/1999, Albany International BV *v.* Stichting Bedrijfspensioenfonds Textielindustrie.

[13] European Court of Justice, C-222/98, Judgement of 21/09/2001, van der Woude *v.* Stichting Beatrixoord.

particular sector or with the specific policy objectives pursued. The challenge facing publicly funded systems, together with increased interest by private insurance companies to develop activities in the health care sector, have given impetus to discussions on regulating the field of voluntary health insurance. It is now considered to play an increasingly important role in complementing the statutory health care system, so further regulatory developments have been suggested to ensure that the market for voluntary health insurance works efficiently and allocates resources in a more equitable manner (Mossialos and Thomson, 2001).

In his European Parliament report Michel Rocard has already advocated the institution at a European level of common rules of general good, applicable to all operators in the field of voluntary health insurance, aiming to preserve solidarity and accessibility in the field of health care. On his later initiative, now as an MEP, the European Parliament adopted a Resolution on supplementary health insurance (European Parliament, 2000), calling on the Commission to examine the possibility of a framework for supplementary health insurance schemes. Referring to the increasing importance of voluntary health insurance in realising the fundamental right of access to quality health care within reasonable time limits, the Resolution suggests some minimum rules to be observed by all private insurers, non-profit as well as for-profit, to prevent discrimination on financial or medical grounds: prohibition on the use of personal medical data (*e.g.* genetic typing) or prior medical screening (except a medical questionnaire), lifelong insurance (with portability), transparency as to foreseeable changes in premiums, organising a pooling system to cover the cost of serious diseases (catastrophic diseases) etc.

Referring to the incorporation into the Community framework of the fundamental right on access to health care and the need to ensure a high level of health protection, the Resolution insists on the need to develop a common view of universal services in the light of the Amsterdam Treaty and calls on the Commission to propose appropriate legislative initiatives aiming at the recognition of a common concept of basic service, based on the Community principle of general interest, enabling every European citizen to have access, in his or her country of residence, to necessary and high-quality care within reasonable time limits.

It seems clear that the concept of general interest in the field of health care extends beyond the scope of "traditional" social security. In its updated Communication on services of general interest in Europe (European Commission, 2000d), the European Commission states, "many activities conducted by organisations performing largely social functions, which are not profit-oriented and which are not meant to engage in industrial or commercial activity, will normally be excluded from the Community competition and internal market rules". Even if the Commission exhibits some reservations in its approach to social services and argues that non-economic services are excluded from the application of competition and internal market rules, this is not likely to create legal certainty for the actors involved in those sectors, especially those being threatened because of their specific role or status.

This problem is also addressed through the debate on services of general interest. This notion covers market and non-market services which the public authorities class as being of general interest and subject to specific public service obligations (European Commission, 2000d). Since the insertion in the Amsterdam Treaty of a special provision on services of general economic interest (Article 16 EC Treaty – ex 7d), the fundamental values underpinning these services are placed on an equal level with the Community's economic principles. Whereas the debate primarily focuses on the economic sectors that are being deliberately liberalised (energy, telecommunication, transport etc.), clearly the concept seems relevant to social sectors. Its aim is to counterbalance competition and internal market rules, where these might jeopardise universal access, high quality and affordability of the service.

Accordingly, the Economic and Social Committee in a recent opinion on private not-for-profit social services in the context of services of general interest in Europe (ESC, 2001) addresses the specific position of "private not-for-profit organisations [...] that are active in the health and social spheres, though where necessary conducting economic activities that are subordinate to their primary social functions". Referring to the role of the general interest of "organised civil society" in protecting the most vulnerable parts of the population and generating social cohesion and solidarity among citizens, the Committee advocates that a legitimate place should be reserved in the EU for social services which strike a balance between those that are entirely public and those that are entirely profit-driven. In order to create more certainty about the application of European competition law, it suggests two options. The first is introducing a general exemption principle for categories of social services provided by private not-for-profit operators in Article 16 of the EC Treaty (ex 7d). The other is to draw up more detailed criteria for competition rules in areas that should be exempted from them.

So far, the whole European legal framework for insurance is essentially based on a logic of free Community-wide competition among insurers whose solvency is guaranteed by the competent authorities of the home Member State, based upon a harmonised set of business conditions and prudential rules. To the extent that rules have been harmonised, governments have agreed no longer to regulate prices and conditions of insurance products, as this could impede fair competition among

European insurers and could jeopardise the financial health of insurance undertakings.

In the field of health care this seriously reduces Member States' possibilities to develop a policy of promoting voluntary health insurance based on solidarity principles. Even though Article 54 of the third non-life insurance Directive, already confirms the possibility of exemption for national arrangements justified by the general good, it seems unlikely that this would meet the regulatory needs felt in different Member States. In order to prevent inequities resulting from a one-sided approach to the insurance market integration process, co-ordination between the different policy areas is needed, especially since Article 152.1 (ex 129.1) of the EC Treaty, introduced by the Amsterdam Treaty (1997), obliges all Community policies "to ensure a high level of health protection".

CHAPTER 7

EU Competition Law
and Health Care Systems

Introduction

A series of judgements by the ECJ have now clarified that while social security systems enjoy some protection they are not entirely exempt
from competition law. This chapter explores the extent to which European competition law applies to activities pursued by institutions within
health care systems. It begins by asking whether, and to what extent,
such institutions are "undertakings" and thus subject to European competition law. Second, it examines the nature and scope of activities that
such an institution is prohibited from performing under European competition law. It then examines the scenario in which if the institution is
considered to be an undertaking and infringes European competition
law, would its action be exempt from the scope of competition law
because it is in the field of health care? Finally, it examines the extent to
which transactions involving health care insurers and providers are
subject to laws relating to financial subsidies.

I. The Status of Health Care Institutions as Undertakings

The EC Treaty does not actually define the term "undertaking". By
custom and practice[1] (European Commission, 1994; Groeben *et al.*,
1999; Grabitz and Hilf, 2001; Lenz, 1999; Emmerich, 2001; Ebsen,
2000) whether something is an undertaking depends on its function.

---

[1] European Court of Justice, C-244/94, Judgement of 16/11/1995, FFSA and others *v.*
Ministère de l'Agriculture et de la Pêche; European Court of Justice, C-41/90,
Judgement of 23/04/1991, Höfner and Elser *v.* Macrotron; European Court of Justice,
C-159/91, Judgement of 17/02/1993, Poucet and Pistre AGF and Cancava, Joined
Case with C-160/91; European Court of Justice, C-364/92, Judgement of 19/01/1994,
SAT Fluggesellschaft *v.* Eurocontrol SAT Airlines; European Court of Justice, C-
55/96, Judgement of 11/12/1997, Job Centre; European Court of Justice, C-115/97,
Judgement of 21/09/1999, Brentjens; European Court of Justice, C-219/97 Judge-
ment of 21/09/1999, Drijvende Bokken.

Thus, an undertaking, within the meaning of European competition law, is any entity that engages in an economic activity, regardless of its legal status and the way it is financed (Weatherill and Beaumont, 1999).

The ECJ has ruled that it is not necessary for an entity to seek to make a profit to be considered as an undertaking[2] (so non-profit or charitable organisations may be considered as undertakings (Schröter, 1999). Similarly, an institution's ownership, legal form, or incorporation under public or private law are not relevant, so the term can apply to publicly owned enterprises as well as to public corporations or other associations engaged in business activities. Finally, undertakings are not limited to individual service providers, such as physicians, (public) hospitals, pharmacists and manufacturers of pharmaceuticals or technology; associations of organisations can also be undertakings.

So when is a health care institution not an undertaking? Essentially, this is when its activities are not economic, but instead are, sovereign, social, non-remunerative, or "purely to meet need". Thus, exemption from competition law arises solely because an entity is not engaged in economic activity. However, there is a widespread but erroneous belief that this exemption is due to the fact that the organisation of social security systems falls under the jurisdiction of the Member States, and thus is a matter for co-ordination rather than harmonisation.

It is true that, under the Treaties, each Member State is free to determine the organisation of its social security system. Issues such as solidarity, compulsory membership, and the distribution of benefits can be decided by Member States. This does not, however, imply that social security systems are beyond the reach of Community law. The ECJ has clearly stated that Member States must observe Community law when organising these systems[3]. Consequently, rules governing competition will apply unless a government structures its system in such a manner that the activities of its institutions can be classed as non-economic (Jones and Sufrin, 2001).

The following section addresses, in turn, each of the reasons why a health care institution might not be considered as an undertaking.

---

[2]   European Court of Justice, C-67/96, Judgement of 21/09/1999, Albany International BV *v.* Stichting Bedrijfspensioenfonds Textielindustrie; European Court of Justice, C-219/97 Judgement of 21/09/1999, Drijvende Bokken; European Court of Justice, C-115/97, Judgement of 21/09/1999, Brentjens; European Court of Justice, C-244/94, Judgement of 16/11/1995, FFSA and others *v.* Ministère de l'Agriculture et de la Pêche.

[3]   European Court of Justice, C-158/96, Judgement of 28/04/1998, Kohll Union des caisses de maladie; European Court of Justice, C-120/95, Judgement of 28/04/1998, Decker *v.* Caisse de maladie des employés privés.

The first factor refers to a health care institution when it is performing a sovereign activity, which is an activity necessarily pursued by the state exercising official authority (Hochbaum, 1999). The limits to such activity were tested in the Höfner and Elser Case[4], which examined provision of employment services by the German Federal Employment Office. Although the Federal Office is a public undertaking operating on the basis of public law, the ECJ regarded this as an economic activity. The Court ruled that simply because employment procurement is normally entrusted to public bodies, it had not always been, and need not necessarily, be carried out by them. As a consequence, it was regarded as an economic activity.

The German Federal government, citing Article 45 EC, had argued that the term "official authority" included all activities through which an institution endowed with state authority interacts with the public by some form of administrative action. The European Commission pointed out that the "exercise of official authority" was a term with a specific meaning in Community law, the content of which did not depend on whether certain activities were performed only by public authorities in some Member States. As private recruitment of executives took place, employment procurement did not involve the exercise of state sovereign power. Thus, an activity that can also be provided by private undertakings as an economic activity cannot be regarded as a sovereign activity.

The judgement in Höfner and Elser does not mean that health care institutions are automatically exempt from the scope of competition law just because they hold sovereign rights (Schulz-Weidner and Felix, 1997). If their activity is to qualify as sovereign, the decisive factor is whether the activity must necessarily by carried out through the exercise of official authority. A sovereign exemption does not apply, even when a body is exercising official authority, if it trades products or services alongside private undertakings that seek to make a profit[5]. Consequently, a state cannot shelter an activity from competition law simply because it is integrated in its sovereign administration (Haverkate and Huster, 1999).

This is illustrated by the example of Germany, where the relationship between health insurance institutions and benefit providers is subject to public law. German health insurance funds have a statutory duty to provide benefits in kind, either through the funds' own institutions or

---

[4] European Court of Justice, C-41/90, Judgement of 23/04/1991, Höfner and Elser *v.* Macrotron.

[5] Advocate General Tesauro (1993) ECR I-661, No.8, and Advocate General Jacobs (1999) ECR I-5751, No.311.

through external benefit providers at the expense of the funds. Payment for benefits obtained can, as in Austria, be on a contractual basis. Germany, in contrast, has chosen to introduce a system in which doctors are admitted to panels by health insurance funds and associations of physicians acting autonomously. Although these bodies conduct this process under public law, they demand services from physicians. Thus they are likely to be considered as private undertakings and, consequently, be submitted to competition law, notwithstanding their acting under public law (Boecken, 2000).

The second possible exemption is where the entity concerned is performing a purely social activity. The definition of social activity has evolved as a result of a series of Court rulings.

In the Poucet and Pistre Cases[6], the ECJ identified provision of insurance by insurance institutions with compulsory membership, organised on the basis of solidarity, as a task with an exclusively social character. To determine the social nature of an activity it established a series of criteria: a social function; the principle of solidarity; disregard for the insured persons' financial situation, their health status at enrolment, and contributions already paid; state control; statutory regulation of benefits; and performance of tasks in conformity with legal provisions. Such institutions are unable to influence the contribution rate, the use of funds, or the scope of benefit provision.

In the Court's view, solidarity exists when contribution payments geared to income and benefits are the same for all recipients, thus leading to redistribution of income and protection for those who would otherwise be disadvantaged by virtue of their financial circumstances or health.

In contrast, the Court has not accepted a social function where social insurance institutions compete with private insurance companies, for example, in the Case of the Fédération française des sociétés d'assurance (FFSA)[7], which involved voluntary supplementary pension insurance. It also considered the provision of compulsory supplementary pension insurance funds to be economic in the Cases of Albany[8],

---

[6] European Court of Justice, C-159/91, Judgement of 17/02/1993, Poucet and Pistre AGF and Cancava. Joined case with C-160/91.

[7] European Court of Justice, C-244/94, Judgement of 16/11/1995, FFSA and others *v.* Ministère de l'Agriculture et de la Pêche.

[8] European Court of Justice, C-67/96, Judgement of 21/09/1999, Albany International BV *v.* Stichting Bedrijfspensioenfonds Textielindustrie.

Brentjens[9], Bokken[10] and Pavlov[11]. These decisions centred on the fact that each system functioned according to the principle of capitalisation. It held that qualification as an economic activity was unaffected even if a social objective was being pursued, there were some aspects of solidarity, or there were restrictions on investments by the social insurance system (Winterstein, 1999).

The consequence of these rulings is that health care institutions pursuing social objectives do not have a blanket exemption from competition law. Instead, activities have to be assessed individually as to whether they are social or economic. This will depend on the objective of the activity in question and the manner in which it is carried out.

As noted above, the Court has held that a health care institution operates in an economic way if it competes with private undertakings. However competition law may also apply in some other circumstances. One example is the abuse of a dominant market position, which occurs where an institution exercises control over other trading partners (Schröter, 1999).

The distinction is whether a given health care institution acts in a manner that is so different from private undertakings that a private company, working in the same way, could not in principle hope to make a profit[12]. Whether the health care institution actually seeks to make a profit is irrelevant. An economic activity can therefore be defined as one that can be carried out to realise a profit, even if this does not actually happen. An activity that is only possible on a non-profit-making basis is different from an economic one because it is not guided by economic motives but, instead, by the principles of solidarity and of social protection (Haverkate and Huster, 1999).

The existence of social protection is indicated by a statutory insurance obligation and disregard of individual risks. The more pronounced the principles of solidarity and social protection, the greater the manifestation of an activity's social character. Whether social or economic criteria predominate is decisive.

The social issues explored so far relate to the supply of insurance benefits, not the purchase of health services. Where the funder of health care (insurance organisation or health authority) acts as a purchaser,

---

[9] European Court of Justice, C-115/97, Judgement of 21/09/1999, Brentjens.
[10] European Court of Justice, C-219/97 Judgement of 21/09/1999, Drijvende Bokken.
[11] European Court of Justice, C-180/98 Judgement of 12/09/2000, Pavlov and others.
[12] Advocate General Tesauro (1993) ECR I-661, No.8, and Advocate General Jacobs (1999) ECR I-5751, No.311.

then different considerations may apply. Obviously, where there is no remuneration, as in tax-based systems with no purchaser-provider split, competition law will not apply. In other situations, each activity must be examined on its merits (Ebsen, 2000); as previously noted, an organisation is not exempt from competition law simply because some of its activities have a social character (Boni and Manzini, 2001; Guibboni, 2001; Evju, 2001).

Where a funder purchases health care on behalf of the population for which it is responsible, this will primarily reflect economic and not social concerns, even when the purpose underlying its activities is to achieve social goals. In the Sacchi Case, paragraph 14[13], the ECJ ruled that although a Member State may have granted, for non-economic reasons of public interest, one or several broadcasting establishments the exclusive right to broadcast television and radio programmes, these establishments are nevertheless subject to competition rules in performing their task if that task involves activities of an economic nature. The decisive issue is purely whether the institution engages in an economic activity in the same way as a private undertaking. It may, however, claim exemption if it can show that the economic task it performs is in the "general interest" and it would be obstructed in doing so by the application of competition law (see later).

A third issue to be taken into account is whether remuneration (the transfer of an identifiable payment) takes place. It does not matter whether payment is made by the recipient of the service or by a third party[14]. In the Höfner and Elser Case[15] the ECJ held that an economic activity existed even though the cost of employment placement was not borne by the job seeker. The decisive factor is whether the service is provided completely free of charge. In the Humbel[16] and Wirth Cases[17], the Court took the view that public education in state schools and universities was not for remuneration. This has been interpreted by some as implying that, by establishing and maintaining a national education system, the state did not seek to engage in profit-making activity, but was merely fulfilling its duties towards its citizens in the social, cultural

---

[13]   European Court of Justice, C-155/73, Judgement of 30/04/1974, Sacchi.

[14]   European Court of Justice, C-352/75 Judgement of 26/04/1988, Bond van Adverteerders *v.* Netherlands State.

[15]   European Court of Justice, C-41/90, Judgement of 23/04/1991, Höfner and Elser *v.* Macrotron.

[16]   European Court of Justice, C-263/86, Judgement of 27/09/1988. Belgian State *v.* Humbel.

[17]   European Court of Justice, C-109/92, Judgement of 07/12/1993. Stephan Max Wirth *v.* Landeshauptstadt Hannover.

and educational spheres by means of a system financed essentially from public funds.

The final ground for exemption from competition law is where the activity is the "mere coverage of need", by the institution concerned and resources obtained are not subsequently traded. This applies to both private and public undertakings, if they are end users and merely cover their personal needs.

Such activities include activities in which the public sector does not compete as a private undertaking with other private undertakings, but only procures marketable products to maintain its own functioning (Bieback, 1999). The state thus merely takes part in the workings of the economy as a consumer; the products and services it demands simply satisfy the relevant authority's own requirements and do not entail any further participation in economic processes (Müllcr-Graff and Zehetner, 1991). Ebsen (2000) takes the view that this applies in tax-financed national health systems, where health care benefits are provided by state authorities as genuine benefits in kind. He compares this with procurement of learning material by schools, which are then distributed to pupils. He does, however, contend that this model of state procurement does not apply to the benefit-in-kind system in German health insurance schemes, for two reasons. First, he argues, what appears as a "benefit in kind" has been converted by the insurance funds to a legal construct, turning the direct economic transaction between benefit providers and the insured into a triangular benefit relationship. Second, he contends that statutory health insurance schemes are organised as provident-provision systems. Insurance funds thus act, in economic terms, as mediators between benefit providers and ultimate recipients. He therefore argues that German health insurance funds cannot be viewed simply as public consumers (Schulz-Weidner and Felix, 1997). He also notes that, although public procurement is not subject to competition law in the narrow sense, it is constrained by regulations governing the award of contracts.

II. Conduct Prohibited by European Competition Law

Where an organisation is considered to be an undertaking, it becomes subject to EU competition law. In these circumstances, certain types of action are prohibited. The two with greatest implications for health care are cartels (Article 81 EC – ex 85) and the abuse of a dominant position in the market (Article 82 EC – ex 86).

An anti-competitive cartel is characterised by one or more of the following features: prohibited forms of co-operation between undertakings, restraint of competition, restraint of trade between Member States, and the existence of a perceptible impact. Prohibited cartel agreements are automatically void under Article 81.2 EC (ex 85.2).

All agreements between undertakings, decisions by associations of undertakings and concerted practices that may interfere with competition are potentially prohibited forms of co-operation. All involve the conscious and deliberate co-operation between several legally independent undertakings that thus strive for, or bring about, co-ordination of their competitive conduct (Schröter, 1999). The term "agreement" includes legally non-binding arrangements (so-called 'gentlemen's agreements') (Stockenhuber, 2001). Decisions by associations of undertakings include recommendations that are binding on their members or are observed by them (Grill, 1999; Stockenhuber, 2001; Schröter, 1999). Concerted practices cover agreements and decisions, which are not legally binding, as well as other forms of conscious and deliberate co-operation among undertakings (Schröter, 1999).

Restraint of competition exists where activities "have as their object or effect the prevention, restriction or distortion of competition within the common market". Thus, competition that would otherwise exist must be impaired by a restriction of the economic freedom of action of one or more parties (Grill, 1999). Article 81 EC (ex 85) protects competition of all types, including not only restrictions and distortions of competition between parties to agreements, but also of competition between each party and third parties. Thus, the prohibition of cartels applies both to "horizontal" agreements that restrict competition between undertakings at the same stage in the economic process and to "vertical" agreements between undertakings operating at different stages of the process which therefore do not compete with each another (Schröter, 1999). The question of whether action that impairs a third parties' freedom to compete constitutes a restraint of competition is unresolved (Schröter, 1999). This prohibition includes distortions of supplier and demand competition and both products and services (Schröter, 1999). With demand competition the key issue is whether the supplier's economic scope of action is restricted (Schröter, 1999).

A restraint of competition must arise, at least partly, from a specified agreement, and the existence of a further restraint as a result of measures undertaken by the state does not mitigate it (Schröter, 1999).

Article 81.1 EC (ex 85.1) lists specific examples of prohibited modes of conduct. These include actions that "directly or indirectly fix purchase or selling prices or any other trading conditions". Prohibited price agreements include fixing prices (Emmerich, 1999; Schröter, 1999), or actions which "limit or control production, markets, technical development, or investment". Their common feature is that there is agreement to restrict competition in terms of quantity and quality (Schröter, 1999).

The ECJ has consistently held that the scale of the impact of restraint of competition must be perceptible (Stockenhuber, 2001; Grill, 1999; Eilmansberger, 2000), so exempting minor cartels. As a consequence, the European Commission has issued a non-binding notice (European Commission, 1997c) that prohibition of cartels will, as a rule, not apply if the aggregated market shares of all parties involved do not exceed 5% in any of the markets concerned (in the case of horizontal agreements) or 10% (in the case of vertical agreements). However, this does not apply if the restraints of competition are especially grave. For horizontal agreements, this is where there are price-fixing agreements, market partitioning arrangements, and restrictions on markets or production; for vertical agreements it is where there are agreements fixing resale prices and territorial protection arrangements (Eilmansberger, 2000).

Although individual ECJ rulings focus on specific cases, it can be inferred from the accumulated case law that the Court also accepts a threshold of 5% of market share (Grill, 1999). The Court does, however, take account of potential as well as actual impact[18].

There are, however, certain ways in which actions that would otherwise be prohibited by Article 81.1 EC (ex 85.1) may be permitted by Article 81.3 EC (ex 85.3). This may occur in cases where the agreement in question contributes to enhancing the production or distribution of products or promoting technical or economic progress. Consumers must be significant beneficiaries. Restriction of competition must, however, be necessary to achieve the desired objectives.

Article 81 EC (ex 85) applies only where undertakings actively promote cartels[19]. If sovereign measures adopted by Member States make a restraint on trade inevitable, the undertakings involved cannot be held responsible (Stockenhuber, 2001).

In a series of decisions, the ECJ has recognised other circumstances in which constraints on trade may be lawful[20]. Many of these involve

---

[18] European Court of Justice, C- 19/77, Judgement of 01/02/1978, Miller v. Commission.

[19] European Court of Justice, C-359/95, Judgement of 11/11/1997, Commission and France v. Ladbroke Racing.

[20] European Court of Justice, C-153/93, Judgement of 09/06/1994. Germany v. Delta Schiffahrts- und Speditionsgesellschaft; European Court of Justice, C-185/91, Judgement of 17/11/1993, Bundesanstalt für den Güterfernverkehr Reiff; European Court of Justice, C-96/94, Judgement of 05/10/1995, Centro Servizi Spediporto v. Spedizioni Marittima del Golfo; European Court of Justice, C-38/97, Judgement of

statutory associations acting in the public interest, especially where the association involved is independent, to a considerable extent, of the undertaking affected, and is pursuing social policy objectives[21].

The second form of prohibited action is abuse of a dominant position on the market. For Article 82 EC (ex 86) to apply it is required that one or more undertakings hold a dominant position within the common market or in a substantial part of it. This is considered to exist if an undertaking's economic position enables it to prevent effective competition, allowing it to act independently of its competitors and its customers (Schröter, 1999)[22]. A group of undertakings may occupy a dominant position even if, while not forming a cartel, they are so closely affiliated that they can effectively act independently of competitors[23]. The market concerned is defined in terms of the product or service involved and the geographical region involved (Schröter, 1999).

Whether a dominant position is being abused is determined by whether the actions of the undertaking are considered to be within the admissible bounds of competition (Grill, 1999). In practice, abuse is restricted to exploitation of trading partners (Jung, 2001; Emmerich, 1999), such as imposing directly or indirectly, unfair prices or other trading conditions or applying different conditions in similar transactions with different parties and so placing them at a competitive disadvantage (termed "exploitative abuse").

Article 82 EC (ex 86) also prohibits the abuse of a dominant market position to obstruct competitors (so-called obstructive abuse) (Emmerich, 2001). This occurs where suppliers or their associations contrib-

---

01/10/1998, Librandi; European Court of Justice, C-35/96, Judgement of 18/06/1998, Commission v. Italy.

[21] European Court of Justice, C-67/96, Judgement of 21/09/1999, Albany International BV v. Stichting Bedrijfspensioenfonds Textielindustrie; European Court of Justice, C-115/97, Judgement of 21/09/1999, Brentjens; European Court of Justice, C-219/97 Judgement of 21/09/1999, Drijvende Bokken.

[22] European Court of Justice, C-41/90, Judgement of 23/04/1991, Höfner and Elser v. Macrotron; European Court of Justice, C-311/84, Judgement of 03/10/1985, CBEM v. CLT and IPB; European Court of Justice, C-179/90, Judgement of 10/12/1991, Merci Convenzionali Porto di Genova v. Siderurgica Gabrielli; European Court of Justice, C-18/88 Judgement of 13/12/1991, RTT v. GB-Inno-BM; European Court of Justice, C-67/96, Judgement of 21/09/1999, Albany International BV v. Stichting Bedrijfspensioenfonds Textielindustrie; European Court of Justice, C-115/97, Judgement of 21/09/1999, Brentjens; European Court of Justice, C-219/97 Judgement of 21/09/1999, Drijvende Bokken.

[23] European Court of Justice, C-393/92, Judgement of 27/04/1994, Gemeente Almelo and others v. Energiebedrijf Ijsselmij; European Court of Justice, C-96/94, Judgement of 05/10/1995, Centro Servizi Spediporto v. Spedizioni Marittima del Golfo.

ute to quality standards in a way that places foreign suppliers at a disadvantage (Hänlein and Kruse, 2000)[24].

The ECJ also considers Article 82 EC (ex 86) to be infringed where an undertaking attempts to extend the monopoly it enjoys in a particular market to other markets without clear justification[25].

Currently the Competition Directorate-General of the Commission is examining the limits within which a pharmaceutical company can use its intellectual property rights to prevent potential newcomers from entering the market. According to commissioner Monti (2001b) there are two main claims that are being examined. The first is related to the Supplementary Protection Certificates. Companies tend to "play around" with dates in order to have the SPCs cover the longest possible time span.

The second claim is that patent holders withdraw and deregister one particular formulation of their drug and have it replaced by another in order to delay market entry of equivalent generic drugs. According to the Directive 65/65/EEC (Council of the European Communities, 1965) on market authorisations, generic manufacturers can obtain a market authorisation under an abridged procedure if there is a "reference product" on the market.

Once again, there are certain exemptions from the prohibition of abuse of a dominant position. Article 82 EC (ex 86) only applies to actions that undertakings take on their own initiative[26]. Consequently, they must have scope to determine their own behaviour which they do not if their behaviour is dictated by national legal provisions.

Other forms of conduct, not stipulated in the examples contained in Article 82 EC (ex 86), may be considered to be abusive under a general clause (refusal to do business) only if further factors apply, including lack of objective justification, non-proportionality, employment of unfair means, or obstruction of remaining competition (Schröter, 1999).

The first exemption from abuse of a dominant position occurs where the undertaking is not acting autonomously. Articles 81 (ex 85) and 82 (ex 86) EC are addressed to undertakings. However, the ECJ has consistently held that Member States must not adopt or retain any measures which impede the practical effectiveness *(effet utile)* of competition

---

[24] European Court of Justice, C-202/88, Judgement of 19/03/1991, France v. Commission.

[25] European Court of Justice, C-18/88 Judgement of 13/12/1991, RTT v. GB-Inno-BM.

[26] European Court of Justice, C-359/95, Judgement of 11/11/1997, Commission and France v. Ladbroke Racing.

rules[27]. This occurs where it requires or favours agreements that are incompatible with Article 81 EC (ex 85)[28]. The key issue is whether an organisation is acting autonomously to create a cartel. The ECJ has held that, where performing the activity is a statutory requirement, the organisation is not autonomous, and therefore its activity is not unlawful[29] (Schröter, 1999).

A related question is whether, when it delegates its role to private organisations, the state gives up this protection[30]. The Court held that it had not in the Reiff and Delta Cases in which the competent public authorities fixed tariffs to promote the general welfare and, when necessary, decided them independently[31]. In the Centro Servizi Spediporto and the Librandi Cases, it based its decisions on the fact that the competent public authorities sought opinions from other public and private institutions[32].

Where there is a question of abuse of a dominant market position by public undertakings, rulings imply that Member States are not only

---

[27]   European Court of Justice, C-66/86 Judgement of 11/04/1989, Ahmed Saeed Flugreisen and others *v.* Zentrale zur Bekämpfung unlauteren Wettbewerbs; European Court of Justice, C-41/90, Judgement of 23/04/1991, Höfner and Elser *v.* Macrotron; European Court of Justice, C-55/96, Judgement of 11/12/1997, Job Centre; European Court of Justice, C-320/91, Judgement of 19/05/1993, Criminal proceedings *v.* Corbeau.

[28]   European Court of Justice, C-66/86 Judgement of 11/04/1989, Ahmed Saeed Flugreisen and others *v.* Zentrale zur Bekämpfung unlauteren Wettbewerbs; European Court of Justice, C- 229/83 Judgement of 10/01/1985, Leclerc *v.* Au blé vert; European Court of Justice, C- 231/83 Judgement of 29/01/1985, Cullet *v.* Leclerc.

[29]   European Court of Justice, C-38/97, Judgement of 01/10/1998, Librandi; European Court of Justice, C-185/91, Judgement of 17/11/1993, Bundesanstalt für den Güterfernverkehr *v.* Gebrüder Reiff; European Court of Justice, C-153/93, Judgement of 09/06/1994. Germany *v.* Delta Schiffahrts- und Speditionsgesellschaft; European Court of Justice, C-96/94, Judgement of 05/10/1995, Centro Servizi Spediporto *v.* Spedizioni Marittima del Golfo.

[30]   European Court of Justice, C-38/97, Judgement of 01/10/1998, Librandi; European Court of Justice, C-267/86 Judgement of 21/09/1988, Van Eycke *v.* ASPA; European Court of Justice, C-185/91, Judgement of 17/11/1993, Bundesanstalt für den Güterfernverkehr Reiff; European Court of Justice, C-153/93, Judgement of 09/06/1994. Germany *v.* Delta Schiffahrts- und Speditionsgesellschaft; European Court of Justice, C-96/94, Judgement of 05/10/1995, Centro Servizi Spediporto *v.* Spedizioni Marittima del Golfo.

[31]   European Court of Justice, C-185/91, Judgement of 17/11/1993, Bundesanstalt für den Güterfernverkehr Reiff; European Court of Justice, C-153/93, Judgement of 09/06/1994. Germany *v.* Delta Schiffahrts- und Speditionsgesellschaft.

[32]   European Court of Justice, C-96/94, Judgement of 05/10/1995, Centro Servizi Spediporto *v.* Spedizioni Marittima del Golfo; European Court of Justice, C-38/97, Judgement of 01/10/1998, Librandi.

prohibited from adopting measures that lead to an infringement of competition law by market-dominating undertakings[33] (Schröter, 1999), but that they must not take any measures that would violate Article 82 EC (ex 86) (Giesen, 1999). It is thus irrelevant whether or not the undertaking concerned was a party to the abuse through an autonomous business act.

The issue of autonomous action arises from the question of whether health care associations form cartels. In many health care systems, institutions form associations that are entrusted with widely differing tasks. For example, they decide on whether to engage with benefit providers or make arrangements with providers' associations. In addition, many recommend standard business conditions to their institutions.

The decisive factor is whether or not such associations have scope for autonomous business activities. This will not be the case, for example, if national regulations stipulate who must be accepted as a benefit provider, so that the association merely enforces statutory regulations without any scope to influence the selection process. Conversely, if anti-competitive co-operation is simply accepted or facilitated by the state then the prohibition on cartels will apply (Stockenhuber, 2001), even where such action is subsequently sanctioned by sovereign measures and declared binding[34].

It is likely that the prohibition of cartels will not apply where decisions can only be taken by health care associations rather than their constituent institutions, or where the structure of the health care system is such that the association and its institutions form a single economic unit. In such cases the institutions lack the economic autonomy needed to enter into a prohibited cartel agreement and their co-operation is not deemed to be a "decision by an association of undertakings". However, while the health care association cannot be accused of creating a prohibited cartel, it may be guilty of abuse of a dominant position.

Conversely, if individual institutions, rather than just the association, are able to make autonomous decisions, a cartel will be created, provided the relevant decisions are binding on the institutions involved, or are observed by them.

---

[33] European Court of Justice, C-66/86 Judgement of 11/04/1989, Ahmed Saeed Flugreisen and others *v.* Zentrale zur Bekämpfung unlauteren Wettbewerbs; European Court of Justice, C-41/90, Judgement of 23/04/1991, Höfner and Elser *v.* Macrotron; European Court of Justice, C-55/96, Judgement of 11/12/1997, Job Centre; European Court of Justice, C-387/93, Judgement of 14/12/1995, Criminal proceedings *v.* Banchero.

[34] European Court of Justice, C-123/83, Judgement of 30/01/1985, BNIC *v.* Clair.

Finally, a resolution adopted by a health care association cannot be deemed to be a prohibited cartel if the members of the institutions involved cannot be regarded as representatives of those institutions. This will be the case if implementation of the resolution takes account of not only the interests of the institutions, but also those of the general public or benefit recipients, as might occur when taking account of the interests of a rural population in determining the distribution of physicians[35]. The same will apply if those participating in the decision are independent of the institutions or if a majority in the decision-making body are representatives of public authorities[36].

There remains the question of the state's responsibility. National regulations that require health care associations to conclude or favour prohibited agreements are incompatible with the Treaties. The state only acts unlawfully if it deprives a regulation of its state character by transferring responsibility for intervening in economic processes to the association. In other words, the state cannot delegate sovereign powers of economic regulation to an association (Schröter, 1999).

Agreements between health care associations and benefit providers are treated in a similar way and are lawful if the statutory provisions allow no scope for autonomous business conduct. The previous comments on state responsibility for actions involving health associations remain valid.

One issue where the question of abuse of a dominant market position has arisen is the policy of restricting the admission of doctors to a panel of providers who have contracts with a health authority. Where health care institutions operate as purchasers of health care, they will often, singly or in association, exercise a monopoly. The question arises as to whether this dominant market position is abused if not all physicians are offered contracts with them. If a restriction on admission is based on the decision of an association of health care purchasers or on an agreement

---

[35] European Court of Justice, C-153/93, Judgement of 09/06/1994. Germany v. Delta Schiffahrts- und Speditionsgesellschaft; European Court of Justice, C-185/91, Judgement of 17/11/1993, Bundesanstalt für den Güterfernverkehr Reiff; European Court of Justice, C-96/94, Judgement of 05/10/1995, Centro Servizi Spediporto v. Spedizioni Marittima del Golfo; European Court of Justice, C-38/97, Judgement of 01/10/1998, Librandi; European Court of Justice, C-35/96, Judgement of 18/06/1998, Commission v. Italy.

[36] European Court of Justice, C-153/93, Judgement of 09/06/1994. Germany v. Delta Schiffahrts- und Speditionsgesellschaft; European Court of Justice, C-185/91, Judgement of 17/11/1993, Bundesanstalt für den Güterfernverkehr Reiff; European Court of Justice, C-96/94, Judgement of 05/10/1995, Centro Servizi Spediporto v. Spedizioni Marittima del Golfo.

between an association and an association of benefit providers, this may constitute a prohibited cartel.

Marhold (Marhold 1995, 1999 and 2001b) argues that, as demand monopolists, health care institutions are obliged to conclude contracts with physicians as they are largely dependent economically on health care institutions because of a lack of other potential markets, and thus a lack of effective demand competition. Excluding physicians from the health care market constitutes an abuse unless the action can be justified (Jung, 2001; Emmerich, 1999; Schröter, 1999; Grill, 1999). Thus, restricted admission of panel doctors is unlawful where the selection process is arbitrary or abusive.

Restricted admission of panel doctors may have adverse effects on patients where it leads to a shortage of physicians, especially where the number of doctors is obviously unable to satisfy the demand for medical services and if recourse to non-admitted physicians is financially disadvantageous to patients[37].

In 1992, the Dutch National Health Insurance Act (NHIA) was amended to make the system more market oriented. The obligation for the NHIA and the Exceptional Medical Expenses Compensation Act to enter into contracts with independent practitioners was removed. The Competition Act was inspired by EU competition law and the Competition Act included a prohibition of agreements and behaviour that restrained competition. Until the Act, health care insurers acted in accordance with the policy of the professional association of health care providers concerning the establishment of new practices. This policy meant that health care providers with established practices decided on the entry of new competitors. If a health care provider had not established a practice in accordance with the rules of the professional group, it could not enter into a contract with the health care insurer (Akyurek-Kievits, 2001).

However, despite the new competition policy, both insurers and professional associations have adhered to the old methods of contracting. This policy had consequences for the provision of care in border regions. On the one hand, it meant that foreign health care providers did not have the opportunity to offer health care in the Netherlands. On the other hand, health care insurers, faced with a shortage of providers in a particular border region were unable to enter into contracts with foreign health care providers (Akyurek-Kievits, 2001). The Dutch Competition Authority (NMA) has rejected this policy and, in doing so, has increased

---

[37] European Court of Justice, C-41/90, Judgement of 23/04/1991, Höfner and Elser *v.* Macrotron.

the opportunities for foreign care providers. The likelihood that European competition rules will be applied has therefore increased. Now that collective negotiations are no longer permitted, a situation has arisen where the health care insurer no longer negotiates with representatives of health care providers in the region. This may be seen as giving the health care insurer a dominant position in the region in which it was originally established (Akyurek-Kievits, 2001).

A second potential exemption arises from Article 86 (2) EC, relating to undertakings entrusted with the operation of services of general economic interest.

The first prerequisite for an exemption is that the undertaking in question is entrusted by the state with services that are of general economic interest. The criteria for determining the "general interest" are defined in Community law[38] (Steinmeyer, 2000; Schulz-Weidner and Felix, 1997) and include health and social protection (European Commission, 1996c). If, in addition, these institutions also become active in economic terms, their activity can be said to consist of providing services of general economic interest.

The appearance of the term "services of general economic interest" not only in Article 86 (2) EC, but also in the newly established Article 16 EC and Article 36 of the Charter of Fundamental Rights of the European Union (European Parliament *et al.*, 2000) confirm that services of general economic interest occupy a special position within the framework of the European Union.

A third potential exemption is where competition rules would obstruct the performance of the task assigned to health care institutions. As the relevant Article limits the application of EC Treaty provisions, this provision is construed restrictively (Hochbaum, 1999). It is not sufficient for the task assigned to a social insurance institution to be merely hampered or impeded by observing competition law (Schulz-Weidner and Felix, 1997; Grill, 1999; Gassner, 2000). This task must be "obstructed", with "obstruction" narrowly defined (Hochbaum, 1999). In the Cases Sacchi[39] and Höfner and Elser[40], the ECJ ruled that the application of the provisions must be incompatible with performance of the particular task. Further clarification came in the Cases Albany[41],

---

[38] European Court of Justice, C-41/83 Judgement of 20/03/1985, Italy *v.* Commission.

[39] European Court of Justice, C-155/73, Judgement of 30/04/1974, Sacchi.

[40] European Court of Justice, C-41/90, Judgement of 23/04/1991, Höfner and Elser *v.* Macrotron.

[41] European Court of Justice, C-67/96, Judgement of 21/09/1999, Albany International BV *v.* Stichting Bedrijfspensioenfonds Textielindustrie.

Brentjens[42] and Bokken[43] where the Court held that an exemption might be valid even if the economic viability of the undertaking is not threatened. Instead, it is sufficient for the application of competition law to prevent the undertaking from performing the tasks assigned to it or to remove certain rights without which it would no longer be economically viable to perform the task. The Commission *v.* France Case[44] introduced the concept of "endangering" performance of a task, with the English and French versions of the judgement using the terms "not be possible" and "faire échec à" (Gassner, 2000) respectively.

The task assigned to health care institutions, as a rule, embraces the provision of accessible, high-quality, low-cost medical care to all those eligible for benefits. Whether a health care institution can only perform this particular task if it contravenes European competition rules will depend on the individual activity concerned, taking account of the specific situation of health care institutions and the special features of the health care market.

The Specific Situation of Health Care Institutions

Health care institutions differ from other undertakings on account of their inherent social role. If this role is so strongly pronounced that it divests the institutions' activities of their economic character, they cannot be considered to be undertakings and so will be exempt from competition law. However, even those activities not classed as "social", in general, include some social elements. These can reduce a health care institution's ability to compete with private undertakings. In its decisions on supplementary pension schemes, the ECJ recognised that such constraints could justify giving these funds an exclusive right to manage these supplementary schemes[45].

There are social aspects to both the supply of insurance and health care benefits. As a rule, their impact on relationships with benefit providers is not sufficient to divest such activities of their economic character, unless they have an absolute obligation to provide benefits in kind.

---

[42] European Court of Justice, C-115/97, Judgement of 21/09/1999, Brentjens.

[43] European Court of Justice, C-219/97, Judgement of 21/09/1999, Drijvende Bokken.

[44] European Court of Justice, C-159/94, Judgement of 23/10/1997, Commission *v.* France; European Court of Justice, C-157/94, Judgement of 23/10/1997, Commission *v.* Netherlands.

[45] European Court of Justice, C-67/96, Judgement of 21/09/1999, Albany International BV *v.* Stichting Bedrijfspensioenfonds Textielindustrie; European Court of Justice, C-219/97 Judgement of 21/09/1999, Drijvende Bokken; European Court of Justice, C-115/97, Judgement of 21/09/1999, Brentjens.

Such an obligation makes their ability to demand services less competitive compared with private health insurance undertakings, since their relationship with benefit providers leaves them less scope for negotiations. Their scope for negotiation is also frequently restricted by the need to safeguard contribution stability.

The special circumstances prevailing in the health care sector mean that the health care market is not subject to pure competition. In the usual competitive market, the purchaser bears the financial consequences of its decision based on need. In the health care market, depending on the precise arrangements in force, patients bear none or only a certain portion of the cost of any benefits they receive. Furthermore, patients are not classic purchasers as they decide on the first step, to consult a doctor, with subsequent decisions on benefits determined, to a considerable extent, by the doctor acting as an agent for the patient.

At least in theory, as the cost is not borne by the patient, he or she may demand excessive services while physicians may use their information advantage to maximise profit and create additional demand, which may occasionally be harmful to health (Kletter, 1994). This is referred to as "moral hazard" and is tackled by admission restrictions, fixed prices and limits on benefit provision (Kletter, 2000). The justification for these restrictions is to avoid an increase in expenditure to the extent that it poses a threat to a health systems' financial viability.

The ECJ has repeatedly recognised the financial viability of social security schemes as grounds for exemption from internal market regulations. For example, in the Duphar Case[46], it held that EU Member States were entitled to regulate drug consumption so as to safeguard the financial situation of their health insurance schemes. In the Cases Kohll[47] and Decker[48] (see also Chapter 4), the Court acknowledged that a threat to the financial viability of social security schemes could justify a restriction of the free movement of goods and services. Finally, as noted earlier, in the Cases Albany[49], Brentjens[50] and Bokken[51], it considered that exemption from competition law was justified if the rights in question

---

[46] European Court of Justice, C-238/82, Judgement of 07/02/1984, Duphar and Others.

[47] European Court of Justice, C-158/96, Judgement of 28/04/1998, Kohll Union des caisses de maladie.

[48] Court of First Instance. T-317/93, Doheny v. Council and Commission.

[49] European Court of Justice, C-67/96, Judgement of 21/09/1999, Albany International BV v. Stichting Bedrijfspensioenfonds Textielindustrie.

[50] European Court of Justice, C-115/97, Judgement of 21/09/1999, Brentjens.

[51] European Court of Justice, C-219/97, Judgement of 21/09/1999, Drijvende Bokken.

were necessary for the institution concerned to perform tasks of general economic interest under economically acceptable conditions.

For health care institutions to resort to, say, anti-competitive price fixing or selective contracting, presupposes that the means are appropriate and proportional. Restriction of the Treaty provisions may not go beyond what is necessary for performance of the task (European Commission, 1976). The Member State need only show that the performance of the particular task is being obstructed; evidence that there is no other way to ensure that the task is performed must be provided by the Commission[52].

Consequently, to the extent that performance of a task is possible without infringing the EC Treaty, health care institutions and national legislators will be bound by it[53] (Emmerich, 2001). Importantly, where a health care institution is unable or unwilling to perform a task assigned to it in a satisfactory manner, there is no scope for exemption from competition law[54]. Thus, a Member State cannot invoke Article 86.2 EC (ex 90.2) to justify restricted admission of panel doctors if the existing system is obviously unable to meet beneficiaries' demand for medical services, whether because it fails to provide adequate geographical coverage or the quality is inadequate. This indicates that assessments of state measures must consider not only cost, but also include qualitative aspects of health care and access to health care benefits. This may have implications in countries with long waiting lists.

Finally, Article 86.2 EC (ex 90.2) requires that the development of trade must not be affected to such an extent as would be contrary to the interests of the Community (Ehricke, 1998). This requires balancing the national interests of the Member State in performing the task in question through a service institution, on the one hand, and the interests of the European Union, on the other (Schröter, 1999). The interests of the Union are inferred from the objectives and principles of the Treaty.

Weighty interests of the Community counterbalance the state's interest in the performance of tasks assigned to health care institutions. Thus, restrictions on the admission of panel doctors may run counter, not only

---

[52] European Court of Justice, C-159/94, Judgement of 23/10/1997, Commission *v.* France.

[53] European Court of Justice, C-155/73, Judgement of 30/04/1974, Sacchi; European Court of Justice, C-258/78 Judgement of 08/06/1982, Nungesser *v.* Commission; European Court of Justice, C-311/84, Judgement of 03/10/1985, CBEM *v.* CLT and IPB.

[54] European Court of Justice, C-41/90, Judgement of 23/04/1991, Höfner and Elser *v.* Macrotron.

to competition law but also to freedom of establishment and freedom to provide services (Pitschas, 1996; Kopetzki, 1999). It is, therefore, important to consider whether the restricted admission of benefit providers is compatible with the fundamental freedoms. A related issue is whether the conditions of contracting discriminate against applicants from other EU Member States (Pitschas, 1996). A conflict of interest will also arise if contracts with benefit providers are subject to territorial limits. This can imply both a restriction of the passive freedom to receive services on the part of the insured and a direct restriction of the active freedom to supply services by benefit providers resident in another EU Member State. It may also act as a bar on imports of medical products. If restriction of benefit providers or price fixing is shown to violate one of the fundamental freedoms, it is likely that the Community interests will prevail (Schröter, 1999).

III. Law on Subsidies

The European Union sees the unjustified provision of subsidies as an important barrier to the development of a single market. Given the many financial transactions in which health care insurers and providers are involved, it is important to understand whether, and to what extent, they may be affected by the relevant laws.

Three decisions by European Courts, two by the ECJ and one by the EFTA Court of Law, have examined whether the setting of premiums in the area of social security violates the ban on financial subsidies. A decision of the ECJ in 1999 examined the deferment of premiums by a health insurance firm in respect of a shipping firm that had sought bankruptcy. Ultimately the bankruptcy proceedings were not averted, despite the deferment of premiums, and it was asked whether the deferment of premiums constituted a prohibited subsidy. Competition had been distorted because the shipper, even though already bankrupt, could continue to run its business because the health insurer did not seek payment, so it was able to compete unfairly with other businesses that did have to pay premiums.

The ECJ interpreted the deferment of premiums as a financial subsidy according to Article 87 (ex 92) Section 1 EC. The issue was whether the organisation received an economic benefit that it would not have received under normal market conditions. The definition of "normal market conditions" depends on the "reasonable investors test". A subsidy does not exist if a private investor would have given financial aid in the same circumstances. If this is not the case, a prohibited subsidy may exist. The ECJ concluded that, in these circumstances, the shipper was unlikely to have been able to attract a loan from a private investor. The sole source of financing was the deferment of health insurance premiums, which were therefore considered to be a prohibited subsidy.

Other decisions have examined state support for certain economic activities through favourable premium payments. The Case of Maribel[55] involved Belgian government programmes that sought to protect some businesses that were especially vulnerable to global competition. Amendments to the legal framework allowed businesses in the transportation, mining, chemical manufacturing, and metallurgy sectors to benefit from reduced premiums, of up to 9,300 Belgian Francs (€ 230) per employee per quarter.

The Commission view that these reductions in social insurance premiums were inadmissible state subsidies was upheld by the ECJ. In a similar case the EFTA Court examined the payment of premiums in Northern Norway where industrial development was encouraged by lower social premiums than in the rest of the country. This, too, was judged by the EFTA Court to be an unlawful subsidy[56]. It is remarkable that Article 87 EC (ex 92) does not recognise an exemption of the scope of the financial subsidies law for the benefit of social institutions. This can attain special importance for the financing of health care institutions.

This may have implications for hospitals where a general deficit is covered without consideration of the performance of this hospital. This could create a distortion of competition between hospitals where such hospitals are considered to be undertakings under competition law.

In November 2001 a ECJ ruling[57] suggested that governmental compensation for public service obligations may not fall under restrictions on state aid. The Case involved a complaint from pharmaceutical manufacturers in France regarding a tax allowance on a form of sales tax that was granted to pharmaceutical wholesalers but not to anyone else. The sales tax was expressly introduced to deal with the fact that wholesalers are under a legal obligation under French health legislation to maintain a stock of all pharmaceutical products. The manufacturers are not under such an obligation and had been involved increasingly in direct sales of their own products to pharmacies. The sales tax was directed at them and wholesalers were exempt from paying it. The new tax and related

---

[55] European Court of Justice, C-75/97, Judgement of 17/06/1999 Kingdom of Belgium *v.* Commission of the European Communities.

[56] EFTA Court. Case E-6/98 Norway *v.* EFTA Surveillance Authority.

[57] European Court of Justice, C-53/00, Judgement of 22/11/2001, Ferring SA.

rebate had the desired effect: direct sales from the companies to the pharmacies were reduced while the wholesalers regained ground.

The pharmaceutical company Ferring challenged the tax under EC law as a form of state aid. It is standard case law that, where a tax advantage/rebate is granted to a selective group this is contrary to Article 87 (ex 92). The ECJ found that the tax rebate was prima facie an aid in that it conferred a selective advantage, but the French government argued that the purpose of the rebate was to offset extra costs that wholesalers incurred in carrying out a public service obligation (in accordance with Article 86.2 EC – ex 90.2) to maintain full range of products in stock. The ECJ ruled that if the tax rebate simply compensated these costs it could not be an aid. It merely allowed the wholesalers to cover their extra-statutorily imposed costs. Hence these firms did not enjoy a competitive advantage over other firms since the effect of the rebate was to neutralise the extra costs. The ECJ went on to rule that if the rebate exceeded the costs this would be a form of state aid and it could not be exempted under Article 86.2.

This is an important ruling because it suggests that governments can provide a form of compensation for public service obligations and this will not fall under restrictions on state aid. The Commission is unhappy because earlier case law suggested Member States still had to notify such schemes and the Commission could apply Article 86.2 (ex 90.2) as an additional exemption to those set out in Article 87.2 (ex 92.2) and 87.3 (ex 92.3), but because of the notification requirement there was still scope for control. The approach of the ECJ now removes this type of "compensation" from the Commission's scrutiny. The Commission is currently seeking to have the matter clarified further via a follow up reference to the full Court.

IV. Public Procurement

European procurement law seeks to ensure equal access for all enterprises to public contracts. The actual procurement procedure is regulated by the service Directive 92/50 (Council of the European Communities, 1992h), the supply Directive 93/36 (Council of the European Communities, 1993d), the public works contracts Directive 93/37 (Council of the European Communities, 1993e), as well as by the sectors Directive 93/38 (Council of the European Communities, 1993f) to co-ordinate the award of contracts by those contracting in the field of water, energy, and traffic supply, as well as in the telecommunications sector. The legal protection possibilities in the procedure of awarding contracts are regulated by the verification Directive 89/665 which co-ordinates the legal and administrative provisions for the application of the verification procedures within the scope of the procurement of public supply and construction contracts (Council of the European Communities, 1989b) and 92/13 which co-ordinates the legal and administrative provisions for the application of the Community rules in the field of the sectors Directive (Council of the European Communities, 1992i).

The Directives set out the need for public contracting to be competitive, non-discriminatory, and maximally transparent. Thus they apply the fundamental freedoms of the EC Treaty to the areas that have held out longest from the market (Schwarze, 2000). The Directives set out verifiable obligations by contract awarders to guarantee the equal treatment of all enterprises applying for public contracts and the transparency of the procurement procedure. The economically most advantageous offer must be awarded the contract, even if it comes from a different Member State (Hermes, 1997). The contractors can invoke their rights at national level[58].

In principle, the procurement Directives cover only those contracts whose estimated total values exceed certain threshold values. Where the threshold value is not reached the special procedural provisions of the Directives are not valid, but the general provisions of the EC Treaty remain applicable (Fruhmann, 1997).

Those awarding contracts that are subject to the Directive include the state, regional (and/or local) authorities, institutions governed by public law, and associations that consist of several of these corporate bodies or institutions[59]. In this connection the term "state" must be understood not in an institutional, but in a functional meaning (Schwarze, 2000). The ECJ also includes in this term such contract awarders that are not formally integrated into the state administration, but are nevertheless active in the name of the state or a regional or local authority[60]. Each institution with a legal personality that was founded for the special purpose of fulfilling non-commercial or non-industrial tasks, but which fulfils the general interest, and is financed or controlled predominantly by the state, regional or local authorities, or other institutions governed by public law is considered to be an institution pursuant to public law[61].

---

[58] European Court of Justice, C-433/93, Judgement of 11/08/1995, Commission *v.* Germany.

[59] Article 1 paragraph 2 of the supply Directive; Article 1 paragraph 2 of the service Directive; Article 1 paragraph 2 of the public works contracts Directive.

[60] European Court of Justice, C-31/87, Judgement of 20/09/1988, Beentjes *v.* Netherlands State.

[61] Article 1 paragraph 2 of the supply Directive; Article 1 paragraph 2 of the service Directive; Article 1 paragraph 2 of the public works contracts Directive.

The term "institution governed by public law" also has to be understood in a functional way. It includes institutions organised according to private law because otherwise it would be possible for Member States to evade the scope of the procurement Directives by transfer of undertakings into private ownership[62] (Hailbronner and Weber, 1997).

Are health care institutions covered by the scope of application of the procurement Directives? As a rule, health care institutions are deemed to be public contract awarders within the meaning of the procurement Directives. In the first instance, those health care institutions that are considered as social according to the criteria developed by the ECJ in relation to competition law are also to be deemed as institutions established for the special purpose of fulfilling tasks of general interest and non-commercial or non-industrial tasks. With regard to qualifying as an institution pursuant to public law it is of no consequence whether the health care institution is active economically as well as socially. The ECJ takes the view that the status of a body governed by public law is not dependent on the relative importance, within its business as a whole, of the meeting of needs in the general interest that do not have an industrial or commercial character[63]. The fact that meeting needs in the general interest constitutes only a relatively small proportion of the activities actually pursued by that entity is irrelevant, provided that it continues to attend to the needs which it is specifically required to meet[64].

The list of institutions governed by public law in Annex I of the public works contracts Directive also contains various national health care institutions. Though not exhaustive, that list is intended to be as complete as possible and is taken into account by the ECJ when checking if the respective tasks have an industrial or commercial character or not[65].

Thus on principle, procurement law is applied when health care institutions make purchases for their own purposes such as equipment and buildings.

---

[62] European Court of Justice, C-360/96, Judgement of 10/11/1998, Gemeente Arnhem and Gemeente Rheden *v.* BFI Holding B.V.

[63] European Court of Justice, C-360/96, Judgement of 10/11/1998, Gemeente Arnhem and Gemeente Rheden BFI Holding; European Court of Justice, C-44/96. Judgement of 15/01/1998, Mannesmann Anlagenbau Austria and others Strohal Rotationsdruck.

[64] European Court of Justice, C-360/96, Judgement of 10/11/1998, Gemeente Arnhem and Gemeente Rheden BFI Holding.

[65] European Court of Justice, C-223/99, Judgement of 10/05/2001, Agorà and Excelsior.

The characterisation of the activities of health care institutions is more problematic in relation to contracts for medical services in systems providing benefits in kind. Such contracts are framework contracts in which the providers of services obligate themselves to provide certain services for patients on account of the institution. This way the health care institution makes available benefits in kind to the patients entitled to them. Then, in case of need, the patient expresses a concrete demand for a service. This demand leads to payment of the remuneration agreed in the framework contract. Consequently, this is a demand on two levels: the health care institution's demand that leads to the framework contract, and, on this basis, the demand for services by the patient. From this one could infer that the actual demand is only made by the patient and not by the health care institution. Consequently, it would not be a demand for services by public contract and therefore the procurement law could not be applied (Köck, 2000).

Notwithstanding this, the ECJ applied procurement law in the Tögel Case[66]. The subject matter was the procurement procedure for a contract concerning ambulance services that was covered by the Service Directive. The contract awarder was an Austrian health insurance carrier. The procurement law remains applicable even when no single contract reaches the financial threshold, if the individual contract forms part of a series of linked contracts whose total value exceeds that set out in the Directive[67].

In the case of health care institutions that provide benefits in kind the ECJ applies the provisions governing the award of public contracts on the first level, *i.e.* on the level of framework agreements between the health care institutions and the performers of services (Mrozynski, 1999). This opinion results in the application of both competition and procurement law. It also finds expression in the jurisdiction of the ECJ. In the previously mentioned Tögel Case[68] it applied the procurement law on the demand by a health insurance carrier for ambulance services. The Sodemare Case[69] dealt with a social assistance carrier's demand for health services. The ECJ did not discuss the status of the social assistance carrier as an undertaking, but still applied the law on competition.

---

[66] European Court of Justice, C-76/97 Judgement of 24/09/1998, Tögel *v.* Niederösterreichische Gebietskrankenkasse.

[67] European Court of Justice, C-79/94 Judgement of 04/05/1995, Commission Greece.

[68] European Court of Justice, C-76/97 Judgement of 24/09/1998, Tögel *v.* Niederösterreichische Gebietskrankenkasse.

[69] C-70/95, Judgement of 17 June 1997, Sodemare and others *v.* Regione Lombardia Sodemare and others.

In order to release the health care institutions from these regulations, a new regulation according to European law would be necessary. This might happen by means of an exemption provision regarding competition provisions in the EC Treaty or by means of an exemption provision in the procurement Directives, depending on what course makes more sense.

Conclusion

This chapter covers a large amount of complex legal argument, much of which has been developed in sectors other than health care but which would appear to have direct relevance to the way that health care is organised within Member States.

It shows that health care organisations are potentially subject to competition law; they may be considered as undertakings and issues such as ownership or profit-seeking status do not affect this. What is important is whether or not they engage in economic activity.

A second important conclusion is that each activity undertaken by an organisation must be judged on its merits; even where most of its activities are deemed to be non-economic, and thus exempt from competition law, it does not follow that everything it does is also exempt.

There are several ways in which activities may qualify as non-economic. They may be sovereign, in other words necessarily performed by the state when exercising official authority. However, the state must show that it is necessary for it to perform this activity, and must exercise caution when delegating its role to other bodies. It may be a social activity, but here it must demonstrate that it involves social protection and is based on the principle of solidarity. It may also be exempt because it involves no identifiable payment or because the activity simply involves the organisation concerned meeting its basic needs to continue to function. However, it is easy to see how poorly considered health care reforms, especially where they introduce market-mechanisms and de-centralisation, might render organisations unexpectedly subject to competition law.

In Europe health care is organised in such a way as to preserve solidarity and promote equitable, effective and efficient treatment. There are many reasons, such as information asymmetry and externalities, why an unrestricted market is unlikely to promote these goals, as is apparent from even a brief examination of the American health care system. In particular, subjecting health care organisations to the full impact of competition law may disrupt the many agreements necessary to provide an equitable distribution of services that is appropriate to population health needs. It risks disadvantaging further the most vulnerable members of society, whose voices are already largely unheard.

In the absence of a clear statement of principles upon which health policy in Europe should be based, the ECJ is bound to base its decisions primarily on the imperative to promote the single market. It does recognise the particular circumstances of health care, such as the need not to undermine national systems, but this chapter demonstrates clearly the need for much more clearly thought out guidance on what the European Union is seeking to achieve when meeting the health needs of its population within a single market.

CHAPTER **8**

Information Technology Law
and Health Care Systems

Introduction

Developments in information and communication technologies (ICT) have serious implications for health and health care systems in the EU. On the one hand, the proliferation of health-related websites on the Internet and the rise of telemedicine[1], or "e-health", are significantly enhancing European consumers' access to information about health and health care. On the other hand, there are growing concerns about the increasing scope of personally identifiable health information about individuals in electronic form, in health databases and through online networks (Hodge *et al.*, 1999).

Since the early 1980s the EU has actively encouraged ICT developments, particularly with regard to the Internet, seeing in them opportunities to create new jobs and provide services more efficiently (Gibbs, 2001). In June 2000, as part of its drive to transform Europe into an information society, the EU launched an initiative known as the eEurope Action Plan 2002 (Council of the European Union and European Commission, 2000). This initiative, largely intended to ensure that European economies do not lose out to international competition in ICT, has three main objectives:

- a cheaper, faster, more secure Internet;
- investment in people and skills;
- stimulation of the Internet (of which "health online" is a key component) (Gibbs, 2001).

Key elements of this action plan include privacy enhancing technologies, harmonised use of smart cards for accessing the Internet and development of best practice in electronic health services.

---

[1] Telemedicine is the delivery of medicine (or health care) to a location distant from the provider.

The European Commission envisages the aim of health protection in the information society as "to improve public health in the European Union, to prevent human illness, diseases and sources of danger to human health via a new generation of computerised clinical systems, advanced telemedicine services and health network applications".[2] It emphasises providing support to health professionals, continuity of care, health service management and intelligent systems, and allowing citizens to assume greater participation in and responsibility for their own health.

While these developments in ICT bring with them a wide range of benefits for consumers and health care providers, they also present new legal challenges that have attracted the attention of policy makers at a global, European and national level. Many issues are not specific to health and health care, so it is not always immediately evident that legislation on ICT has implications for the provision of health care. From a health care perspective, however, the most directly relevant legal issues involve questions of consumer protection in three areas: the privacy of identifiable health data (maintaining confidentiality and ensuring data protection); the reliability and quality of health information provided electronically; and tort based liability. Issues that indirectly impact on health care, in so far as they affect health databases, website operators and providers of telemedical services, include ownership and intellectual property rights, and secure transfer of information and financial transactions.

I. Current EU Legislation

In recent years the EU has adopted various legal measures to address all of these issues, the most relevant of which are summarised in table 8.1.

---

[2]   http://europa.eu.int/information_society/ topics/health/index_en.htm.

**Table 8.1: EC Directives with Consequences
for the Information Society**

Date	Directive	Title
1985	85/374/EEC	Liability for defective products
1993	93/42/EEC	Medical devices
1995	95/46/EC	Protection of individuals with regard to the processing of personal data and on the free movement of such data
1996	96/9/EC	Legal protection of databases
1997	97/7/EC	Protection of consumers in respect of distance contracts
1997	97/66/EC	Processing of personal data and the protection of privacy in the telecommunications sector
1999	99/93/EC	A Community framework for electronic signatures
2000	2000/31/EC	Certain legal aspects of information society services, in particular electronic commerce, in the Internal Market

A. Data Protection

Confidentiality is vital to any medical exchange. In order to maintain confidentiality in electronic medical exchanges, regardless of the medium employed, computer and telecommunications systems must be secure, all those who handle information must have a high duty of confidentiality, and patients must have the option of verifying any information that is held about them (Rigby, 1999). Rapid developments in information technology and the purposes to which personal data are put necessitate new safeguards. Some are, however, pessimistic about whether privacy can be ensured in this new information society (Raab, 1997). At the EU level the following measures have been taken with the aim of ensuring confidentiality in data processing:

- EU Directive 95/46/EC on the protection of individuals with regard to the processing of personal data and on the free movement of such data (European Parliament and Council of the European Union, 1995);

- EU Directive 97/66/EC concerning the processing of personal data and the protection of privacy in the telecommunications sector (European Parliament and Council of the European Union, 1997b).

Directive 95/46/EC aims to "protect the fundamental rights and freedoms of natural persons, and in particular their right to privacy with respect to the processing of personal data" (Article 1.1). A related aim is to harmonise data protection legislation in order to facilitate "the free flow of personal data between Member States" of the EU (Article 1.2) (Allaert and Barber, 1998). Protection is to be provided to the highest standard available under national law within the EU, rather than being a compromise of average standards of national protection (Chalton, 1997).

Building on the principles enshrined in the Council of Europe's 1981 Convention for the Protection of Individuals with regard to Automatic Processing of Personal Data (Council of Europe, 1981), the Directive gives individuals basic rights of consent (Article 7), verification and correction (Article 12). Each Member State must create an independent public authority to supervise personal data protection and organisations processing data must appoint a "data controller" who must register with the relevant public authority. The Directive applies to all data, including manually held records containing personal information (Smith, 1996), but data collected for "purely personal" or "household purposes" are outside the scope of the Directive. Data must be processed fairly and lawfully; collected for specified, explicit and legitimate purposes and not further processed in a way incompatible with those purposes; accurate, kept up to date (in certain circumstances), relevant and not excessive given the purposes for which they are stored; and kept in a form which permits identification of individual data subjects only for as long as necessary for the purposes for which the data were originally collected (Article 6).

The Directive also requires adequate measures to be taken to ensure the security of stored data (although greater health relevant guidance on such measures is given in the Council of Europe Recommendation No. R (97) 5 on the protection of medical data) (Rigby, 1999). Article 25 restricts the transfer of personal data outside the EU except where third countries ensure "an adequate level of protection", as judged by the standards of the Directive. So far, the United States has been found not to provide an adequate level of protection, posing potential problems for US businesses, particularly those with European operations (Ballon, 2001). In July 2000 the EU and the US Department of Commerce reached agreement on a "safe harbour framework" to allow individual companies to operate on the basis of a system that certifies their provision of adequate data protection as defined by Article 25.[3]

The sensitivity of personal health data is recognised in Article 8 regarding the processing of special categories of data, which is prohibited unless safeguards are in place (Allaert and Barber, 1998). Special categories include information revealing racial or ethnic origin, political opinions, religious or philosophical beliefs or trade union membership or disclosing details of a person's health or sexual orientation. Although the Directive identifies health data as a special category and generally

---

[3]   http://www.export.gov./safeharbor.

prohibits their processing unless an individual has given his explicit consent to do so. There are exemptions to this including when (Price-WaterhouseCoopers, 2001):

- processing of health data is necessary to carry out rights of organisations under employment law;
- the individual is physically or legally incapable of giving his consent;
- the data are expressly made public by the individual;
- processing of data is required for the purposes of preventive medicine, medical diagnosis, the provision of care or treatment or the management of health services, and where those data are processed by a health professional subject to national law or rules established by national competent bodies to the obligation of professional secrecy.

Where personal health data are recorded for research or other purposes, but not used directly in the process of delivering health care, the key issue is of confidentiality; however, where information systems relate to the active treatment of patients, the issue is of the integrity and availability of the patient data required (Allaert and Barber, 1998).

The degree of harmonisation that the Directive can achieve has been questioned, partly because the Directive gives Member States substantial scope for derogation, and partly because it does not apply to the processing of personal data in the course of any activity that falls outside the scope of EU law, although this is not defined by the Directive (Chalton, 1997). In spite of the October 1998 deadline for Member State action, France, Germany, Ireland and Luxembourg have yet to pass legislation implementing the Directive.[4]

Directive 97/66/EC regulates privacy in telecommunications (European Parliament and Council of the European Union, 1997b). It extends certain privacy rights to legal as well as natural persons and applies to data processed in connection with the provision of telecommunications services in public telecommunications networks, in particular via ISDN (Rigby, 1999). In 1999 the European Commission launched a review of the current telecommunications framework, leading to a proposal for a new Directive aimed at adapting Directive 97/66/EC (European Parliament and Council of the European Union, 1997b) (Pérez Asinari and Louveaux, 2001). The proposal for a Directive concerning the processing of personal data and the protection of privacy in the electronic communications sector aims to impose on all electronic communications

---

[4] http://europa.eu.int/comm/internal_market/en/dataprot/law/impl.htm.

services (rather than just telecommunications services) the same rules that apply to offline services. It states that the Directive "should be adapted to developments in the markets and technologies for electronic communications services in order to provide an equal level of protection of personal data and privacy for users of publicly available electronic communications services, regardless of the technologies used" (Recital 3). The use of the broader term "electronic communications services" suggests that the proposed Directive goes beyond Directive 97/66/EC, but it is important to note that the existing Directive already applies to the Internet, so the proposed Directive is not as radical a change as might have been expected (Pérez Asinari and Louveaux, 2001).

A criticism of the proposed Directive is that its scope is limited to the provision of electronic communications services "for remuneration", which suggests that Internet providers that provide free access do not fall within the scope of the Directive.

B. Ownership of Data and Intellectual Property Rights

Although the data protection Directive (95/46/EC) (Council of the European Union, 1995) specifies that data should only be used for the purpose stated when collected, this duty is interpreted more widely in the area of health care, and further data processing for scientific research purposes may be acceptable, even if not originally declared to the data subject, so long as appropriate care to ensure confidentiality is taken (Recital 34) (Rigby, 1999).

Directive 96/9/EC on the legal protection of databases attempts to address the issue of who actually owns health related data by improving the previously weak copyright protection for databases (European Parliament and Council of the European Union, 1996). Although it is argued that the Directive effectively set the global agenda for national and international database protection, going beyond the protection afforded to databases in other areas of the world, notably the United States (Thakur, 2001), it is not entirely clear to what extent this increases the protection available to owners of health related databases (Rigby, 1999). Thakur also points out several weaknesses in the Directive, arguing that it fails in a number of respects to qualify as an optimum global model.

C. Security and Electronic Signatures

The electronic signature is a key tool in ensuring confidentiality, integrity and authenticity in the transfer of data between electronic sources (Rigby, 1999; Allaert and Barber, 1998). It is therefore vital for building consumer confidence in and maximising the opportunities presented by e-commerce (Roscam Abbing, 2000). Although a whole range of electronic signature tools exist and are widely used, legally they were not widely recognised within the EU prior to the European Commission's Directive on a Community framework for electronic signatures, which aims to establish a legal framework for electronic signatures in order to create a homogenous technology-neutral background for the operation of electronic signatures issued through certification service providers anywhere in the EU (European Parliament and Council of the European Union, 1999).

Commentators have, however, noted a number of weaknesses in the Directive. First, it does not provide a basis for dealing with electronic, as opposed to paper documents and further legislation is necessary to allow electronically signed documents to be treated in exactly the same way as paper documents (Rigby, 1999). Specifically, some national laws still require certain health related documents, such as prescriptions, to be produced on paper. Because the Directive does not cover the conclusion of contracts or other non-contractual acts (Article 1), Member States are not required to address these issues (Rigby, 1999). Finally, the legal issues regarding electronic signatures largely fall on health care providers rather than telecommunications service providers.

D. Consumer Protection in Distance Selling

EU Directive 97/7/EC on the protection of consumers in respect of distance contracts seeks to protect consumers (as natural persons and not in a commercial or professional capacity) from the risks that may arise when they are unable to examine goods prior to purchase or to see the supplier's premises, as is usually the case with telemedicine and use of the Internet (European Parliament and Council of the European Union, 1997a). Suppliers are required to comply with the duties outlined in the Directive in situations where they use one or more means of distance communication to conclude a contract. These duties include the consumer's right to written information about the supplier and the goods or service, and the right to withdraw from the contract within seven working days from the time at which the written information is supplied, without penalty and without giving any reason. Although this Directive is the EU's key legal text applicable to contracts concluded at a distance, critics claim that it does not provide EU consumers with comprehensive protection, particularly as protection is only granted where contracts are concluded (and concluded at a distance), and does not afford protection to consumers merely surfing the Internet (Salaün, 2000).

E. Electronic Commerce

The Directive on electronic commerce complements the existing laws protecting consumers in the EU and concerns three areas: general information to be provided; commercial communications; and contracts. In terms of general information, the Directive goes beyond the distance selling Directive by requiring information such as: the name, address and email address of the service provider; the trade register (where applicable) with which the service provider is registered; any activity subjected to an authorisation scheme (where applicable); and (where applicable) the professional body with which the service provider is registered, the professional title granted by the Member State, and the VAT number (Article 5). Prices and essential terms and conditions should also be mentioned (Article 5). For commercial communications the new Directive also goes beyond the distance selling Directive in requiring the service provider to identify clearly: the commercial nature of the communication; the person on whose behalf the communication is made; and (where authorised) promotional offers such as discounts, premiums, gifts, competitions and games. The electronic commerce Directive completes the distance selling Directive by defining exactly when a contract is concluded and by informing consumers of the procedure for correcting handling errors (Salaün, 2000) (see also Chapter 5).

F. Liability

A further aspect of consumer protection is concerned with preventing consumers from harm by imposing duties on suppliers and producers of goods and services. There have been several EU level initiatives to promote this aspect of consumer protection, although there is currently no EU level legislation that directly states the liability of the telemedicine practitioner, although patients can seek compensation when injured as a result of telemedical treatment under existing laws on medical negligence (Rigby, 1999).

Two EU Directives do, however, afford consumers some protection in the area of product liability. EU Directive 85/374/EEC on product liability establishes the general principle that the producer is liable for damages (Council of the European Communities, 1985). In order to establish liability there must be a defect in the product and harm to the consumer, regardless of whether or not the defect is the result of negligence on the part of the producer. The Directive further stipulates that when the producer cannot be identified, liability will fall on the supplier, so a patient injured by a defective telemedical product would have cause for action against the producer, if identifiable, or the medical practitioner. Because medical practitioners are also consumers, they can take action against the supplier or producer if an injury arose through the use of a defective product used in a reasonable and responsible way. The duties imposed by the Directive highlight the importance of stringent product testing, quality control and risk monitoring (Rigby, 1999).

EU Directive 93/42/EEC on medical devices supplements Directive 85/374/EEC by forcing producers of medical devices to comply with the standards set by the European Committee on Standardisation (CEN) and the European Committee for Electrotechnical Standardisation (CENELEC) (Council of the European Communities, 1993b). The Directive covers a wide range of medical products (although it is restricted to devices that are in immediate contact with the human body so it does not cover all telemedical devices), including medical imaging devices (Rigby, 1999).

G. Quality

The tension between access and quality is central to e-health technologies (Terry, 2001). e-Health breaks down the traditional single point, gatekeeper model of access, allowing multiple entry points and the direct distribution of information to patients (Terry, 2000). Health related websites are currently among the most frequently accessed sites on the Internet. However, while these technologies may increase access to information and decrease the cost of obtaining it, they present serious issues in terms of quality assurance. The quality of information on the Internet is extremely variable and, at the present time, European consumers have very few resources with which to assess quality and authenticity, which may generate public concern and thus inhibit the Internet's usefulness (Eysenbach and Diepgen, 1998; Silberg *et al.*, 1997; Rodrigues, 2000). A study undertaken to assess the reliability of health information on the Internet, looking at parent-oriented web pages relating to home management of feverish children, found that only a few websites provided complete and accurate information for this common condition, suggesting an urgent need to check health information on the Internet for accuracy, completeness and consistency (Impicciatore *et al.*, 1997).

The quality of health information is particularly important because poor or inappropriate information could result in serious injury or even death. However, ensuring quality is a complex issue, raising the following questions:

– What constitutes quality?
– How can it be assessed?
– How can consumers be guided to the best available information?

- How can consumers be helped in appraising information? (Roscam Abbing, 2000)

In the case of the Internet, the issue is further complicated by practical constraints and the currently limited capacity of regulators to exert control over operations in "cyberspace". However, leaving aside these technical and philosophical debates regarding the advantages, disadvantages and possibilities of regulating the Internet, the EU has launched several initiatives to improve the quality of health related websites.

II. EU Initiatives: Self-regulation

As well as legislative measures, the EU has promoted voluntary self-regulation as a means of improving the quality and scope of e-health.

"Health online" forms a part of the EU's eEurope Action Plan 2002 (under the objective of stimulating the use of the Internet) and involves the implementation (by the end of 2002) of an infrastructure to provide user-friendly, validated and interoperable systems for medical care, disease prevention and health education through national and regional networks connecting citizens, practitioners and authorities online (Liikanen, 2001). Further action includes:

- Developing quality criteria for health related websites to boost consumer confidence in the use of such sites and foster best practice in the development of sites and to form the basis of future policy tools for assuring the quality of information, such as user guides, voluntary codes of conduct, trust marks, accreditation systems etc. The European Commission aims to publish a code of good practice for health websites in 2002. The Commission emphasises that it is not trying to establish a central EU marking system for websites because it does not have the staff, finance or the legal basis to do so (Watson, 2002). However, it is doubtful whether a basic code of practice will have any effect and a more rigorous system may have to be implemented.

- Identifying and disseminating best practice in e-health services to assist purchasing departments in decision-making and establishing benchmarking criteria (as soon as possible in 2002);

- Establishing a series of data networks to assist with informed health care planning in Member States (by the end of 2002);

- Drafting a communication on legal aspects of e-health to clarify which existing legislation has an impact on e-health in order to remove some of the uncertainties expressed by industry about the legal aspects of such commercial activity.

MedCERTAIN is another recently launched project (medPICS Certification and Rating of Trustworthy and Assessed Health Information on the Net) funded by the EU under the Action Plan for Safer Use of the Internet with the aim of developing a technical and organisational infrastructure for a pilot system allowing consumers to access meta-information about health related websites and health information providers, including disclosure information from health providers and the opinions of external evaluators (both associations and individual experts) (Eysenbach *et al.*, 2001). It is hoped that this system will promote consumer confidence by enabling consumers to assess the quality and reliability of information provided on the Internet. The model adopted by MedCERTAIN combines:

- consumer education;
- encouragement of best practice among information providers;
- self labelling;
- external evaluation.

While these initiatives are welcome, the difficulties inherent in assuring quality should not be underestimated (Wilson, 2001).

For example, developing quality criteria such as trust marks and accreditation systems to rate or label websites (a key element of "health online" and MedCERTAIN) can be problematic. In order to operate efficiently and effectively, rating systems should be set up where the following conditions can be satisfied: the rating system or label should be clearly explained to consumers (for example, through a hyperlink to the rating system's own website); the label should guarantee the identity of the service provider; only a limited number of labels should be developed; labelling should be undertaken on a voluntary basis and defined in collaboration with professional and consumer associations; the label should take into account existing legal standards as a minimum; it should be surrounded by adequate security measures (Salaün, 2000).

The use of quality ratings can, however, expose those involved to legal challenges in three areas (Terry, 2000). First, e-health providers may lodge complaints about negative ratings; second, the rating body might award a positive rating to an e-health provider that subsequently injured a third party; and third, a rating body might face liability for its own web misconduct. There are a number of examples of legal action against rating bodies in the United States (Terry, 2000). Rating bodies and the legal authorities that endorse them will need to implement effective risk management strategies to ensure that they do not jeopardise their worthwhile attempts to improve the quality of e-health and reduce information asymmetry.

Codes of conduct and out-of-court dispute settlements are other elements of developing quality criteria under "health online". Article 16 of the electronic commerce Directive (European Parliament and the Council of the European Union, 2000) also specifies that Member States should encourage the drawing up of codes of conduct at European level, by trade, professional and consumer associations or organisations, so as to enforce the principles set down in Articles 5 to 15 of the Directive, and that these codes should be accessible by electronic means in the community languages. Codes of conduct can be an effective means of enhancing consumer confidence, but they may need to be accompanied by sanctions against providers that do not comply with a code's principles. Furthermore, a provider should not be allowed to make reference to a code without complying with its principles.

Article 17 of the electronic commerce Directive states that Member States should ensure that "in the event of disagreement between an information society service provider and the recipient of the service, their legislation does not hamper the use of out-of-court schemes, available under national law, for dispute settlement, including appropriate electronic means". Alternative methods of dispute resolution are seen as a complement to the judicial system and aim to provide a solution better adapted to the particularities of electronic communication than traditional Court procedures. As the Directive notes, out-of-court dispute settlement could be especially useful for disputes on the Internet because of their low transactional value and the size of the parties involved, who might otherwise be deterred from using legal procedures. Again, however, this type of settlement should not take place unless certain conditions are fulfilled, including: adequate consumer information; the explicit consent of both parties to submit the dispute to a third party; the participation of consumer associations in the establishment of rules and/or in the resolution procedure; the ensured neutrality and competence of the third party; and compliance with the legal requirements regarding consumer protection (Salaün, 2000).

Conclusion

The EU has taken a number of measures to protect consumers in the information society, both legislative and non-legislative. Many of these measures indirectly affect certain aspects of health care systems, in so far as they concern data and database protection, security in electronic transfers, distance selling, product liability and quality control. As few were initiated with health care in mind, they may suffer from weaknesses that reduce their effectiveness when applied to health care. Some of the non-legislative initiatives do directly concern the quality and scope of e-health, largely through voluntary or self-regulatory action, and while these initiatives are welcome, their task is compounded by the complexities involved in ensuring quality on the Internet. Furthermore, the growth of electronic commerce creates challenges for health policy, as recognised by the Council of Ministers' call for information technology to be implemented within the health sector in ways that promote social inclusion.

e-Health breaks down the traditional gatekeeper model of access to health care, allowing direct distribution of information to patients. However, the quality of information on the Internet is variable; while the Internet could increase access to information and decrease the costs of obtaining it, quality assurance issues have to be seriously addressed.

CHAPTER 9

The Way Forward

This book began by outlining the case for a shared European vision of how health care should be organised. It recognised that Member States vary considerably in the detailed organisation of their health care systems but, underlying all of them, is a common model based on social solidarity and universal coverage. This model has several important features that distinguish health care from a normally traded good. In particular, the European social model is based on a complex system of cross-subsidies, from rich to poor, from well to ill, from young to old, and from single people to families and from workers to the non-active. This model has continued to attract overwhelming popular support, reflecting the historical forces from which it emerged and the deeply rooted values of solidarity in Europe. It also recognises that a market for health care is inevitably imperfect; individuals may not always be in the best position to assess their health needs, whether because they are unaware of the nature of their health need or are simply unable to voice it effectively. Health care is increasingly complex, creating major information asymmetries that open up scope for exploitative opportunistic behaviour by providers and therefore an effective system of regulation and oversight is needed. For these reasons, all industrialised countries have taken an active role in the organisation of health care. As a consequence, Member States have explicitly stated, in the Treaties, that the organisation and delivery of health services and medical care remains a matter of national competence.

Nevertheless, many individual elements of health care are, entirely reasonably, subject to market principles. With the exception of some vaccines and drugs with specialised applications related to national security, governments generally do not produce or distribute pharmaceuticals. Health facilities purchase equipment, whether clinical or otherwise, on the free market. Both medical equipment and technology are freely traded on the international market. Many health professionals are self-employed, engaging in contracts with health authorities or funds. Patients may obtain treatment outside the statutory health care system, either in their own country or abroad. All of these matters are entirely legitimate subjects for applications of the internal market; indeed the fundamental freedoms enshrined in the Treaty require that such transactions are transparent and non-discriminatory.

This situation creates certain difficulties. Policies developed to sustain the principle of solidarity, with its complex system of cross-subsidies, are especially vulnerable to policies whose roots are in market principles. Unregulated competition in health care will, almost inevitably, reduce equity because of the incentive to select those whose health needs are least, making it difficult or expensive for those in greatest need to obtain cover. Risk adjustment systems can be established but are far from perfect, especially in an intensely competitive environment. Cost containment policies may be based on restricting supply, such as the number of health facilities. This may be undermined if patients can require their funders to pay for treatment elsewhere. Policies that address the issue of information asymmetry may involve selective contracting with providers but this requires the existence of agreed uniform standards. Concerns about information asymmetry have also caused European governments to reject policies that may seem, superficially, to redress this asymmetry, such as direct-to-consumer advertising of pharmaceuticals, on the basis of empirical evidence that it is often misleading and drives up health care costs while bringing few if any benefits to patients. However, this is clearly an interference with the working of the market. In other words, even for those elements of health care that are covered by internal market provisions, Member States and the European Union have stated explicitly that the effects of the market must be constrained.

At present, therefore, health and social policy in Europe is being developed in an extremely disconnected fashion. Member States decide the goals they wish to pursue, such as equity and more effective care, and must then find mechanisms by which to do this that are consistent with European law. Much of the relevant European law has emerged from rulings that have either arisen from considerations in other sectors or, by addressing only the issues in a single case, leave major issues of applicability unresolved. As a consequence, health policy makers are confronted with a mass of contradictory advice from those who take either a restricted or expansive view of the scope of European law in health care.

The evolving issue of free movement of patients is instructive. The Kohll and Decker rulings of the ECJ forced the Luxembourg social security system to reimburse unauthorised health care in another Member State on the basis of the Community principles of free movement of services and goods. This made it clear that social security systems, even if a matter of national competence, were not exempt from European law. Following from the later Cases of Smits and Peerbooms, the ECJ clarified that all medical services, including hospital treatment, fall within the definition of services according to the EC Treaty, since in one way or another the provider is remunerated for the delivered service. The fact that reimbursement was claimed under the Dutch health insurance system, which operates through a benefits in-kind approach, was not considered relevant.

Even if the ECJ considered that requiring prior authorisation in all cases in which health care is delivered in another Member State constitutes a barrier to free movement of services and goods, it accepted in the Smits-Peerbooms Cases that it was a necessary and reasonable measure to guarantee a balanced and accessible supply of hospital services. However, the Court would only accept such an exemption to the principle of free movement of services if the criteria applied to grant the authorisation were objective and non-discriminatory *vis-à-vis* providers established in another Member State. In that respect, it found the Dutch authorisation conditions not to be compatible with the principle of equal treatment, because they are likely to favour Dutch providers.

While not completely outlawing the use of a prior authorisation system, the Court rulings have radically restricted Member States' discretion to determine their own policies by requiring that their decisions are necessary, proportional and based on objective and non-discriminatory criteria. Furthermore, in the Vanbraekel ruling, the ECJ considered that if authorisation is given – or is wrongly refused – the patient should be granted the best possible reimbursement tariff, either that of the home country or that of the providing state. By linking EEC Regulation 1408/71, on which cover for health care abroad has been traditionally based, with the free provision of services, the ECJ seems to have created difficulties for this system of co-ordination.

The jurisprudence of the ECJ has created important uncertainties. Given the centrality of EEC Regulation 1408/71 in the free movement of patients, these decisions have robbed it of much of its certainty. Consequently it seems necessary to undertake a revision of the whole legal framework regulating access to health care across the European Union. Since the issue is now attracting much attention – especially in countries where patients are confronted with waiting lists and other difficulties with access, and key actors are experimenting with new ways of meeting patients' expectations, including across borders, some guidance is needed.

The situation with regard to free movement of professionals also creates difficulty. The relevant Directives arose at a time when a qualification, once awarded, essentially provided a lifetime right to practice. This is increasingly no longer the case and several Member States are instituting mechanisms to restrict registration to those fulfilling certain continuing education requirements. It is far from clear how these are to be treated within the existing legal framework. Furthermore, the principle of mutual recognition, upheld in the Kohll Case, effectively precludes the possibility that training programmes in one country may be of a different standard from that in another, despite extensive evidence that this is so.

There is now a jurisdictional gap in the regulation of health professionals in Europe, with enhanced national regulatory structures but an absence of co-ordination at a European level. For many reasons, professional self-regulation prevails in Europe but the bodies involved nationally often have additional functions, which may include education, the establishment of professional standards, a trade union function, or others. Unfortunately, in those European bodies that do exist, these roles are often confused.

The pharmaceutical sector creates numerous difficulties as the international dimension is so much greater than for many of the other issues considered here and the challenge of balancing trade and health policy concerns is especially acute. One example is direct-to-consumer advertising where there is strong commercial pressure to permit it but sound health policy reasons to reject it. The EU institutions have created a framework in which the supply of medicines has been harmonised along common lines to the benefit of drug manufacturers (and intermediate suppliers who source their products – parallel imports – from different markets within the EU) even in the face of intellectual property rights. European law and policy has had much less direct impact on the demand side. Pricing and reimbursement controls, as demand side management techniques, are only marginally impacted upon by EU law – whether primary Treaty rules or secondary harmonising legislation. Proxy-demand side controls on doctors' prescribing, wholesalers and pharmacists' margins are outside the remit of EU pharmaceutical policies. However, e-health and e-commerce could provide many possibilities to break down the traditional single gatekeeper model of access, allowing multiple entry points and the direct distribution of information to patients. Whether this will allow the Commission to influence proxy-demand and demand more directly remains to be seen.

Issues also arise in relation to medical devices. While they have contributed greatly to the benefits achieved by health systems, there are inevitable risks that have led governments to establish post-marketing surveillance systems. Although a new European post-market monitoring protocol has been created, many problems remain. The national differences in both reporting and implementation, raise questions of how to obtain convergence without compromising health and safety of patients in countries that now have stricter provisions, in other words to avoid regulating down to the lowest common denominator, while still supporting industrial policy. Such national differences will ensure that postmarketing surveillance of medical devices in the EU remains a complicated and difficult process.

Voluntary health insurance is increasingly important in some countries as a means of obtaining access to quality health care within a reasonable time. Here, European policy is dominated by the objective of integrating insurance markets. The existing Community legal framework is based essentially on the logic of free Community-wide competition among insurers whose solvency is supervised and guaranteed by competent authorities in the home Member State, based upon a harmonised set of insurance business conditions and prudential rules. Governments' discretion to materially regulate prices and conditions of insurance products is seriously reduced as this could impede fair competition among European insurers and could jeopardise the financial health of insurance undertakings. In the field of health care this constrains Member States' options to expanding the role of voluntary health insurance while maintaining principles of solidarity. Article 54 of the third non-life insurance Directive, introducing the possibility of exemption based on the general good, is unlikely to meet the regulatory needs felt in different Member States.

The growth of electronic commerce also creates challenges to health policy, as recognised by the Council of Ministers' call for information technology to be implemented in the health sector in ways that promote social inclusion. The EU has taken a number of measures to protect consumers in the information society, both legislative and non-legislative. Many of these measures indirectly affect certain aspects of health care systems, in so far as they concern data and database protection, security in electronic transfers, distance selling, product liability and quality control. Few were initiated with health care in mind so they may face problems in achieving their full potential in the health sector.

The application of competition law in the field of health care is also problematic. While many of the transactions within statutory systems may be exempt on social grounds, health authorities must be aware of the possibility of removing this protection through deregulation and privatisation. There are many circumstances in which health care organisations may be considered as undertakings, regardless of issues such as ownership or profit-seeking status. What is important is whether or not they engage in economic activity. For this, each activity undertaken by an organisation must be judged on its merits; even where most of its activities are deemed to be non-economic, and thus exempt from competition law, it does not follow that everything it does is also exempt.

211

While it is unnecessary to go through all of the issues raised in previous chapters, it is apparent that there are many other areas in which health policy and the promotion of the single market can either conflict or, more often, create ambiguities.

Many of these challenges arise from the growing role of the ECJ. Its role is to interpret the application of EU law in specific circumstances but these interpretations then establish precedents that are applied in different circumstances. Alter points out that

> if Member States cannot sway the interpretation of the ECJ, they may still be able to change the European law itself. This would not necessarily be an affront to the ECJ, nor would it necessarily undermine the Court's legitimacy. The political system is supposed to work by having legislators draft and change laws, and Courts apply laws (Alter, 2001).

However, the reality of the joint-decision trap makes it extremely difficult to reverse the ECJ advances based directly on an EC Treaty. Though in theory it should have been easier to change Regulations and Directives because of the possibilities offered by qualified majority voting (Tsebelis and Garrett, 2001), in practice few ECJ interpretations have provoked legislative action to reverse the thrust of the decision.

> This is because most ECJ's decisions […] affect Member States differently, so there is no coalition of support to change disputed legislation […]. After enough time passes, and enough protests or attempts to challenge ECJ jurisprudence lead nowhere, political passivity sets in […]. Inertia undermines the political will to effect change, and passivity is taken as a sign of tacit support (Alter, 2001).

As Dehousse (1995) has emphasised

> The tendency toward juridification may help to weaken the legitimacy of the integration process as a whole. The European Union is already suffering from a form of 'political deficit' to the extent that such actors as the political parties, the trade unions or even the media, whose actions often act as a reference point for national voters, are generally weak at European level.

Dehousse argues that by camouflaging conflicts of interest and replacing partisan conflicts with supposedly neutral debates on the interpretation of law, the EU considerably weakens the political process and offers opportunities to opponents of integration to claim that citizen's democracy is replaced by a form of "judicial democracy". Nonetheless, Dehousse also points out that the same process may be seen in a more positive light because litigation at European level can enable European citizens to protect their rights against decisions of national administrations. However, "ECJ rulings may easily be perceived as intrusions calling into question the choices and traditions of national communities" (Dehousse, 2000).

So what is to be done? This review suggests that a European health policy would bring considerable benefits, by setting out more explicitly an agreed position among Member States on what they are seeking to achieve through their health care systems. The evidence reviewed in Chapter 1 suggests that there is likely to be sufficient agreement to reach a common position, at least at the level of principles, although this does not imply that there is not considerable room for reform. However, difficulties may arise when attempting to develop more detailed policies, given the wide diversity of arrangements in place in Member States to deliver health care.

The challenge that the EU faces is that its secondary legislation, such as Directives and Regulations, and the Court's interpretation of them, must be based on what is in the Treaties. However, as this book has shown, the social character of European health systems is not embedded in the Treaties. Consequently, if the European social model is not to be undermined inadvertently by the inappropriate application of EU law designed to meet needs in other sectors or a piecemeal series of ECJ judgements on health care, it will be necessary to agree on a statement of fundamental principles of general interest that enshrine the goals of European health systems, that balance the internal market with social goals, and that can be incorporated into a future Treaty.

However, this is itself insufficient to achieve the benefits that closer European integration offers for health care systems. A system of open co-ordination, in which there are formally established means to learn from the experience of others while taking account of national circumstances, provides an opportunity to promote best practice, increasing exchange of information on what works and what does not, and in what circumstances. In many cases it will be possible to develop shared approaches to common problems but this development respects historical, political and cultural diversity and does not force the harmonisation of processes that, while pursuing the same goal, are organised in ways that are incompatible with each other.

An open method of co-ordination will make some of the challenges posed by the internal market for health cares systems more explicit. It will also provide a framework within which they can be addressed and appropriate legal responses, including possible Treaty revisions, debated.

These procedures will, however, take time and it is apparent that action is needed now. Consequently, it is of the utmost importance that the EU establishes, as soon as possible, a system that can monitor the impact of EU law on health care systems on a continuing basis.

Chronological Table of Cases

Rulings by the European Court of Justice and Court of First Instance can be read in full at www.europa.eu.int/cj/en/jurisp/index.htm.

European Court of Justice

Case C-26/62, Judgement of 5 February 1963, Van Gend en Loos *v.* Nederlandse Administratie der Belastingen.

Case C-6/64, Judgement of 3 June 1964, Costa *v.* E.N.E.L.

Case C-155/73, Judgement of 30 April 1974, Sacchi.

Case C-8/74, Judgement of 11 July 1974, Procureur du Roi *v.* Benoît and Gustave Dassonville.

Case C-15/74, Judgement of 31 October 1974, Centrafarm B.V. and Adriaan de Peijper *v.* Sterling Drug Inc.

Case C-43/75, Judgement of 8 April 1976, Defrenne *v.* Sabena (Defrenne II).

Case C-352/75, Judgement of 26 April 1988, Bond van Adverteerders *v.* Netherlands State.

Case C-85/76, Judgement of 13 February 1979, Hoffmann-La Roche *v.* Commission.

Case C-19/77, Judgement of 1 February 1978, Miller *v.* Commission.

Case C-117/77, Judgement of 16 March 1978, Bestuur van het algemeen Ziekenfonds Drenthe-Platteland *v.* Pierik I.

Case C-120/78, Judgement of 20 February 1979, Rewe-Zentral A.G. *v.* Bundesmonopolverwaltung für Branntwein (Cassis de Dijon).

Case C-182/78, Judgement of 31 May 1979, Bestuur van het algemeen Ziekenfonds Drenthe-Plattoland *v.* Pierik II.

Case C-258/78, Judgement of 8 June 1982, Nungesser *v.* Commission.

Case C-187/80, Judgement of 14 July 1981, Merck *v.* Stephar and Exler Merck & Co. Inc.

Case C-238/82, Judgement of 7 February 1984, Duphar and Others *v.* The Netherlands State.

Case C-286/82, Judgement of 31 January 1984, Graziana Luisi and Giuseppe Carbone *v.* Ministero del Tesoro. Joined Case with C-26/83.

Case C-229/83, Judgement of 10 January 1985, Leclerc *v.* Au blé vert.

Case C-231/83, Judgement of 29 January 1985, Cullet *v.* Leclerc.

Case C-123/83, Judgement of 30 January 1985, BNIC *v.* Clair.

Case C-41/83, Judgement of 20 March 1985, Italy *v.* Commission.

Case C-224/84, Judgement of 15 May 1986, Johnston *v.* Chief Constable of the Royal Ulster Constabulary.

Case C-311/84, Judgement of 3 October 1985, CBEM *v.* CLT and IPB.

Case C-263/86, Judgement of 27 September 1988. Belgian State *v.* Humbel.

Case C-267/86, Judgement of 21 September 1988, Van Eycke *v.* ASPA.

Case C-62/86, Judgement of 3 July 1991, AKZO *v.* Commission.

Case C-66/86, Judgement of 11 April 1989, Ahmed Saeed Flugreisen and others *v.* Zentrale zur Bekämpfung unlauteren Wettbewerbs.

Case C-31/87, Judgement of 20 September 1988, Beentjes *v.* The Netherlands State.

Case C-18/88, Judgement of 13 December 1991, RTT *v.* GB-Inno-BM.

Case C-202/88, Judgement of 19 March 1991, France *v.* Commission.

Case C-353/89, Judgement of 25 July 1991, Commission *v.* Netherlands.

Case C-159/90, Judgement of 4 October 1991, Society for the Protection of Unborn Children Ireland *v.* Grogan and others.

Case C-179/90, Judgement of 10 December 1991, Merci Convenzionali Porto di Genova *v.* Siderurgica Gabrielli.

Case C-41/90, Judgement of 23 April 1991, Höfner and Elser *v.* Macrotron.

Case C-6/90, Judgement of 19 November 1991, Francovich and Bonifaci and others *v.* Italian Republic. Joined Case with C-9/90.

Case C-159/91, Judgement of 17 February 1993, Poucet and Pistre AGF and Cancava. Joined Case with C-160/91.

Case C-185/91, Judgement of 17 November 1993, Bundesanstalt für den Güterfernverkehr *v.* Gabrüder Reiff.

Case C-320/91, Judgement of 19 May 1993, Criminal proceedings *v.* Corbeau.

Case C-97/91, Judgement of 3 December 1992, Oleificio Borelli *v.* Commission.

Case 109/92, Judgement of 7 December 1993, Stephan Max Wirth *v.* Landeshauptstadt Hannover.

Case C-364/92, Judgement of 19 January 1994, SAT Fluggesellschaft *v.* Eurocontrol SAT Airlines.

Case C-393/92, Judgement of 27 April 1994, Gemeente Almelo and others *v.* Energiebedrijf Ijsselmij.

Case C-153/93, Judgement of 9 June 1994, Germany *v.* Delta Schiffahrts- und Speditionsgesellschaft.

Case C-387/93, Judgement of 14 December 1995, Criminal proceedings *v.* Banchero.

Case C-433/93, Judgement of 11 August 1995, Commission *v.* Germany.

Case C-55/94, Judgement of 30 November 1995, Reinhard Gebhard *v.* Consiglio dell'Ordine degli Avvocati e Procuratori di Milano.

Case C-157/94, Judgement of 23 October 1997, Commission *v.* the Netherlands.

Case C-159/94, Judgement of 23 October 1997, Commission *v.* France.

Case C-238/94, Judgement of 26 March 1996, Garcia and others *v.* Mutuelle de Prévoyance sociale dAquitaine and others.

Case C-244/94, Judgement of 16 November 1995, FFSA and others *v.* Ministère de l'Agriculture et de la Pêche.

Case C-333/94, Judgement of 14 November 1996, Tetra Pak *v.* Commission.

Case C-79/94, Judgement of 4 May 1995, Commission *v.* Greece.

Case C-96/94, Judgement of 5 October 1995, Centro Servizi Spediporto *v.* Spedizioni Marittima del Golfo.

Case C-120/95, Judgement of 28 April 1998, Decker *v.* Caisse de maladie des employés privés.

Case C-267/95, Judgement of 5 December 1996, Merck *v.* Primecrown and Beecham *v.* Europharm.

Case C-359/95, Judgement of 11 November 1997, Commission and French Republic *v.* Ladbroke Racing.

Case C-70/95, Judgement of 17 June 1997, Sodemare and others *v.* Regione Lombardia Sodemare and others.

Case C-158/96, Judgement of 28 April 1998, Kohll *v.* Union des caisses de maladie.

Case C-35/96, Judgement of 18 June 1998, Commission *v.* Italy.

Case C-360/96, Judgement of 10 November 1998, Gemeente Arnhem and Gemeente Rheden *v.* BFI Holding B.V.

Case C-44/96, Judgement of 15 January 1998, Mannesmann Anlagenbau Austria and others Strohal Rotationsdruck.

Case C-55/96, Judgement of 11 December 1997, Job Centre.

Case C-67/96, Judgement of 21 September 1999, Albany International BV *v.* Stichting Bedrijfspensioenfonds Textielindustrie.

Case C-76/97, Judgement of 24 September 1998, Tögel Niederösterreichische Gebietskrankenkasse.

Case 115/97. Judgement of 21 September 1999, Brentjens.

Case C-219/97, Judgement of 21 September 1999, Drijvende Bokken.

Case C-38/97, Judgement of 1 October 1998, Librandi.

Case C-75/97, Judgement of 17 June 1999, Kingdom of Belgium *v.* Commission of the European Communities.

Case C-76/97, Judgement of 24 September 1998, Tögel *v.* Niederösterreichische Gebietskrankenkasse.

Case C-206/98, Judgement of 18 May 2000, Commission *v.* Belgium.

Case C-222/98, Judgement of 21 September 2001, van der Woude *v.* Stichting Beatrixoord.

Case C-180/98, Judgement of 12 September 2000, Pavlov and others.

Case C-239/98, Judgement of 16 December 1999, Commission *v.* Republic of France.

Case C-368/98, Judgement of 12 July 2001, Vanbraekel and others.

Case C-376/98, Judgement of 5 October 2000, Federal Republic of Germany *v.* European Parliament and Council of the European Union.

Case C-411/98, Judgement of 3 October 2000, Ferlini.

Case C-1/99, Judgement of 11 January 2001, Kofisa Italia.

Case C-157/99, Judgement of 12 July 2001, Smits and Peerbooms.

Case C-223/99, Judgement of 10 May 2001, Agorà and Excelsior.

Case C-226/99, Judgement of 11 January 2001, Siples.

Case C-385/99, Pending Case, Müller-Fauré and van Riet.

Case C-424/99, Judgement of 27 November 2001, Commission of the European Communities *v.* Republic of Austria.

Case C-53/00, Judgement of 22 November 2001, Ferring *v.* ACOSS.

Case C-298/01, Pending Case, Commission *v.* Germany.

Case C-322/01, Pending Case, Deutscher Apothekerverband.

Court of First Instance

Case T-83/91, Judgement of 6 October 1994, Tetra Pak International SA *v.* Commission of the European Communities.
Case T-41/96, Judgement of 26 October 2000, Bayer *v.* Commission of the European Communities.

EFTA Court

Case E-6/98R, 11 December 1998, Norway *v.* EFTA Surveillance Authority.

Bibliography

Abraham, J. and Lewis, G. (1998), "Secrecy and Transparency of Medicines Licensing in the EU", *Lancet*, No.352, pp.480-482.

Akyurek-Kievits, H.E. (2001), "The Dutch Health Insurance Sector and EU Competition Law", Paper presented at the conference organised during the Belgian Presidency of the European Union on "European Integration and Health Care Systems: A Challenge for Social Policy", Ghent, 7-8 December 2001.

Albedo (1995), "At Last, A Real European Milestone", *Pharmaceutical Technology Europe*, December 1995, pp.8-11.

Allaert, F.-A. and Barber, B. (1998), "Some Systems Implications of EU Data Protection Directive", *European Journal of Information Systems*, Vol.7, No.1, March 1998, pp.1-4.

Allen, J. (2001), "Ensuring Suality of Health Care Providers within the Single Market", Paper presented at the conference organised during the Belgian Presidency of the European Union on "European Integration and Health Care Systems: A Challenge for Social Policy", Ghent, 7-8 December 2001.

Altenstetter, C. (1992a), "Health Care in the European Community", in Hermans, H. E. G. M. *et al.* (eds.), *Health Care in Europe after 1992*, Dartmouth, Leiden.

Altenstetter, C. (1992b), "Health Policy Regimes and the Single European Market", *Journal of Health Politics, Policy and Law*, Vol.17, No.4, pp.813-846.

Altenstetter, C. (1999), "European Integration and National Governance: A Comparative Analysis of the Implementation of EU Regulatory Policy on Medicinal Products" (Preliminary Report), Paper presented to the ECSA Sixth Biennial International Conference, Pittsburgh, 2-5 June 1999.

Altenstetter, C. (2001a), "EU and Medical Devices Regulation in the Member States", Paper delivered at the conference organised during the Belgian Presidency of the European Union on "European Integration and Health Care Systems: A Challenge for Social Policy", Ghent, 7-8 December 2001 (unpublished).

Altenstetter, C. (2001b), "EU Policies on the Regulation of Medical Goods and Equipment", Paper presented to the 29th ECPR Joint Session of Workshops, Workshop No.15 "Health Governance in Europe: Europeanisation and New Challenges in Health Policies", Grenoble, 6-11 April 2001.

Alter, K. J. (2001), *Establishing the Supremacy of European Law*, Oxford University Press, Oxford.

Ballon, I. C. (2001), "E-Commerce and Internet Law: A Primer", Paper presented at the 2nd Annual Spring Meeting of the State Bar of California, La Jolla, 27-29 April 2001 (www.calbar.org/buslaw/spring2001/ballonpt00.htm).

Bangemann, M. (1997), "Completing the Single Pharmaceuticals Market", *Euro-health*, Vol.3, No.1, pp.22-23.

Bartlett, W., Roberts, J. A. and Le Grand, J. (1998), *A Revolution in Social Policy Quasi-market Reforms in the 1990s*, Policy Press, Bristol.

Baum, F. (1999), "Social Capital: is it Good for your Health? Issues for a Public Health Agenda", *Journal of Epidemiology and Community Health*, No.53, pp.195-196.

Belcher, P. (1997), "Amsterdam 1997: New Dawn for Public Health?", *Eurohealth*, Vol.3, No.2, pp.21-23.

Belcher, P. and Mossialos, E. (1997), "Health Priorities for the European Intergovernmental Conference", *British Medical Journal*, No.314, pp.1637-38.

Bergmark, A. (2000), "Solidarity in Swedish Welfare – Standing the Test of Time?", *Health Care Analysis*, No.8, pp.395-411.

Betten, L. (1998), "The Democratic Deficit of Participatory Democracy in Community Social Policy", *European Law Review*, Vol.23, No.1, pp.20-36.

Bieback, K. J. (1999), "Die Kranken- und Pflegeversicherung im Wettbewerbsrecht der EG", *Europäisches Wirtschafts- und Steuerrecht*, No.10, pp.361-372.

Blendon, R. J., Leitman, R., Morrison, I. and Doneland, K. (1990), "Satisfaction with Health Systems in Ten Nations", *Health Affairs*, Summer, pp.185-192.

Boecken, W. (2000), "Rechtliche Schranken für die Beschaffungstätigkeit der Krankenkassen im Hilfsmittelbereich nach der Publizierung des Vertragsrechts – insbesondere zum Schutz der Leistungserbringer vor Ungleichbehandlungen", *Neue Zeitschrift für Sozialrecht*, No.6, pp.269-277.

Boni, S. and Manzini, P. (2001), "National Social Legislation and EC Antitrust Law", *World Competition*, Vol.24, No.2, pp.239-255.

Bosco, A. (2000), "Are National Social Protection Systems under Threat? Observations on the Recent Case Law of the Court of Justice", *Notre Europe*, Paris.

Bowe, D. (1995), "EU Health Policy – Fact or Fiction?", *Eurohealth*, Vol.1, No.3, pp.24-25.

Brazier, M., Lovecy, J. and Moran, M. (1993), "Professions, Doctors and Europe: The Lessons", *European Business Journal*, Vol.5, No.4, pp.36-40.

Brittan, L. (1992), "Making a Reality of the Single Market: Pharmaceutical Pricing and the European Economic Community", Paper presented to the Institute of Economic Affairs Conference on Pharmaceutical Policies in Europe, London, December 1992.

Brown, K. (1995), "Government to Demand Curb on European Court", *Financial Times*, 2 February 1995.

Bundesaufsichtsamt für das Versicherungswesen (2001), *Submission to the European Commission's Study on Voluntary Health Insurance in the EU*, Bundesaufsichtsamt für das Versicherungswesen, Berlin.

Busse, R. (2001a), "Interesting Times in German Health Policy", *Eurohealth*, Vol.7, No.3, pp.7-8.

Busse, R. (2001b), *Voluntary Health Insurance in Germany: A Study for the European Commission*, European Observatory on Health Care Systems, Madrid.

Busse, R., Wismar, M. and Berman, P. (2002), *The European Union and Health Services – The Impact of the Single European Market on Member States*, IOS Press, Amsterdam.

Cadreau, M. (1991), "An Economic Analysis of the Impacts of the Health Systems of the European Single Market", in Kyriopoulos, J. *et al.* (eds.), *Health Systems and the Challenge of Europe after 1992*, Lambrakis Press, Athens.

CEA (1997), *Health Insurance in Europe 1997*, Comité européen des assurances, Paris.

Chai, J. (2000), "Medical Device Regulation in the United States and the European Union: A Comparative Study", *Food and Drug Law Journal*, No.55, pp.57-80.

Chalmers, D. (1997), "Judicial Preferences and the Community Legal Order", *Modern Law Review*, Vol.60, No.2, pp.164-199.

Chalton, S. (1997), "The Transposition into UK Law of EU Directive 95/46/EC (the Data Protection Directive)", *International Review of Law, Computers and Technology*, No.11, pp.25-32.

Christiansen, T. (1996), "A Maturing Bureaucracy? The Role of the Commission in the Policy Process", in Richardson, J. (ed.), *European Union Power and Policy-Making*, Routledge, London.

Church, C. (1996), "European Integration Theory in the 1990s", *European Dossiers Series*, No.33, University of North London, London.

Coheur, A. (2001), "Cross-border Care: New Prospects for Convergence", Paper presented at the conference organised during the Belgian Presidency of the European Union on "European Integration and Health Care Systems: A Challenge for Social Policy", Ghent, 7-8 December 2001.

Coopers & Lybrand (1994), "Intellectual Property", A report on EC commentaries, as cited in Chaudhry P.E. and Walsh M.G. (1995), "International Property Rights: Changing Levels of Protection under GATT, NAFTA and the EU", *Columbia Journal of World Business*, January 1995.

Cornelissen, R. (1996), "The Principle of Territoriality and the Community Regulations on Social Security", *Common Market Law Review*, No.3.

Council of Europe (1981), Convention for the Protection of Individuals with regard to Automatic Processing of Personal Data, Council of Europe, Strasbourg.

Council of the European Communities (1965), Council Directive 65/65/EEC of 26 January 1965 on the approximation of provisions laid down by Law, Regulation or Administrative Action relating to proprietary medicinal products, OJ P 022, 9 February 1965, pp.0369-0373.

Council of the European Communities (1973), First Council Directive 73/239/EEC of 24 July 1973 on the co-ordination of laws, Regulations and administrative provisions relating to the taking-up and pursuit of the business of direct insurance other than life assurance, OJ L 228, 16 August 1973.

Council of the European Communities (1975a), Council Directive 75/362/EEC of 16 June 1975 concerning the mutual recognition of diplomas, certificates and other evidence of formal qualifications in medicine, including measures to facilitate the effective exercise of the right of establishment and freedom to provide services, OJ L 167, 30 June 1975, pp.0001-0013.

Council of the European Communities (1975b), Council Directive 75/363/EEC of 16 June 1975 concerning the co-ordination of provisions laid down by law, Regulation or administrative action in respect of activities of doctors, OJ L 167, 30 June 1975, pp.0014-0016.

Council of the European Communities (1975c), Council Decision 75/364/EEC of 16 June 1975 setting up an Advisory Committee on Medical Training, OJ L 167, 30 June 1975, pp.0017-0018.

Council of the European Communities (1981), Council Regulation 2793/81/EEC of 17 September 1981 amending Regulation (EEC) 1408/71 on the application of social security schemes to employed persons and their families moving within the Community and Regulation (EEC) 574/72 fixing the procedure for implementing Regulation (EEC) 1408/71, OJ L 275, 29 September 1981.

Council of the European Communities (1984), Council Directive 84/450/EEC of 10 September 1984 relating to the approximation of the laws, Regulations and administrative provisions of the Member States concerning misleading advertising, OJ L 250, 19 September 1984, pp.0017-0020.

Council of the European Communities (1985), Directive 85/374/EEC of 25 July 1985 on the approximation of laws, Regulations and administrative provisions of the Member States concerning liability for defective products, OJ L 210, 7 August 1985, pp.0029-0033.

Council of the European Communities (1986), Council Directive 86/457/EEC of 15 September 1986 on specific training in general medical practice, OJ L 267, 19 September 1986.

Council of the European Communities (1988), Second Council Directive 88/357/EEC of 22 June 1988 on the co-ordination of laws, Regulations and administrative provisions relating to direct insurance other than life assurance and laying down provisions to facilitate the effective exercise of freedom to provide services and amending Directive 73/239/EEC, OJ L 172, 4 July 1988.

Council of the European Communities (1989a), Council Directive 89/105/EC of 21 December 1988 relating to the transparency of measures regulating the pricing of medicinal products for human use and their inclusion in the scope of national health insurance systems, OJ L 40, 11 February 1989.

Council of the European Communities (1989b), Council Directive 89/665/EEC of 21 December 1989 on the co-ordination of the laws, Regulations and administrative provisions relating to the application of review procedures to the award of public supply and public works contracts OJ L 395, 30 December 1989, pp.33-35.

Council of the European Communities (1990), Council Directive 90/385/EEC of 20 June 1990 on the approximation of the laws of the Member States relating to active implantable medical devices, OJ L 189, 20 July 1990, pp.17-36.

Council of the European Communities (1992a), Council Recommendation 92/442/EEC of 27 July 1992 on the convergence of social protection objectives and policies, Official Journal of the European Communities 1992, OJ L 245, 26 August 1992.

Council of the European Communities (1992b), Council Directive 92/27/EEC of 31 March 1992 on the labelling of medicinal products for human use and on package leaflets, OJ L 113, 30 April 1992.

Council of the European Communities (1992c), Council Directive 92/26/EEC of 31 March 1992 concerning the classification for the supply of medicinal products for human use, OJ L 113, 30 April 1992.

Council of the European Communities (1992d), Council Directive 92/25/EEC of 31 March 1992 on the wholesale distribution of medicinal products for human use, OJ L 113, 30 April 1992.

Council of the European Communities (1992e), Council Regulation 1768/92/EEC of 18 June 1992 concerning the creation of a supplementary protection certificate for medicinal products.

Council of the European Communities (1992f), Council Directive 92/28/EEC of 13 March 1992 on the advertising of medicinal products for human use, OJ L 113, 30 April 1992.

Council of the European Communities (1992g), Council Directive 92/49/EEC of 18 June 1992 on the co-ordination of laws, Regulations and administrative provisions relating to direct insurance other than life assurance and amending Directives 73/239/EEC and 88/357/EEC (third non-life insurance Directive), OJ L 228, 11 August 1992.

Council of the European Communities (1992h), Council Directive 92/50/EEC of 18 June 1992 relating to the co-ordination of procedures for the award of public service contracts, OJ L 209, 24 July 1992, pp.1-24.

Council of the European Communities (1992i), Council Directive 92/13/EEC of 25 February 1992 coordinating the laws, Regulations and administrative provisions relating to the application of Community rules on the procurement procedures of entities operating in the water, energy, transport and telecommunications sectors OJ L 076, 23 March 1992, pp.14-20.

Council of the European Communities (1993a), Council Directive 93/16/EEC of 5 April 1993 to facilitate the free movement of doctors and the mutual recognition of their diplomas, certificates and other evidence of formal qualifications, OJ L 165, 7 July 1993.

Council of the European Communities (1993b), Directive 93/42/EEC of 14 June 1993 concerning medical devices, OJ L 169, 12 July 1993, pp.1-43.

Council of the European Communities (1993c), Council Regulation 2309/93/EEC of 22 July 1993 laying down Community procedures for the authorisation and supervision of medicinal products for human and veterinary use and establishing a European Agency for the Evaluation of Medicinal Products, OJ L 214, 24 August 1993, pp.0001-0021.

Council of the European Communities (1993d), Council Directive 93/36/EEC of 14 June 1993 co-ordinating procedures for the award of public supply contracts, OJ L 199, 9 August 1993, pp.1-53.

Council of the European Communities (1993e), Council Directive 93/37/EEC of 14 June 1993 concerning the co-ordination of procedures for the award of public works contracts, OJ L 1999, 9 August 1993, pp.54-83.

Council of the European Communities (1993f), Council Directive 93/38/EEC of 14 June 1993 co-ordinating the procurement procedures of entities operating in the water, energy, transport and telecommunications sectors OJ L 1999, 9 August 1993, pp.84-138.

Council of the European Union (1993g), Council Directive 93/104/EC of 23 November 1993 concerning certain aspects of the organisation of working time OJ L 307, 13 December 1993, pp.0018-0024.

Council of the European Union (1995), Directive 95/46/EC on the protection of individuals with regard to the processing of personal data and on the free movement of such data, OJ L 281, 23 November 1995, pp.3-50.

Council of the European Union (1996), Consolidated version: Council Regulation 118/97/EC of 2 December 1996 amending and updating Regulation 1408/71/EEC on the application of social security schemes to employed persons, to self-employed persons and to members of their families moving within the Community and Regulation 574/72/EEC laying down the procedure for implementing Regulation 1408/71/EEC, OJ L 28, 30 January 1997, pp.0001-0229.

Council of the European Union (1999), Council conclusions of 17 December 1999 on the strengthening of co-operation for modernising and improving social protection, OJ C 8, 12 January 2000, pp.7-8.

Council of the European Union and European Commission (2000), "eEuropa 2002 – An Information Society For All", Action Plan prepared by the Council and the European Commission for the Feira European Council (19-20 June 2000), Brussels, 14 June 2000.

Craig, P. and de Burca, B. (1998), *EC Law*, Oxford University Press, Oxford.

Cram, L. (1996), "Integration Theory and the Study of the European Policy Process", in Richardson, J. (ed.), *European Union Power and Policy-making*, Routledge, London.

Curwen, P. (1992), "Social Policy in the European Community in Light of the Maastricht Treaty", *European Business Journal*, Vol.4, No.4, pp.17-26.

de la Porte, C., Pochet, P. and Room, G. (2001), "Social Benchmarking, Policy Making and New Governance in the EU", *Journal of European Social Policy*, Vol.11, No.4, pp.291-307.

Dehousse, R. (1995), "Constitutional Reform in the European Community: Are there Alternatives to the Majoritarian Avenue?", *West European Politics*, No.18, pp.118-136.

Dehousse, R. (2000), "Integration through Law Revisited: Some Thoughts on the Juridification of the European Political Process", in Snyder, F. (ed.), *The Europeanisation of Law; the Legal Effects of European Integration*, Hart Publishing, Oxford.

Department of Health and Children (2001), *Submission to the European Commission's Study on Voluntary Health Insurance in the European Union*, Department of Health and Children, Dublin.

Deutsch, K. (1966), "Communication Theory and Political Integration", in Jacob, P. and Toscano, J. (eds.), *The Integration of Political Communities*, JP Lippincott & Co, Philadelphia.

Dewulf, L. (2000), "DTC via the Internet: An Overview", *Pharmaceutical Physician*, September 2000, pp.12-14.

Dinan, D. (1994), *Ever Closer Union? An Introduction to the European Community*, Macmillan Press Ltd, Basingstoke.

Dreyfus, M. and Gibaud, B. (eds.) (1995), *Mutualités de tous les pays. Un passé riche d'avenir*, Mutualité française, Paris.

Dukes, G. (1996), "Drug Regulation and the Tradition of Secrecy", *The International Journal of Risk and Safety in Medicine*, Vol.9, No.3, pp.143-149.

Duranton, M., Zouaq, A. and Pilón, J. (2001), "Mutual Benefit Societies: Solutions in Europe, North-Africa and Latin America", in Ron, A. and Scheil-Adlung, X. (eds.), *Recent Health Policy Innovations in Social Security*, International Social Security Series, Vol.5, ISSA, Transaction, London, pp.253-266.

Durkheim, E. (1984), *The Division of Labour in Society*, Macmillan, Basingstoke.

EBRD (1999), *Transition Report 1999*, European Bank for Reconstruction and Development, London.

Ebsen, I. (2000), "Öffentlich-rechtliches Handeln von Krankenkassen als Gegenstand des Wettbewerbsrechts? Probleme materiellrechtlicher und kompetenzrechtlicher Koordinierung", in Igl, G. (ed.), *Das Gesundheitswesen in der Wettbewerbsordnung*, Verlag Chmielorz, Wiesbaden, pp.22-38.

EFPIA (1999), *The Pharmaceutical Industry in Figures – Key Data* (1999 Update), European Federation of Pharmaceutical Industries and Associations, Brussels.

EGA (2000), *EGA Position on Is Marketed Problem*, European Generics Association, Brussels.

EHMA (1994), *European Union and Health*, European Healthcare Management Association, Dublin.

EHMA (2001), "Dutch Court rejects Smits-Peerbooms Cases", *EU Shortcuts 2001*, No.18, European Health Management Association, Dublin, pp.1-2.

Ehricke, U. (1998), "Zur Konzeption von Article 37 I und Article 90 II EGV", *Zeitschrift für Europäisches Wirtschaftsrecht*, No.24, pp.741-747.

Eichener, V. (1997), "Effective European Problem-solving: Lessons from the Regulation of Occupational Safety and Environmental Protection", *Journal of European Public Policy*, No.4, pp.591-608.

Eilmansberger, T. (2000), *Europarecht II. Das Recht des Binnenmarkts: Grundfreiheiten und Wettbewerbsrecht*, Orac-Verlag, Wien.

El-Agraa, A. (1994), *The Economics of the European Community* (4th Edition), Harvester-Wheatsheaf, London.

Emmerich, V. (1999), *Kartellrecht* (8th Edition), CH Beck-Verlag, München.

Emmerich, V. (2001), "Wettbewerbsregeln. Article 81 und 82 EGV", in Dauses, M. A. (ed.), *Handbuch de EU-Wirtschaftsrechts*, Volume 2, loose-leaf edition, CH Beck-Verlag, München.

Engels, F. (1987), *The Condition of the Working Class in England*, Penguin, Harmandsworth.

Epstein, R., Lenard, T., Miller, H., Tollinson, R., Kip Viscusi, V. and Wardell, W. (1996), *Advancing Medical Innovation: Health, Safety and the Role of Government in the 21st Century*, The Progress and Freedom Foundation, Washington.

ESC (1998), Opinion of the Economic and Social Committee on the Communication from the Commission on modernising and improving social protection in the European Union (COM (97) 102 final of 3 December 1997), OJ C 73, Vol.41, 9 March 1998, pp.1-10.

ESC (2001), Own-initiative opinion of the Economic and Social Committee on private not-for-profit social services in the context of services of general interest in Europe, CES 1120/2001, 12 September 2001.

Esping-Andersen, G. (1996), "After the Golden Age? Welfare State Dilemmas in a Global Economy", in Esping-Andersen, G. (ed.), *Welfare States in Transition: National Adaptations in Global Economies*, Sage, London.

EUCOMED (1999), *EUCOMED Response to the Commissions Green Paper on the Product Liability Directive*, EUCOMED, Brussels.

European Commission (1976), Commission Decision of 26 July 1976 relating to a Proceeding under Article 85 of the EEC Treaty (IV/28.980 – Pabst & Richarz/BNIA), OJ L231 of 21 August 1976, pp.0024-0029.

European Commission (1994), Decisions of 13 July 1994 (Commission Decision 94/601/EC relating to a proceeding under Article 85 of the EC Treaty (IV/C/33.833 – Cartonboard, OJ 1994 L 243, p.1) and 27 July 1994 (Commission Decision 94/599/EC relating to a proceeding pursuant to Article 85 of the EC Treaty (IV/31.865 – PVC).

European Commission (1995a), Report from the Commission to the Council, the European Parliament and the Economic and Social Committee on the Integration of Health Protection Requirements in Community Policies, COM (1995) 196 final of 25 May 1995.

European Commission (1995b), "Inauguration of the European Agency for the Evaluation of Medicinal Products", *Press Release* DN IP/95/64, 26 January 1995.

European Commission (1996a), Green Paper on Commercial Communications in the Internal Market, COM (96) 192-C4-0365/96, Brussels.

European Commission (1996b), Insurance: Infringement Proceedings against Germany and Spain, 1 August 1996, http://europa.eu.int/comm/internal_market/en/finances/infr/760.htm.

European Commission (1996c), Notice from the Commission on "Services of General Interest in Europe" (COM (96) 443, final version), OJ C 281 of 26 September 1996, paragraphs 69 and 73, pp.3-12.

European Commission (1997a), Modernising and Improving Social Protection in the European Union, COM (1997) 102 final of 12 March 1997.

European Commission (1997b), Proposal for a Council Recommendation on the suitability of blood and plasma donors and the screening of donated blood in the European Community, Brussels, COM (97) 605 final of 17 November 1997.

European Commission (1997c), Notice on Agreements of Minor Importance, OJ C 372 of 9 December 1997.

European Commission (1999a), Communication from the European Commission "A Concerted Strategy in Order to Modernise Social Protection", COM (1999) 347 final of 14 July 1999.

European Commission (1999b), Green Paper – Liability for Defective Products, COM (1999) 396 final of 28 July 1999.

European Commission (2000a), Diplomas: Commission Pursues Infringement Cases Concerning Health Professions, 11 January 2000, DG Markt (http://europa.eu.int/ com/internal_market/en/people/infr/2k-11.htm).

European Commission (2000b), Communication from the European Commission on the European Community Health Strategy, Proposal of a Programme of Action of Community Action in the Field of Public Health (2001-2006), COM (2000) 285 of 16 May 2000.

European Commission (2000c), "Freedom to Provide Services and the General Good in the Insurance Sector", Commission Interpretative Communication C (1999) 5046, 2 February 2000 (http://europa.eu.int/comm/internal_market/en/ finances/insur/5046en.pdf).

European Commission (2000d), Communication from the Commission "Services of General Interest in Europe", COM (2000) 580 C5-0 2000/0580 (INC), (http://europa.eu.int/comm/consumers/policy/developments/serv_gen_int/serv_gen _int05_en.pdf).

European Commission (2001a), Communication from the Commission to the Council, the European Parliament, the Economic and Social Committee and the Committee of the Regions on the Future of Health Care and Care for the Elderly: Guaranteeing Accessibility, Quality and Financial Viability, COM (2001) 723 final of 5 December 2001.

European Commission (2001b), "The Internal Market and Health Systems", Report of the High Level Committee on Health, Health and Consumer Protection Directorate-General, Luxembourg, 17 December 2001.

European Commission (2001c), Free movement of goods: Commission tackles obstacles in Greece and Denmark, *Press Release* IP/01/428, Brussels, 22 March 2001.

European Commission (2001d), "Commission Prohibits Glaxo Wellcomes Dual Pricing System in Spain", *Press Release* IP/01/661, Brussels, 8 May 2001.

European Commission (2001e), Commission Calls for the Tax Discrimination in Favour of French Mutual and Provident Societies to be Brought to an End, European Commission, Brussels.

European Council (1992), Edinburgh European Council, *Presidency Conclusions* (http://www.pio.gov.cy/docs/euro/european_union/european_council/concl_19921 211.htm).

European Parliament (2000), Resolution of the European Parliament on supplementary health insurance, December 2000, 2000/2009 (INI).

European Parliament (2001), Answer given by Mr. Liikanen on behalf of the Commission, E-1941/01EN, 1 October 2001.

European Parliament and Council of the European Union (1995), Directive 95/46/EC of the European Parliament and of the Council of 24 October 1995 on the protection of individuals with regard to the processing of personal data and on the free movement of such data, OJ L 281, 23 November 1995, pp.31-50.

European Parliament and Council of the European Union (1996), Directive 96/9/EC of the European Parliament and of the Council of 11 March 1996 on the legal protection of databases, OJ L 077, 27 March 1996, pp.20-28.

European Parliament and Council of the European Union (1997a), Directive 97/7/EC of the European Parliament and of the Council of 20 May 1997 on the protection of consumers in respect of distance contracts, OJ L 144, 4 June 1997, pp.19-27.

European Parliament and Council of the European Union (1997b), Directive 97/66/EC of the European Parliament and of the Council of 15 December 1997 concerning the processing of personal data and the protection of privacy in the telecommunications sector, OJ L 024, 30 January 1998, pp.1-8.

European Parliament and the Council of the European Union (1998), Directive 98/79/EC of the European Parliament and of the Council of 27 October 1998 on in vitro diagnostic medical devices, OJ L 331, 7 December 1998, pp.1-37.

European Parliament and Council of the European Union (1999), Directive 99/93/EC on a Community framework for electronic signatures, OJ L 013, 19 January 2000, pp.12-20.

European Parliament and the Council of the European Union (2000), Directive 2000/31/EC of the European Parliament and of the Council of 8 June 2000 on certain legal aspects of information society services, in particular electronic commerce, in the Internal Market ("Directive on electronic commerce"), OJ L 178, 17 July 2000, pp.1-16.

European Parliament, Council of the European Union and European Commission (2000), Charter of Fundamental Rights of the European Union, OJ C 364/01, 18 December 2000.

European Parliament and Council of the European Union (2001), Council Directive 2001/19/EC of the European Parliament and of the Council of 14 May 2001 amending Council Directives 89/48/EEC and 92/51/EEC on the general system for the recognition of professional qualifications, OJ L 206, 31 July 2001, pp.0001-0051.

European Parliament and Council of the European Union (2002), Decision of the European Parliament and of the Council of adopting a programme of Community action in the field of public health (2003-2008), PE-CONS 3627/02, 15 May 2002.

Evju, S. (2001), "Collective Agreements and Competition Law. The Albany Puzzle, and van der Woude", *The International Journal of Comparative Labour Law and Industrial Relations*, Summer 2001, pp.165-184.

Eysenbach, G. and Diepgen, T. L. (1998), "Towards Quality Management of Medical Information on the Internet: Evaluation, Labelling, and Filtering of Information", *British Medical Journal*, No.317, pp.1496-1502.

Eysenbach, G., Køhler, C., Yihune, G., Lampe, K., Cross, P. and Brickley, D. (2001), "A Framework for Improving the Quality of Health Information on the World-wide-web and Bettering Public (e-)health: The MedCERTAIN Approach", in Haux, R., Patel, V. and Hasmann, A. (eds.), Medinfo01, Proceedings of the Tenth World Congress on Medical Informatics, pp.1450-1454.

Fillon, J. C. (1999), "La citoyenneté de l'Union européenne et la coordination des régimes de sécurité sociale", *Journal des Tribunaux du Travail*, No.747, 20 October 1999, Brussels, pp.393-403.

Finley, S. D. (2001), "Direct-to-consumer Promotion of Prescription Drugs: Economic Implications for Patients, Payers and Providers", *Pharmacoecon*, No.19, pp.109-119.

Flora, P. and Alber, J. (1982), "Modernization, Democratisation, and the Development of Welfare States in Western Europe", in Flora, P. and Heidenheimer, A. (eds.), *In the Development of Welfare States in Europe and America*, Transaction Publishers, New Brunswick NJ.

Flynn, P. (1997), "Reactions to the Treaty of Amsterdam", *Eurohealth*, Vol.3, No.2, pp.2-3.

Flynn, P. (1998), "The Future of EU Public Health Policy", Speech delivered at UK Presidency conference on developing EU public health policy, London, 19 May 1998.

Freeman, S. (1994), "Health Care Provision in the EC", *AIDA Information Bulletin*, No.47, pp.120-22.

Fruhmann, M. (1997), "Europarecht und organisationsrechtliche Ausgestaltung des Vergaberechtsschutzes", *Ecolex*, pp.210-214.

Gambardella, A., Orsenigo, L. and Pammolli, F. (2000), "Global Competitiveness in Pharmaceuticals: A European Perspective", Report prepared for the Directorate-General Enterprise of the European Commission (http://dg3.eudra.org/F2/pharmacos/docs/Doc2000/nov/comprep_nov2000.pdf).

Ganslandt, M. and Maskus, K. E. (2001), Parallel Imports of Pharmaceutical Products in the European Union (unpublished).

GAO (1996), "Medical Device Regulation: Too Early to Assess European Systems Value as Model for FDA", *Report GAO/HEHS-96-65*, General Accounting Office, Washington DC.

Garattini, S. and Bertele, V. (2001), "Adjusting Europe's Drug Regulation to Public Health Needs", *Lancet*, No.358, pp.64-67.

Gassner, U.M. (2000), "Nationaler Gesundheitsmarkt und europäisches Kartellrecht", *VSSR*, No.2, pp.121-148.

Gibbs, D. (2001), "Harnessing the Information Society? European Union Policy and Information and Communication Technologies", *European Urban and Regional Studies*, No.8, pp.73-84.

Giesen, R. (1999), *Die Vorgaben des EG-Vertrages für das Internationale Sozialrecht*, Nomos-Verlag, Baden-Baden.

Glass, N. (2001), "European Commission May Reform Drug Advertising Legislation", *Lancet*, Vol.358, No.9278, page 306.

Goldstein, M. (1998), "Advertising Prescription only Drugs", *Lancet*, No.351, page 1583.

Gopal, K. (2001), "World News and Analysis: Task Masters", *Pharmaceutical Executive*, May 2001, pp.26-38.

Grabitz, E. and Hilf, M. (eds.) (2001), *Das Recht der Europäischen Union*, Volume I: EUV/EGV, loose-leaf edition, CH Beck-Verlag, München.

Grill, G. (1999), "Artikelen 81 und 82", in Lenz C. O. (ed.), *EG-Vertrag* (2nd Edition), Bundesanzeiger, Helbing & Lichtenhahn, Ueberreuter, Köln, Basel, Genf, München, Wien.

Groeben, H., Thiesing, J. and Ehlermann, C.D. (1999) (eds.), *Kommentar zum EU-/EG-Vertrag*, Volume 2/I (5th Edition), Nomos-Verlag, Baden-Baden.

Guibboni, S. (2001), "Social Insurance Monopolies in Community Competition Law and the Italian constitution: 'Practical' Convergences and 'Theoretical' conflicts", *European Law Journal*, Vol.7, No.1, pp.69-94.

Haas, E. (1968), *The Uniting of Europe* (2nd Edition), Stanford University Press, Stanford.

HAI Europe (2001), HAI Europe Criticises EC Moves towards DCTA and Calls for Evidence of Health Benefit, Health Action International (http://www.haiweb.org/campaign/DTCA/EC%20release%20170701.htm).

Hailbronner, K. and Weber, C. (1997), "Die Neugestaltung des Vergabewesens durch die Europäische Gemeinschaft", *Europäisches Wirtschafts- und Steuerrecht*, No.3, pp.73-83.

Haltern, U. (1995), "Intergovernmentalism as a Way of European Governance", in Weiler, J., Ballmann, A., Haltern, U., Hofmann, H. and Mayer, F. (eds.), *Certain Rectangular Problems of European Integration*, PrOJt IV/95/02, Directorate-General for Research, European Parliament, Brussels.

Ham, C. (1991), "The European Community and UK, Health and Health Services", in Harrison, A. (ed.), *Health Care UK 1991*, Kings Fund Institute, London.

Hancher, L. (2000), "EC Competition Law, Pharmaceuticals and Intellectual Property: Recent Developments", in Goldberg, R. and Lonbay, J. (eds.), *Pharmaceutical Medicine, Biotechnology and European Law*, Cambridge University Press, Cambridge, pp.76-90.

Hancher, L. (2001a), "The Pharmaceuticals Market Competition and Free Movement – Actively Seeking Compromises", Paper delivered at the conference organised during the Belgian Presidency on "European Integration and Health Care Systems: A Challenge for Social Policy", Ghent, 7-8 December 2001.

Hancher, L. (2001b), "Pricing European Pharmaceuticals: Can the Commission untie the Gordian Knot?", *Eurohealth*, Vol.7, No.2, pp.23-25.

Hänlein, A. and Kruse, J. (2000), "Einflüsse des Europäischen Wettbewerbsrechts auf die Leistungserbringung in der gesetzlichen Krankenversicherung", *Neue Zeitschrift für Sozialrecht*, No.4, pp.165-176.

Hantrais, L. (2000), *Social Policy in the European Union*, McMillan Press Ltd, London.

Hatzopoulos, V. (2000), "Recent Developments of the Case Law of the European Court of Justice in the Field of Services", *Common Market Law Review*, No.37, pp.43-82.

Hatzopoulos, V. (2002), "National Health Systems and EC Rules on State Aids and Public Procurement", in Mossialos, E., McKee, M. and Baeten, R. (eds.), *The Impact of EU Law on Health Care Systems*, P.I.E.-Peter Lang, Brussels.

Haverkate, G. and Huster, S. (1999), *Europäisches Sozialrecht*, Nomos-Verlag, Baden-Baden.

Hermans, H. E. G. M. (1998), "Mobility and Free Establishment of Doctors: What is the Present Practice in Europe? What Should Happen in Medical Education to Facilitate?", MED-NET Conferences 1998, Anthology of presentations 4.3 (http://www.med-net.nl/network/conference/1998-1999/lille-maastr-4-3.htm).

Hermans, H. E. G. M. (2000), "Cross-border Health Care in the European Union: Recent Legal Implications of Decker and Kohll", *Eval Clin Practice*, No.6, pp.431-439.

Hermes, G. (1997), "Gleichheit durch Verfahren bei der staatlichen Auftragsvergabe", *JZ*, No.19, pp.909-915.

Hermesse, J. (1999), "The Opening of Frontiers to Patients: What Economic Consequences?", Proceedings AIM International Symposium Health Care without Frontiers within the European Union?, AIM, Brussels.

Hervey, T. (1998), *Europan Social Law and Policy*, Longman, London.

Hervey, T. (2002), "The Legal Basis of European Community Public Health Policy", in Mossialos, E., McKee, M. and Baeten, R. (eds.), *The Impact of EU Law on Health Care Systems*, P.I.E.-Peter Lang, Brussels.

Hochbaum, I. F. (1999), "Article 90", in Groeben, H., Thiesing, J. and Ehlermann, C.D. (eds.), *Kommentar zum EU-/EG-Vertrag*, Volume 2/I (5th Edition), Nomos-Verlag, Baden-Baden.

Hodge, J. G., Gostin, L.O. and Jacobson, P.D. (1999), "Legal Issues concerning Electronic Health Information: Privacy, Quality, and Liability", *The Journal of the American Medical Association*, No.282, pp.1466-1471.

Hoffman, J. and Wilkes, M. (1999), "Direct to Consumer Advertising of Prescription Drugs: An Idea whose Time Should not Come", *British Medical Journal*, No.318, pp.1301-1302.

Hoffmann, S. (1966), "Obstinate or Obsolete? The Fate of the Nation State and the Case of Western Europe", *Daedalus*, No.95, pp.892-908.

House of Commons (1999), *Trade and Industry – 8th Report, Trade and Industry Committee, House of Commons*, The Stationery Office, London.

Huelshoff, M. (1992), "European Integration after the SEA: The Case of the Social Charter", *Political Research Quarterly*, Vol.46, No.3, pp.619-640.

ICER (2001), "Werkgroep zorgstelsel", *Eindrapport*, Interdepartmentale Commissie Europees Recht, 3 April 2001.

Impicciatore, P., Pandolfini, C., Casella, N. and Bonati, M. (1997), "Reliability of Health Information for the Public on the World Wide Web: Systematic Survey of Advice on Managing Fever in Children at Home", *British Medical Journal*, No.314, page 1875.

IMS Health (2002), *US physicians responsive to patient requests for brand-name drugs*, IMS Health, Fairfield.

ISDB (2001), "European Medicines Evaluation Agency", *International Society of Drug Bulletins Newsletters*, Vol.15, No.1, pp.11-13.

Jackson, C. (1995), "European Public Health Policy", *Eurohealth*, Vol.1, No.1, pp.11-14.

Jamison, J., Butler, M., Clarke, P., McKee, M. and Oneill, C. (2001), *Cross-border Co-operation in Health Services in Ireland*, Centre for Cross-Border Studies, Armagh.

Jessop, B. (1990), *State Theory: Putting Capitalist States in their Places*, Polity Press, Cambridge.

Jinks, C., Ong Bio, B. and Patum, C. (2000), "Mobile Medics? The Mobility of Doctors in the European Economic Area", *Health Policy*, No.54, pp.45-64.

Joffe, M. (1993), "Future of European Community (EC) Activities in the Area of Public Health: European Public Health Alliance", *Health Promotion International*, Vol.8, No.1, pp.53-61.

Johnson, C. (2001), The US-EU Recognition Agreement: Its Implications for the United States Medical Device Industry. Medical Device and Diagnostic Industry Magazine, May 2001, (http://www.devicelink.com/mddi/archive/01/05/003.html).

Jones, A. and Sufrin, B. (2001), *EC Competition Law*, Oxford University Press, Oxford.

Jung, C.H.A. (2001), "Article 82 EGV", in Grabitz, E. and Hilf, M. (eds.), *Das Recht der Europäischen Union*, Volume I: EUV/EGV, loose-leaf edition, CH Beck-Verlag, München.

Kaesbach, W. (2001), "Pharmaceutical Policies in Germany and European Competition Law", Paper delivered at the conference organised during the Belgian Presidency of the European Union on "European Integration and Health Care Systems: A Challenge for Social Policy", Ghent, 7-8 December 2001.

Kanavos, P. (1999), "Financing Pharmaceuticals in Transition Economies", *Croatian Medical Journal*, Vol.40, No.2, pp.244-259.

Kanavos, P. (2000), "The Single Market for Pharmaceuticals in the European Union in Light of European Court of Justice Rulings", *Pharmacoecon*, No.18, pp.523-532.

Kapteyn P.J.G. and Verloren van Themat P. (1995), *Inleiding tot het recht van de Europese Gemeenschappen. Na Maastricht*, Kluwer, Deventer.

Kay, A. (2000), Speech delivered to the Roundtable on Global Competitiveness in Pharmaceuticals organised by the European Commission, 11 December 2000, as cited in European Generic medicines Association, "More Generic Competition Would Help EU Pharmaceutical Market", *Press Release*, 13 December 2000.

Kesteloot, K., Pocceschi, S. and van der Schueren, E. (1995), "The Reimbursement of the Expenses for Medical Treatment Received by 'transnational' patients in EU-countries", *Health Policy*, Vol.33, No.1, pp.43-57.

Kinsella, R. and Cully, A.J. (2001), "Risk Equalisation – The Health Insurance (Amendment) Bill 2001 and the Irish PMI Market", *Irish Financial Services Law Journal*, Vol.II, No.2, pp.5-10

Kletter, M. (1994), "Kostenerstattung und Sachleistungsvorsorge", *Soziale Sicherheit*, No.1, pp.27-37.

Kletter, M. (2000), "Das VfGH-Erkenntnis zur Kostenerstattung", *Soziale Sicherheit*, No.7/8, pp.704-714.

Köck, S. (2000), "Die Auswirkungen des EG-Wettbewerbsrechts auf die öster-reichische Sozialversicherung", in Tomandl, T. (ed.), *Der Einfluß europäischen Rechts auf das Sozialrecht,* Braumüller Verlag, Wien, pp.27-60.

Kopetzki, C. (1999), "Rechtsfragen der vertragsärztlichen Stellenplanung in Öster-reich", in Jabornegg, P., Resch, R. and Seewald, O. (eds.), *Der Vertragsarzt im Spannungsfeld zwischen gesundheitspolitischer Steuerung und Freiheit der Be-rufsausübung,* Manz-Verlag, Wien, pp.31-58.

Kranz, H. (1999), "Basis for Switching", Paper delivered to Joint Annual Meeting of AESGP and WSMI (Workshop: Effective Rx-to-OTC switching), Berlin, 9-12 June 1999.

Lahure, J. (1997), "Public Health in the European Union under the Luxembourg Presidency", *Eurohealth,* Vol.3, No.2, pp.9-11.

Lane, R. (1993), "New Community Competences Under the Maastricht Treaty", *Common Market Law Review,* No.30, pp.939-979.

Lauridsen, M. and Lund, M. (1996), "Public Health in the European Union – Status and Perspective", *Eurohealth,* Vol.2, No.1, pp.24-26.

Lawson, V. (2001), "Competitiveness, Innovation and New Market Dynamics", *Eurohealth,* Vol.7, No.2, pp.15-18.

Leidl, R. (1990), "1992 and the Challenge for Health Systems", Paper prepared for EC/WHO EURO Workshop on the Future of Health Services Research.

Leidl, R. (1991), "How Will the Single European Market Affect Health Care?", *British Medical Journal,* No.303, pp.1081-1082.

Lenz, C.O. (ed.) (1999), *EG-Vertrag* (2nd Edition), Bundesanzeiger, Helbing & Lichtenhahn, Ueberreuter, Köln, Basel, Genf, München, Wien.

Light, D. (1996), "Does Medical Care Have to be Rationed?", AIM International Conference, 3-4 October 1996, "Paying for Health: The New Partnership", AIM, May 1997, pp.11-22.

Light, D. (1998), "Keeping Competition Fair for Health Insurance. The Irish Beat Back Risk-rated Policies", *American Journal of Public Health,* No.88, pp.745-748.

Liikanen, E. (2001), Speech 01/354 delivered by Enterprise Commissioner, Erkki Liikanen on the Commissions proposal to review pharmaceutical legislation, 18 July 2001.

Lipsky, M.S. and Taylor, C.A. (1997), "The Opinions and Experiences of Family Physicians Regarding Direct-to-consumer Advertising", *Fam Pract,* Vol.45, No.6, pp.495-499.

Lonbay, J. (2000), "The Free Movement of Health Care Professionals in the Euro-pean Community", in Goldberg, R. and Lonbay, J. (eds.), *Pharmaceutical Medi-cine, Biotechnology and European Law,* Cambridge University Press, Cambridge.

Mabbet, D. (2000), "Social Regulation and the Social dimension in Europe: The Example of Insurance", *European Journal of Social Security,* No.2/3, pp.241-257.

Macarthur, D. (2001), "Parallel Trading of Medicines: The Case for a Fair Deal", *Consumer Policy Review,* Vol.11, No.1, pp.6-10.

Majone, G. (1993), "The European Community between Social Policy and Social Regulation", *Common Market Studies*, Vol.31, No.2, pp.152-170.

Majone, G. (1996), "The Rise of Statutory Regulation in Europe", in Majone, G. (ed.), *Regulating Europe*, Routledge, London.

Marhold, F. (1995), "Europäischer Wettbewerb im Gesundheitswesen", in Tomuschat, C., Kötz, H. and von Maydell, B. (eds), *Europäische Integration und nationale Rechtskulturen*, Carl Heymanns Verlag, Köln, Berlin, Bonn, München, pp.451-462.

Marhold, F. (1999), "Das europäische Wirtschaftsrecht und die Gesundheitsleistungen – Auswirkungen", in Palm, W. (ed), *Gesundheitsleistungen ohne Grenzen in der Europäischen Union?* Brüssel, pp.48-54.

Marhold, F. (2001a), "The Relation between Primary and Secondary EC-Legislation", in Austrian Federal Ministry of Social Security and Generations (ed.), *The EC-Treaty and Regulation 1408/71*, Austrian Federal Ministry of Social Security and Generations, Vienna, pp.16-29.

Marhold, F. (2001b), "Auswirkungen des Europäischen Wirtschaftsrechts auf die Sozialversicherung", in Theurl, E. (ed.), *Der Sozialstaat an der Jarhtausendwende*, Physica-Verlag, Heidelberg, pp.234-246.

Marmor, T.R. (2000), *The Politics of Medicare*, Aldine de Gruyter, Hawthorne NY.

Mazey, S. (1996), "The Development of the European Idea: From Sectoral Integration to Political Union", in Richardson, J. (ed.), *European Union Power and Policy-Making*, Routledge, Oxford.

Mazey, S. and Richardson, J. (1993), *Lobbying in the European Community*, Oxford University Press, Oxford.

McKee, M. and Fulop, N. (2000), "On Target for Health? Lessons from 15 Years of Health Targets in Europe", *British Medical Journal*, No.320, pp.327-328

McKee, M. and Mossialos, E. (2000), "Seattle and the World Trade Organisation: The Potential Implications", *Journal of the Royal Society of Medicine*, No.93, pp.109-110.

McKee, M., Mossialos, E. and Belcher, P. (1996), "The Influence of European Law on National Health Policy", *Journal of European Social Policy*, Vol.6, No.4, pp.263-286.

MDA (2000), *Annual Report and Accounts 2000-2001*, Medical Devices Agency, The Stationery Office, London.

Merkel, B. (1995), "The Public Health Competence of the European Community", *Eurohealth*, Vol.1, No.1, pp.21-22.

Merkel, B. and Hübel, M. (1999), "Public Health Policy in the European Community", in Holland, W. and Mossialos, E. (eds.), *Public Health Policies in the European Union*, Ashgate, Aldershot.

Miller, H. (2000), "Americans Are Dying for FDA Reform", *Hoover Institution Weekly Essays*, 9 April 2000.

Ministerie van Volksgezondheid, Welzijn en Sport (2001), Vraag aan bod. Hoofdlijnen van vernieuwing van het zorgstelsel, Tweede Kamer, 2000-2001, 27855, No.1-2 (http://www.zorgaanzet.nl/materiaal/Vraag_aan_bod.pdf).

Mittrany, D. (1966), *A Working Peace System*, Quadrangle, Chicago.

Monti, M. (2001a), "Competition and the Consumer: The Case of Pharmaceutical Products", Speech by Mario Monti European Commissioner for Competition Policy in EC Competition Day, Antwerpen, 11 October 2001.

Monti, M. (2001b), "EC antitrust policy in the pharmaceutical sector", Mario Monti – Alliance Unichem Conference, Brussels, 26 March 2001.

Moravcsik, A. (1995), "Liberal Intergovernmentalism and Integration: A Rejoinder", *Common Market Studies*, Vol.33, No.4, pp.611-628.

Mossialos, E. (1998), *Citizens and Health Systems: Main Results from a Eurobarometer Survey*, European Commission, Luxembourg.

Mossialos, E. and Abel-Smith, B. (1996), "The Regulation of the European Pharmaceutical Industry", in Stavridis, S. *et al.* (eds.), *New Challenges to the European Union: Policies and Policy-making*, Dartmouth, Aldershot.

Mossialos, E. and Le Grand, J. (eds.) (1999), *Health Care and Cost Containment in the European Union*, Ashgate, Aldershot.

Mossialos, E. and Permanand, G. (2000), "Public Health in the European Union: Making it Relevant", *LSE Health Discussion Paper*, No.17, January 2000.

Mossialos, E. and McKee, M. (2001), "Is a European Healthcare Policy Emerging?", *British Medical Journal*, No.323, page 248.

Mossialos, E. and Permanand, G. (2002), "EU Law and Pharmaceuticals", *LSE Health and Social Care Working Paper*, London.

Mossialos, E. and Thomson, S. (2001), "Voluntary Health Insurance in the European Union", *LSE Health Discussion Paper*, No.19, May 2001.

Mossialos E. and Thomson, S. (2002), "Voluntary Health Insurance in the EU", *International Journal of Health Services*, Vol.32, No.1, pp.19-88.

Mountford, L. (2000), *Health Care without Frontiers? The Development of a European Market in Health Services?*, Office of Health Economics, London.

Mrozynski, P. (1999), "Der Einfluß des Wettbewerbs- und Vergaberechts in Europa auf die Erbringung von Sozialleistungen", *Sozialer Fortschritt*, No.9, pp.221-228.

Müller-Graff, P.C. and Zehetner, F. (1991), *Öffentliche und privilegierte Unternehmen im Recht der Europäischen Gemeinschaften*, WISO, Linz.

Nemeth, K. (2001), "European Insurance Law: A Single Insurance Market?", *Working paper*, No.2001/04, European University Institute, Florence.

Neunreither, K. (1998), "Governance without Opposition: The Case of the European Union", *Government and Opposition*, Vol.33, No.4, pp.419-441.

NHS (2000), "Pharmacy in the Future – Implementing the NHS Plan", A programme for pharmacy in the National Health Service, London, September 2000 (http://www.doh.gov.uk/pdfs/pharmacyfuture.pdf).

Nickless, J. (2001), "A Guarantee of Similar Standards of Medical Treatment across the EU: Were the European Court of Justice Decisions in Kohll and Decker Right?", *Eurohealth*, Vol.7, No.1, pp.16-18.

Nickless, J. (2002), "The Impact of the EU Internal Market on Social Health Care", in Mossialos, E., McKee, M. and Baeten, R. (eds.), *The Impact of EU Law on Health Care Systems*, P.I.E.-Peter Lang, Brussels.

Palm, V. (2002), "Voluntary Health Insurance and EU Insurance Directives: between Solidarity and the Market", in Mossialos, E., McKee, M. and Baeten, R. (eds.), *The Impact of EU Law on Health Care Systems*, P.I.E.-Peter Lang, Brussels.

Palm, W., Nickless, N., Lewalle, H. and Coheur, A. (2000), "Implications of Recent Jurisprudence on the Co-ordination of Health Care Protection Systems", Summary Report produced for the European Commission Directorate-General for Employment and Social Affairs, Association Internationale de la Mutualité (AIM), Brussels.

Payer, L. (1989), *Medicine and Culture*, Victor Gollancz, London.

Pecosolido, B.E., Boyer, C. and Tsui, W.Y. (1985), "Medical Care in the Welfare State: A Cross-national Study of Public Evaluations", *Journal of Health and Social Behaviour*, No.26, pp.276-297.

Pérez Asinari, M.V. and Louveaux, S. (2001), "Processing of Personal Data and the Protection of Privacy", Research Paper ECLIP II: Electronic Commerce Legal Issues Platform (http://www.eclip.org/documentsII/research/personaldata_privacy.pdf).

Permanand, G. and Mossialos, E. (2001), "The Politics of Regulation in the EU Pharmaceutical Industry: A Case of Reconciling Contrasting Objectives and Conflicting Interests", Paper presented to the 29th ECPR Joint Session of Workshops, Workshop No.15, "Health Governance in Europe: Europeanisation and New Challenges in Health Policies", Grenoble, 6-11 April 2001.

Peterson, J. (1995), "Decision Making in the European Union: Towards a Framework for Analysis", *Journal of European Public Policy*, No.2, pp.69-93.

Pfaff, M. and Wassener, D. (2000), "Germany", *Journal of Health Politics, Policy and Law*, No.25, pp.907-14.

Pierson, P. (1998), "The Path to European Integration: A Historical-Institutionalist Analysis", in Sandholtz, W. and Stone Sweet, A. (eds.), *European Integration and Supranational Governance*, Oxford University Press, Oxford.

Pieters, D. and van den Bogaert, S. (1997), *The Consequences of European Competition Law for National Health Policies*, Maklu Uitgevers, Antwerp.

Pieters, D. (1999), De Nederlandse zorgverzekering in het licht van het recht van de EG, Achtergrondstudie in opdracht van de Raad voor de volksgezondheid en Zorg bij het RVZ-advies Europa en gezondheidszorg, Zoetermeer.

Pitschas, R. (1996), "Heilberufe im Europäischen Gesundheitsrecht. Der Einfluß des Gemeinschaftsrechts auf die Ausübung von Heilberufen in Österreich", in Tomandl, T. (ed.), *Sozialrechtliche Probleme bei der Ausübung von Heilberufen*, Braumüller Verlag, Wien, pp.1-28.

Pollack, M. (1997), "Delegation, Agency, and Agenda Setting in the European Community", *International Organization*, Vol.51, No.1, pp.99-134.

Poullier, J.-P. and Sandier, S. (2000), "France", *Journal of Health Politics, Policy and Law*, No.25, pp.899-205.

PricewaterhouseCoopers (2001), HealthCast 2001 (http://www.pwchealth.com/ehq.shtml).

Prodi, R. (1999), Intervention of Mr. Prodi, Cologne European Council, 3 June 1999 (http://www.europa.eu.int/comm/commissioners/prodi/speeches/designate/030699 _en.htm).

Puchala, D. (1972), "Of Blind Men, Elephants and International Integration", *Common Market Studies*, No.X/3, pp.267-284.

Raab, C.D. (1997), "Co-producing Data Protection", *International Review of Law Computers and Technology*, No.11, pp.11-24.

Randall, E. (2001), *The European Union and Health Policy*, Palgrave, Hampshire and New York.

Reichard, S. (1996), "Ideology Drives Health Care Reforms in Chile", *Journal of Public Health Policy*, No.17, pp.80-98.

Richards, J. (2000), "Medical Issues within a European Dimension", *Europa*, Vol.4, No.1.

Richards, T. and Smith, R. (1994), "How Should European Health Policy Develop? A Discussion", *British Medical Journal*, No.309, pp.116-121.

Richter, E. (2001), "Regelung vor dem Aus", *Pharmazeutische Zeitung*, Vol.146, No.5, pp.18-19.

Rigby, M. (ed.) (1999), *Taking Health Telematics into the 21st Century*, Radcliffe Medical Press, Abingdon.

Robertson, G. (1992), "A Social Europe: Progress through Partnership", *European Business Journal*, Vol.4, No.4, pp.10-16.

Rocard, M. (1999), "Mission mutualité et droit communautaire", Rapport de fin de mission, Paris, May 1999.

Rodrigues, R.J. (2000), "Ethical and Legal Issues in Interactive Health Communications: A Call for International Cooperation", *Journal of Medical Internet Research*, Vol.2, No.1, e8, March 2000.

Roscam Abbing, H.D.C. (2000), "Internet, the Patient and the Right to Care for Health", *European Journal of Health Law*, No.7, pp.221-228.

Salaün, A. (2000), "Consumer Protection Issues", *ECLIP*, Esprit Project 27028, 13 January 2000 (http://www.eclip.org/documents/deliverable_2_1_3_consumer_ protection_2.pdf).

Saltman, R. and Figueras, J. (1997), *European Health Care Reform: Analysis of Current Strategies*, World Health Organization, Copenhagen.

Sandier, S. and Ulmann, P. (2001), *Voluntary Health Insurance in France: A Study for the European Commission*, ARgSES/CNAM, Paris.

Sansgiry, S., Sharp, W.T. and Sansgiry, S.S. (1999), "Accuracy of Information on Printed over-the-counter Drug Advertisements", *Health Marketing Quarterly*, Vol.17, No.2, pp.7-18.

Sbragia, A. (ed.) (1991), *Euro-politics*, Brookings Institution, Washington D.C.

Scharpf, F. (1996), "Negative and Positive Integration in the Political Economy of European Welfare States", in Marks, *et al.* (eds.), *Governance in the European Union*, SAGE Publications, London.

Scharpf, F. (1997), "The Problem-solving Capacity of Multi-level Governance", *Journal of European Public Policy*, Vol.4, No.4, pp.520-538.

Schilling, T. (1995), "Subsidiarity as a Rule and a Principle, or: Taking Subsidiarity Seriously", *The Jean Monnet Chair Working Paper*, No.10/95, Harvard Law School.

Schröter, H. (1999), "Arts 85-89", in Groeben, H., Thiesing, J. and Ehlermann, C.D. (eds.), *Kommentar zum EU-/EG-Vertrag*, Volume 2/I (5th Edition), Nomos-Verlag, Baden-Baden.

Schulz-Weidner, W. and Felix, F. (1997), "Die Konsequenzen der europäischen Wirtschaftsverfassung für die österreichische Sozialversicherung", *Soziale Sicherheit*, No.12, pp.1120-1160.

Schwarze, J. (2000), "Die Vergabe öffentlicher Aufträge im Lichte des europäischen Wirtschaftsrechts", *Zeitschrift für Europäisches Wirtschaftsrecht*, No.5, pp.133-144.

Segest, E. (1997), "Consumer Protection and the Free Movement of Medical Practitioners in the European Union", *European Journal of Health Law*, No.4, pp.267-272.

Shechter, Y. (1998), "Interests, Strategies, and Institutions: Lobbying in the Pharmaceutical Industry of the European Union", Ph.D. Dissertation, University of London, London School of Economics & Political Science.

Silberg, W.M., Lundberg, G. and Musacchio R.A. (1997), "Assessing, Controlling, and Assuring the Quality of Medical Information on the Internet: Caveant Lector et Viewor – Let the Viewer Beware", *The Journal of the American Medical Association*, No.277, pp.1244-1245.

Simmons & Simmons (2001), E-Pharmacy. *Simmons & Simmons Pharmaceutical and Medical Newsletter* May 2001, No.32, pp.1-3.

Smee, C. (2000), "United Kingdom", *Journal of Health Politics, Policy and Law*, No.25, pp.945-51.

Smith, M., Graham, R. and Wrong, M. (1999), "Prodi Makes Food Safety a Priority for the EU", *Financial Times*, 6 October 1999.

Smith, M.F. (1996), "Data Protection, Health Care, and the New European Directive", *British Medical Journal*, No.312, pp.197-198.

Spurgeon, D. (1999), "Doctors Feel Pressurised by Direct to Consumer Advertising", *British Medical Journal*, No.319, page 1321.

Starnes, L. (2000), "European Healthcare E-Commerce Takes Off" (http://www.inpharm.com/netfocus/trends/articles_002.html).

Starr, P. (1982), *The Social Transformation of American Medicine*, BasicBooks, New York.

Stein, H. (1997), "The Treaty of Amsterdam & Article 129: A Second Chance for Public Health in Europe?", *Eurohealth*, Vol.3, No.2, pp.4-8.

Steinmeyer, H.D. (2000), *Wettbewerbsrecht im Gesundheitswesen. Kartellrechtliche Beschränkungen in der gesetzlichen Krankenversicherung*, Erich Schmidt Verlag, Berlin.

Stockenhuber, P. (2001), "Article 81 EGV", in Grabitz, E. and Hilf, M. (eds.), *Das Recht der Europäischen Union*, Volume I: EUV/EGV, loose-leaf edition, CH Beck-Verlag, München.

Stone Sweet, A. and Caporaso, J. (1998), "From Free Trade to Supranational Polity: The European Court and Integration", in Sandholtz, W. and Stone Sweet, A. (eds.), *European Integration and Supranational Governance*, Oxford University Press, Oxford.

Sullivan, R. (2000), "Direct-to-consumer Advertising: The Future of Europe", *Journal of the Royal Society of Medicine*, No.93, pp.400-401.

Sussex, J. (2001), "Cross-border Healthcare: Hoing Nowhere", *Health Services Journal*, Vol.111, No.5754, pp.24-25.

Terry, N. (2000), "Rating the 'Raters': Legal Exposure of Trustmark Authorities in the Context of Consumer Health Informatics", *Journal of Medical Internet Research*, No.2, Vol.2, No.3, e18, September 2002.

Terry, N. (2001), "Access *vs* Quality Assurance: The E-health Conundrum", *The Journal of the American Medical Association*, No.285, page 807.

Thakur, N. (2001), "Database Protection in the European Union and the United States: The European Database Directive as an Optimum Global Model?", *Intellectual Property Quarterly*, No.1, pp.100-133.

Tsebelis, G. and Garrett, G. (2001), "The Institutional Determinants of Supranationalism in the European Union", *International Organisation*, No.5592, pp.357-90.

Tsoukalis, L. (1998), "The European Agenda: Issues of Globalization, Equity and Legitimacy", *Jean Monnet Chair Papers*, No.98/49, European University Institute, Florence.

Turner, A. (2001), *Just Capital: The Liberal Economy*, Macmillan, London.

UK Consumers Association (2001), "Promotion of Prescription Drugs: Public Health or Private Profit?", Briefing Paper (www.which.net/campaigns/health/dtca.pdf).

van der Mei, A. P. (2001), "Free Movement of Persons within the European Community: Cross-border Access to Public Benefits", Ph.D. Thesis, University of Maastricht, Maastricht.

van Herten, L.M. and van de water, H.P.A. (2000), "Health Policies on Target? Review on Health Target Setting in 18 European Countries", *European Journal of Public Health*, No.10 (suppl.), pp.11-16.

Van Raepenbusch, S. (1997), "Le champ d'application personnel du règlement n°1408/71 et la citoyenneté européenne: du travailleur migrant au citoyen européen", *Journal des Tribunaux du Travail*, No.665, Brussels, 10 January 1997, pp.1-7.

Vand der Linden, M. (1996), *Social Security Mutualism. The Comparative History of Mutual Benefit Societies*, Peter Lang, Bern.

Vandenbroucke, F. (2002), "Foreword", in Esping-Andersen, G., Gallie, D., Hemerijck, A. and Myles, J. (eds.), *A New Welfare Architecture for Europe?*, Oxford University Press, Oxford.

Viehbacher, C. and Benbow, A. (2001), "The G10: An Opportunity to Improve Competitiveness and Benefit Patients", *Eurohealth*, Vol.7, No.2, pp.21-22.

Wallace, H. and Wallace, W. (eds.) (2000), *Policy-Making in the European Union*, Oxford University Press, Oxford.

Watson, R. (1994), "European Union Puts Health at Centre of New Policy", *British Medical Journal*, No.308, page 1530.

Watson, R. (2001), "News Roundup: EC moves towards direct to consumer advertising", *British Medical Journal*, No.323, page 184.

Watson, R. (2002), "European Commission to Publish a Code of Practice for Websites", *British Medical Journal*, No.324, page 567

Weatherill, S. and Beaumont, P. (1999), *EU Law*, Penguin Books, London.

Weiler J A. (1994), "Quiet Revolution: The European Court of Justice and Its Interlocutors", *Comparative Political Studies*, No.26, pp.510-534.

Wessels, W. (1998), "Comitology: Fusion in Action. Politico-administrative Trends in the EU System", *Journal of European Public Policy*, Vol.5, No.2, pp.209-34

Williams, S. (1990), "Sovereignty and Accountability in the European Community", *Political Quarterly*, Vol.61, No.3, pp.299-317.

Wilson, P. (2001), "A Report on the eEurope Action Plan 2002 – An Information Society for All", *La Revue des Samu*, No.XXIII, pp.267-270

Wincott D. (1996), "The Court of Justice and the European policy process", in Richardson, J. (ed.), *European Union Power and Policy-Making*, Routledge, London, pp.170-184.

Winterstein, A. (1999), "Nailing the Jellyfish: Social Security and Competition Law", *ECLR*, No.6, pp.324-333 (http://europa.eu.int/comm/competition/speeches/text/sp2001_029_en.pdf).

Withers, S.D. (1996), "The Concept of General Good in European Jurisprudence, in Competition and Solidarity. Can they Co-exist in Europes Health Care Systems?", AIM-symposium, pp.91-97.

Yataganas, X. (2001), "Delegation of Regulatory Authority in the European Union. The Relevance of the American Model of Independent Agencies", *Harvard Jean Monnet Working Paper*, 2001.

Index

243

Green Paper on Producer
Liability, 132
health policy, 19, 41, 63–64
ICT, 132, 194, 197, 202
insurance, 153, 154, 155–56
parallel trade, 129–30, 131
pharmaceuticals and medical
devices, 105, 109, 110, 142,
144
policy-making, 29, 30, 69, 71
pricing and reimbursement,
119–21, 123
professional qualifications, 79
social protection, 39, 67
subsidies, 186
see also Health and Consumer
Protection Directorate
European Commission *v.*
Austria, 120–21
European Commission *v.* France,
181
European Committee for
Electrotechnical
Standardisation (CENELEC),
201
European Committee on
Standardisation (CEN), 201
European Convention for the
Protection of Human Rights
and Fundamental Freedoms,
121
European Court of Justice (ECJ),
15, 23, 28, 29, 30–31, 51–52,
53, 72, 86
cartels, 173
competition law, 160, 175–76
dominant market position
abuse, 174
free movement of patients, 85,
86–102, 208–9
free movement of services,
209
general good, 154

intellectual property rights,
108, 125
parallel trade, 123, 126–30
pharmaceuticals and medical
devices, 105, 106, 107, 117,
118–19, 144
public procurement, 187–90
role, 46, 53–56, 212–13
single market, 191
social security systems, 166,
182–83
subsidies, 184–86
undertakings, 160, 165
voluntary health insurance,
151
European Economic Community
(EEC), 28, 57
European Federation of
Pharmaceutical Industry
Associations (EFPIA), 125
European Free Trade Area
(EFTA), 111
Court of Law, 184, 185
European Generics Association
(EGA), 123
European Healthcare
Management Association
(EHMA), 97
European integration, 44–45, 56
ECJ role, 55–56, 107
intergovernmentalism, 47–50
neo-functionalism, 45–47
positive and negative, 50–53
single market, 69
European Parliament, 18, 29, 70–
71
European Public Assessment
Reports (EPARs), 114, 115
European social model, 21, 41,
207
challenges, 73
development, 31–35
political embodiment, 38–41

Smith, M. F., 196
Smith, R., 60, 67
Smits-Peerbooms Case, 92–97,
   99, 100, 209
social activities, 168–70, 181–82,
   190
social and ecological dumping,
   46, 52
Social Charter, 38, 60
social insurance systems, 15, 21,
   27, 33, 36, 37
social protection, 21, 34, 104
Social Protection Committee, 19,
   40
social security, 23, 30–31
   and voluntary health
      insurance, 151–52
   free movement of people, 83
Sodemare Case, 91, 92, 189
soft law, 30
   see also Decisions; Recom-
      mendations
solidarity, 24, 34, 48, 190, 207
   and market principles, 22, 72,
      208
   and voluntary health
      insurance, 148–49, 211
   ECJ rulings, 168–69
sovereign activities, 166, 167
Spain
   doctors' mobility, 80
   parallel trade, 128–29
   patents, 126
   voluntary health insurance,
      148
SPCs *see* Summary of Product
   Characteristics
spill over, 45–47, 49, 51
Spurgeon, D., 137
stage working, 31
Starnes, L., 134
Starr, P., 33
state liability, 54–55

Stein, H., 68
Steinmeyer, H. D., 180
Stephar Case, 128, 129
Stockenhuber, P., 172, 173, 177
Stone Sweet, A., 51
subsidiarity, 59, 61, 62, 70
   pharmaceuticals and medical
      devices, 107, 109, 122
subsidies, 184–86
substitutive voluntary health
   insurance, 147–48, 152–54
substitutive voluntary health
   insurance (VHI), 147
Sufrin, B., 166
Sullivan, R., 136
Summary of Product
   Characteristics (SPCs), 114,
   115, 126, 135
Supplementary Protection
   Certificates, 129, 175
supplementary voluntary health
   insurance, 18, 147, 148, 154–
   56, 161
supranationality, 51, 56
supremacy, 55, 107
Sussex, J., 102
Sweden
   approval ratings, 36
   free movement of patients, 85
   market reforms, 37
   medicines advertising, 135
   online pharmacies, 134
   parallel trade, 124
   purchaser/provider split, 36
   voluntary health insurance,
      148
Switzerland
   approval ratings, 36
   online pharmacies, 134

taxation, unfair competition,
   158–60
Taylor, C. A., 137

About the Authors

Elias Mossialos

Brian Abel-Smith Reader in Health Policy, Department of Social Policy, London School of Economics and Political Science and Research Director, European Observatory on Health Care Systems.

Martin McKee

Professor of European Public Health, London School of Hygiene and Tropical Medicine and Research Director, European Observatory on Health Care Systems.

Willy Palm

Director, Association Internationale de la Mutualité (AIM), Brussels, Belgium.

Beatrix Karl

Assistant Professor, Institute for Labour Law and Social Law of the Karl-Franzens-University Graz, Austria and Visiting Fellow, Max-Planck-Institute for Foreign and International Social Law, Munich, Germany.

Franz Marhold

Professor, Institute of Labour Law and Social Security Law, Karl-Franzens-University, Graz, Austria.

"Work & Society"

This series analyses the development of employment and social policies, as well as the strategies of the different social actors, both at national and European levels. It puts forward a multi-disciplinary approach – political, sociological, economic, legal and historical – in a bid for dialogue and complementarity.

"Work & Society" is not confined to the social field *stricto sensu*, but also aims to illustrate the indirect social impacts of economic and monetary policies. It endeavours to clarify social developments, from a comparative and a historical perspective, thus portraying the process of convergence and divergence in the diverse national societal contexts. The manner in which European integration impacts on employment and social policies constitutes the backbone of the analyses.

Series Editor: Philippe POCHET, Director of the Observatoire social européen *(Brussels) and Digest Editor of the* Journal of European Social Policy.

Recent Series Titles

N° 41– *L'aide au conditionnel. La contrepartie dans les mesures envers les personnes sans emploi en Europe et en Amérique du Nord*, Pascale DUFOUR, Gérard BOISMENU & Alain NOËL (2003) en coéd. avec les PUM, 248 p., ISBN 90-5201-198-2

N° 40– *Protection sociale et fédéralisme. L'Europe dans le miroir de l'Amérique du Nord*, Bruno THÉRET (2002) en coéd. avec les PUM, 495 p., ISBN 90-5201-107-9

No.39– *The Impact of EU Law on Health Care Systems*, Martin MCKEE, Elias MOSSIALOS & Rita BAETEN (eds.) (2002, 2nd printing 2003) 314 p., ISBN 90-5201-106-0.

No.38– *EU Law and the Social Character of Health Care*, Elias MOSSIALOS & Martin MCKEE (2002, 2nd printing 2004), 259 p., ISBN 90-5201-110-9.

No.37– *Wage Policy in the Eurozone*, Philippe POCHET (ed.), Observatoire social européen (2002), 286 p., ISBN 90-5201-101-X.

N° 36– *Politique salariale dans la zone euro*, Philippe POCHET (ed.), Observatoire social européen (2002), 309 p., ISBN 90-5201-100-1.

No.35– *Regulating Health and Safety Management in the European Union. A Study of the Dynamics of Change*, David WALTERS (ed.), SALTSA (2002), 346 p., ISBN 90-5201-998-3.

No.34– *Building Social Europe through the Open Method of Co-ordination*, Caroline DE LA PORTE & Philippe POCHET (eds.), SALTSA–Observatoire social européen (2002, 2nd printing 2003), 311 p., ISBN 90-5201-984-3.

N° 33– *Des marchés du travail équitables ?*, Christian BESSY, François EYMARD-DUVERNAY, Guillemette DE LARQUIER & Emmanuelle MARCHAL (eds.), Centre d'Études de l'Emploi (2001), 308 p., ISBN 90-5201-960-6.

No.32– *Trade Unions in Europe. Meeting the Challenge*, Deborah FOSTER & Peter SCOTT (eds.) (2003), 200 p., ISBN 90-5201-959-2.

No. 31– *Health and Safety in Small Enterprises. European Strategies for Managing Improvement*, David WALTERS, SALTSA (2001), 404 p., ISBN 90-5201-952-5.

No. 30– *Europe – One Labour Market?*, Lars MAGNUSSON & Jan OTTOSSON (eds.), SALTSA (2002), 306 p., ISBN 90-5201-949-5.

No. 29– *From the Werner Plan to the EMU. In Search of a Political Economy for Europe*, Lars MAGNUSSON & Bo STRÅTH (eds.), SALTSA (2001), 526 p., ISBN 90-5201-948-7.

N°28– *Discriminations et marché du travail. Liberté et égalité dans les rapports d'emploi*, Olivier DE SCHUTTER (2001), 234 p., ISBN 90-5201-941-X.

No. 27– *At Your Service? Comparative Perspectives on Employment and Labour Relations in the European Private Sector Services*, Jon Erik DØLVIK (ed.), SALTSA (2001), 556 p., ISBN 90-5201-940-1.

N°26– *La nouvelle dynamique des pactes sociaux*, Giuseppe FAJERTAG & Philippe POCHET (dir.), Observatoire social européen–European Trade Union Institute (2001), 436 p., ISBN 90-5201-927-4.

No. 25– *After Full Employment. European Discourses on Work and Flexibility*, Bo STRÅTH (ed.) (2000), 302 p., ISBN 90-5201-925-8.

N°24– *L'Europe syndicale au quotidien. La représentation des salariés dans les entreprises en France, Allemagne, Grande-Bretagne et Italie*, Christian DUFOUR et Adelheid HEGE, IRES (2002), 256 p., ISBN 90-5201-918-5.

N°23– *Union monétaire et négociations collectives en Europe*, Philippe POCHET (ed.), SALTSA–Observatoire social européen (1999), 284 p., ISBN 90-5201-916-9.

No. 22– *Monetary Union and Collective Bargaining in Europe*, Philippe POCHET (ed.), SALTSA–Observatoire social européen (1999), 284 p., ISBN 90-5201-915-0.

No. 21– *The Regulation of Working Time in the European Union (Gender Approach) – La réglementation du temps de travail en Europe (Perspective selon le genre)*, Yota KRAVARITOU (ed.), European University Institute, (1999), 504 p., ISBN 90-5201-903-7.

The Impact of EU Law on Health Care Systems
Martin MCKEE, Elias MOSSIALOS & Rita BAETEN (eds.)

The expanding scope of European law in areas that impinge on health care, coupled with a greater awareness by individuals and organisations within the European Union of the rights that this confers on them, has created new tensions. It throws into relief the challenge of ensuring that progress in developing an internal market enhances rather than undermines consumer safety and social protection. Resolving this challenge has become more important as the social dimension of what was first conceived as primarily an economic union has become more prominent.

In December 2001 the Belgian presidency of the European Union convened a conference in Ghent on the implications of European law for the social nature of health care. Two complementary books emerged from this process. This volume provides an in-depth analysis of some of the most important issues facing health policy makers in Europe. Leading commentators present a range of perspectives from the legal profession on the current situation and prospects for the future, providing a detailed map of the often-labyrinthine body of European law and how it impacts on health care.

Contributors: Christa Altenstetter, Rita Baeten, Leigh Hancher, Vassilis G. Hatzopoulos, Tamara K. Hervey, Yves Jorens, Beatrix Karl, Martin McKee, Elias Mossialos, Jason Nickless, Willy Palm

* * *

Martin MCKEE is Research Director of the European Observatory on Health Care Systems and Professor of European Public Health at the London School of Hygiene and Tropical Medicine.

Elias MOSSIALOS is Research Director of the European Observatory on Health Care Systems and Brian Abel-Smith Reader in Health Policy, Department of Social Policy, London School of Economics and Political Science.

Rita BAETEN is Researcher at the Observatoire social européen. She worked for several years as a policy adviser on health care issues at the Cabinet of Belgian ministers of Public Health and Social Affairs.

P.I.E.-Peter Lang, Brussels, 2002, 314 p., ISBN 90-5201-106-0.

Peter Lang – The website

Discover the general website of the Peter Lang publishing group:

www.peterlang.net

You will find

– an online bookshop of currently about 21,000 titles from the entire publishing group, which allows quick and easy ordering
– all books published since 1992
– an overview of our journals and series
– contact forms for new authors and customers
– information about the activities of each publishing house

Come and browse! We look forward to your visit!